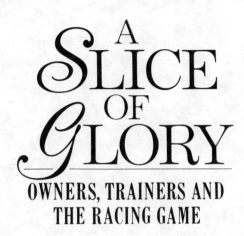

A SLICE OF GLORY

OWNERS, TRAINERS AND
THE RACING GAME

A SLICE OF GLORY

OWNERS, TRAINERS AND THE RACING GAME

Elizabeth Walton

STANLEY PAUL

LONDON SYDNEY AUCKLAND JOHANNESBURG

Stanley Paul & Co. Ltd
An imprint of Random Century Group

20 Vauxhall Bridge Road, London SW1V 2SA

Random Century Australia (Pty) Ltd
20 Alfred Street, Milsons Point, Sydney 2061

Random Century New Zealand Limited
PO Box 40–086, Glenfield, Auckland 10

Century Hutchinson South Africa (Pty) Ltd
PO Box 337, Bergvlei 2012, South Africa

First published 1992

Photoset by Raven Typesetters, Ellesmere Port

Printed and bound in Great Britain by
Mackays of Chatham PLC, Chatham, Kent

A catalogue record of this book is available from the British Library
ISBN 0–09–174920–4

In Memory
of
Aubrey Myerson Q.C.

Photographic acknowledgement

The author and publishers would like to thank the following for the use of their copyright photographs: Gerry Cranham, George Selwyn, *Racing Post*, Trevor Jones and Tony Edenden.

Contents

A Game of Opinions

The object of racing is to win; winning is everything, and second is nowhere.

The essence of racing is uncertainty.

It soon becomes clear to the innocent bystander taking a look at the amazingly bruising business of owning and training racehorses that it is a supreme test of character against the depredations of which it is worthwhile to keep Trollope's dictum echoing always in the back of the mind. 'If you must have your vitals eaten into – have them eaten into like a man.'

A trainer needs the dedication of a priest, the eye of a stockman and the mentality of a street trader; the owner needs trust, patience and money to waste – money to tear up and scatter recklessly to the four winds.

'It's a bloody hard game,' warns long-time owner the Duke of Devonshire. 'But it's a labour of love,' adds debutant owner and advertising executive, Graham Treglown. Toby Balding, who has twice trained the winner of the Grand National, says, 'It's a way of life; never think of it as a job,' and former champion trainer Nicky Henderson agrees: 'You're always under pressure; one never gets complaisant about it. On the good days when it goes right, it is very very special. There's nothing like it in the world.'

The Jockey Club dipped its toe into the murky waters of populism in 1969 and relaxed its rules on the ownership of racehorses so that owners now come from an infinitely wider section of the public than could ever have been thought possible even thirty years ago, and the industry has expanded as a consequence. Not everyone is happy; Newmarket trainer Tom Jones has aired his views in the *Sporting Life*. 'Like a fading tart racing

1

seems well set on the downward path from the proud title of the Sport of Kings,' he lamented. 'Where, I wonder, will the poor old darling end up?'

She is, at the moment of writing, in a crisis.

'Obituaries are premature,' top trainer Luca Cumani says. 'Racing will exist in one form or another; racing existed before '61, before legislation was introduced for off-course betting, before there was any subsidy or money coming from the Levy Board. So it can always revert to that. It can always contract – it will contract. It will probably not be as flourishing and as high-quality as it has been in the last ten years again.' He puts a heavy emphasis on his last word. Does that matter? I ask. 'Yes,' comes the forceful reply.

Leading racehorse veterinary surgeon Mike Burrell strips the matter back to first principles. 'A candid view? I think racing missed out on the last recession because the Arab money came in at about that time and cushioned it – nobody really felt it – and whereas the rest of industry in Britain was having a serious slimming-down programme during that last recession, racing had a good ten years. We're now in a situation where the current recession is hitting something which expanded too fast and none too wisely, and the whole thing is going to slim down, and come out leaner and fitter and better.'

Everyone knows what's wrong with racing, of course.

The Jockey Club is worse than the Politburo under Brezhnev; that's what's wrong with racing. It's the level of prize money – that's what's wrong: it's too low to encourage the owners. And the bookmakers: they're not putting *anything* in, whatever they may say. That's what's wrong with racing. Going racing has become too expensive . . . The local stewards – they're blind and bungling amateurs. The way the races are framed; the Arabs; it's treated so carelessly by the government – that's what's wrong. Racing stinks; it's totally corrupt and it comes by and large from the jockeys. That's what's wrong. They stop and start their horses as it suits them. The media coverage is appalling; there are too many bad race-courses, too many bad breeders, too many bad trainers and too many bad horses. The owners are crap. That's what's wrong with racing . . .

Racing is a great game of opinions and this inferno of certainties came from some of the men and women who are professionally involved, the particular irony being that they are all convinced English racing is the best in the world. Their concern is for its future and ways in which to safeguard its pre-eminence.

'It has its salvation in its own hands and always has had,' says the much-respected racecourse bookmaker, John Pegley. 'I think you've got a great problem with racing because the situation is that racing is broken up into little groups who are all speaking with their own interests at heart, and maybe not the overall interest of the racing business.' Jim Old, a trainer given to blunt speaking, would agree. 'Everybody's pulling in different directions – greed – they all want their own little bit. In the film *Lawrence of Arabia*, when Lawrence meets Omar Sharif who's shot his guide at the well, he makes a brilliant speech about the Arabs and if you substitute the racing world for them, I think that about sums it up. "So long as the Arabs fight tribe against tribe – so long they will be a little people", he said. "Greedy, barbarous and cruel. A silly people . . ." That's the way I see it.'

Adding the spice of class consciousness without which no English story would be complete, a member of the Jockey Club supplies a final detail. 'The bookmakers have a tremendously good political lobby; they've done their work in the past. Also, they know how to present themselves – they're streetwise. And when it comes to talking about racing, and this is a pretty snobbish thing, we send Lord Hartington and Sir Nevil Macready and the upper classes who are not pushed for cash to deal with the all-party racing committee at Westminster. They are *incredibly* able, but it's the image that's wrong.'

A Slice of Glory is a true story, for racing with its strong characters, intriguing plot, picturesque setting and brisk timing has no need of fiction; but occasionally a name or two will be omitted in order to protect both the innocent and the guilty.

CHAPTER ONE

'It's all go'

The lithe blonde wearing a chiffon blouse, a sun-tan and a suggestion of celebrity is standing on the steps of the weighing room at Sandown Park intent on putting over her message.

'I want to ride,' she says. 'I want to *really* ride.' No one could doubt her determination. 'I mean . . . I can *ride*,' she continues, 'but I want to *really* ride.'

As she clasps her hands fervently before her it seems that Suzanne Dando has a yen to ride Thoroughbred racehorses, but the Eighties imprecation 'I want' is curiously dated and falls rather flat. No one takes her on. Minutes before she was posing for the photographers beside the pre-parade ring with a grey horse taken from the racecourse stables. She had removed her dark glasses for the cameras. 'And that's all I'm taking off,' she announced archly. The horse was called Absolution.

'Who *is* Suzanne Dando . . . ?' asks someone with the predictability of a second-rate barrister.

This is the Variety Club's thirty-third annual race meeting, one of the major fund-raising events for the children's charity. Twelve thousand people crowd on to the London track and a profit of £100,000 is confidently expected. A good many game girls with faces not much given to expressions of surprise are out for an airing with their flash escorts. Older women with maquillage gleaming like barley sugar sport expensive clothes and even more pricey jewellery. Sharp haircuts and well-exercised legs make them look much younger from the back than from the front, and the noise of their chatter ('Did you get that suit retail or wholesale?') lends the occasion the feel of an evening in Drury Lane – an air very far removed from Whitbread

4

Day, or any of Sandown's more seriously equine meetings.

With consummate and practised ease one man enters fully into the spirit of things.

'Find me two nubile nineteen-year-olds!' rings out his command. 'And bring them down to the start.'

Sir John Guise, late of the King's Own Hussars and a Wykehamist whose baronetcy was founded in 1783, is now employed by the Jockey Club as a Starter. His job is to ensure that all the runners are at the start and are assigned the correct draw. The day's high humidity and hot sunshine have led him sensibly to abandon his jacket, but the sight of a shirt-sleeved Starter has raised some murmurings of dissent from those whose Establishment hobbles fit more tightly. He threatens to remove his shirt in addition and the critics are silenced.

'The fun about racing,' he enthuses, 'is that you're dealing with very very nice people all the time. It's a fun sport.' His appointment back in 1968 necessitated an interview at Portman Square.

'I was interviewed by two dukes,' he recalls, 'and I *think* the two dukes had been out to a rather good lunch! It was three o'clock in the afternoon! Eventually Tom Blackwood felt it incumbent on him to enquire of their Graces, each of whom was at the end of a long table, if they wished to ask any questions of the applicant. One of them livened into action, peered at me, and said, "Yes. I want to ask one question. Ask Guise if he can afford to do the job."' Sir John's rasping laughter fills the room. 'It was a sensible question, because in those days you got paid practically nothing, and unless you had some money of your own, there was absolutely no point in going into racing.' He was actually paid £1,500 a year. 'The expenses were £6 a day and you had to buy your own car, pay all your hotel bills, petrol – the lot.'

Nevertheless, he remembers those days with affection. 'It's not as much fun as it used to be: everybody tramping in and out of Portman Square. It was more fun, and it worked extremely well say fifteen or twenty years ago without all the rules and regulations. Nowadays there are too many people running racing.

'In the old days, when I started, if you made a complete cock-up, you used to ring up David Weatherby who was Secretary of the Jockey Club in the morning and say, "Look David, I'm dreadfully sorry, but I made a nonsense at Windsor last night," and he'd say, "Don't do that again." Now – if something goes wrong – you end up with a file of correspondence like that,' and his hands complete with the perpetual cigarette move apart to indicate the measure of his despondency.

5

'This is the only job in racing where you've got to make an instant decision, and you have to be right. Any other official's job . . . the Judge looks at the photograph, the Stewards' Secretary advises the Stewards, the Clerk of the Scales looks after the rules if there's any doubt about anything, the handicapper's in trouble . . . We actually have to get it right. What you've got to remember is there are thirteen hundred betting shops with people shovelling their money across the counter; it's not just the crowd out there,' he says, waving the cigarette at the punters beyond the weighing room. 'If you make a mistake and leave the odds-on favourite in jumping facing the wrong way, tens of thousands of people lose an absolute fortune! You're talking in probably millions of pounds. So we try not to make mistakes.' He pauses. 'But we do!' He chuckles softly to mock human frailty, and the cigarette end is flung out of the window.

It is not the weight of this responsibility which is propelling Sir John towards an early retirement. 'It's the driving in the winter. Heaving up and down the motorways. You leave in the dark in the morning and you drive back in the pitch dark. Most of us are always there two hours before the first race which may be at 12.15.'

What makes it all worthwhile for Sir John is the horses.

'I love horses,' he says. 'I was in a Cavalry regiment after all, and I've ridden all me life – until I got kicked in the back at Folkestone. At the six-furlong start. I got two hind legs absolutely straight in the small of my back which the jockeys thought was extremely funny until they realized I was totally unconscious, and not very well!'

Sir John joined his regiment from Sandhurst. 'I just missed the War,' he says, his words resounding with triumph. 'By the time they'd trained me it'd just finished! We had our own pack of hounds out there, and we did absolutely nothing at all. We just went hunting, show jumping, hunter trialling, racing . . .' His eyes are wide in recognition of his singular good fortune. 'I've had a marvellous life: I can't think of a better one. Fifteen years in the best regiment in the British Army, and twenty-five years in racing.'

Ten minutes before the start of each race, Sir John and his assistant of the day Mrs Judy Grange leave their table beside the scales in the weighing room, and a Racecourse Technical Services minibus delivers them down to the start.

'I do 188 racing days a year,' says Judy Grange. 'Sir John does less.'

'Oh shut up!' he yells, provoking them both into a gale of laughter before he takes up the story. 'There's a lot of travelling days as well, and one very rarely gets a weekend off. Of course you never get Bank Holidays or Boxing Days: the busiest days of the year.'

The Baroness Trumpington, who is not only Minister of State for Agriculture ('I'm delighted the performance horse comes under my tender, loving care') but also a Steward at Folkestone, had cast some doubts on the joys of being a Starter.

'Why anyone wants to be a Starter to me is a mystery,' she said. 'Having got them all in, all you see is a lot of bottoms disappearing into the distance. You don't see the race.' Her *basso profundo* gasped out its disbelief. 'And there's a queue of people wanting to be Starters . . .'

But do you ever see a race? I ask at Sandown.

'Oh, good Lord yes,' Judy Grange interjects briskly. 'At Bath, Chester – depending on the course . . .'

'You *would* butt in . . .' More barracking cuts her short. 'I should like to say I entirely disapprove of lady officials, and particularly lady Starters!' More wheezing laughter.

'You see what we have to put up with, don't you? We're all in dead men's shoes. When the likes of Sir John retires, we all move up a notch.'

What did you do before?

'Now *that's* a good question . . .' Sir John's antiphonal is *sotto voce*.

'I was a trainer's secretary.'

And how long have you been doing it?

'Too long . . .', he murmurs.

'About eight years. And every race is different.'

'It'll actually get serious when we get down to the start,' says Sir John as the bus rattles over the good to firm going. 'When you walk on to the racecourse you're on duty and all the jockeys call me Sir John at the start. And if they don't . . .' No further explanation was necessary. 'But after the last race if I pull into a pub and all the jockeys are there, I'll drink with them all night!'

Before the horses arrive at the start, the stalls are tested and they clang shut as Mrs Grange with her neat hat and sensible divided skirt allots the horses to handlers, the odd numbers preceding the even numbers into the stalls.

'The starting stalls are a considerable art: one's got to know how every horse is going to behave,' says Sir John. 'The bad ones we know are going to come out on their knees, or rear over backwards, go in last. The stubborn ones go in first.'

Yards away, the trains rip past to and from central London, and the topic of conversation amongst the handlers is the all-important question of the going, and how many horses had broken down at Newton Abbot during the last meeting there. One handler gives his personal opinion.

'It was good on the first day, firm the second day and hard on the third day.'

7

'They should start the jumping season later,' says another. 'It shouldn't be allowed.'

'Why haven't we got any horses?' asks the Starter, and eventually the six superior two-year-old runners for the 3.10 Graduation Race canter towards his jurisdiction. This is a moment of great appeal for the *aficionado*, Lady Trumpington.

'I tell you,' she said, her eyes full of dreams beyond Whitehall, 'it's the nearest thing to heaven you can imagine. As a Steward, you go out sometimes to the start for the two-year-old races to see how they behave down there, and if it's a lovely day, it's dead quiet; there isn't a sound excepting vague horsey noises, and the chaps who put them in the stalls who are so *nice* to them. The way they talk to them . . . "Come along my little darling . . ." They're sweet. They just must love their horses to do it because they *are* so nice to them.'

The bay filly Feminine Wiles carries the hopes of Robert Sangster, and her first-season trainer, Peter Chapple-Hyam. He will be standing alone somewhere to watch the performance of this half-sister to his stellar juvenile Dr Devious, and he is, by his own admission, feeling very nervous. 'You do get a little bit worried . . .', he says. 'I hate failure, I really do. I like everything to be 100 per cent every time a horse goes to the racecourse so that it's ready to run for its life.' This 28-year-old from Leamington Spa has restored the fortunes of Mr Sangster who dominated the English Turf before the arrival of the Arab owners relegated him to a supporting role. The honours on this particular occasion are, however, destined for that more seasoned campaigner Henry Cecil and owner Sheikh Mohammed.

The starting operation conducted under Sir John Guise's control was a marvel of efficiency. 'It's not always as simple as that, I can tell you!' he laughs. Some small degree of drama had been introduced by three men sauntering across the track as the runners quit the stalls.

'This is just not acceptable!' says an excitable official to Sir John.

'Bloody dangerous,' he growls in concurrence.

'If we have an accident, we haven't a leg to stand on . . .'

The Starter duly delivers a message to that effect to the Clerk of the Course, Nick Cheyne, and then collects the draw for the next race.

The weighing room echoes to the non-stop action of a race meeting in progress. Les Holt is in charge of getting the jockeys out on time for each race.

'It's all go,' he says, his stiff suit hardly appropriate for the room's steamy temperature even for a man who spent his life before retirement in a foundry. 'We're all old!' he laughs, referring to his fellow officials who check the jockeys are weighing in and out and have the correct number cloths. They also guard the jockeys' room from penetration by owners and trainers. 'They're not allowed in there,' he says darkly.

The Stewards' Secretary, another straight-backed Army man, Captain Stopford, is stalking about the room making sure everyone obeys the rules. One trainer is about to incur his wrath. 'I've put two calls out for him already . . . Really, this is no way to behave.'

'When I applied for this job,' explains Sir John, 'most racing officials came out of the Army. They were absolutely ideal. They were the right age and one had a certain amount of authority.'

'Do you believe a *word* he says?' asks the Captain, permitting himself a smile.

'You want to keep your mouth shut or you'll get the sack!' admonishes the Starter.

Almost before there is time to draw breath, the minibus is bumping and grinding its way down to the start of another race. Above its rattling, a girl passenger delivers a startling non-sequitur.

'It's not as bad as the Isle of Wight railway,' she says. How the Starter's back endures these journeys is hard to tell but he stares into his cigarette smoke and touches in another detail to his picture. 'Occasionally the trainers get angry with the Starter . . .' He feigns amazement. 'They obviously get upset when we withdraw their horses at the start – and incidentally, I have got Vodkatini off *every* time – but next day, one's the best of friends again. No animosity!' He pauses. 'Apart from one or two exceptions I refuse to name!' He shakes with laughter and disembarks from the bus. Judy Grange hands him a stirrup leather.

'The bumper race . . . whoever finished last lost a leather.'

This race for amateur riders was the talk of the day for the experts among the crowd. A seventeen-year-old schoolgirl called Sarah Vigors, the daughter of an ex-trainer, had taken the honours in her racecourse debut aboard a nine-year-old chestnut carrying top weight called Gilderdale who had survived a nerve-racking objection from Amanda Harwood, who was riding for her father, trainer Guy Harwood. A year before, Sarah Vigors' brother had won the same race partnering the same horse. 'Must be some kind of all-time record,' says the Starter, who the previous evening had been the guest of Gilderdale's owner, Dan Abbott.

'The old horse has done frightfully well over the years,' says Sue Abbott, wife of the owner and a member of the Jockey Club, 'but he hasn't paid for himself. Last season he won three times and was placed twice, and he won £17,500 in prize money – but he hasn't paid for himself. We're miles away

9

from the ideal that a horse should cover its training costs with three wins. Miles away.' John Biggs, Director-General of the Racehorse Owners' Association, bemoans the fact that the racehorse owner is taken for granted in Britain. 'I think the thing that upsets people more than anything is that you get a good horse like Gilderdale – and you must bear in mind that the majority of owners are not going to have *that* many good horses in the whole of their racing lives – and even with this good horse, it will still cost you money. That is *infuriating*. Infuriating . . .'

At Sandown, everyone was delighted for the horse, the rider and the owner. 'I'm delighted he won – despite the objection,' says Dan Abbott, leaning from his great height. It transpires that Guise and Abbott had put in a spot of anticipatory celebration the night before in the absence of Mrs Abbott, who is fishing in Scotland. 'Susie was away . . . we had to fend for ourselves.' Sir John is ready to be decorated for bravery. 'At 11 o'clock I said I wanted to go to bed, and he said, "No you can't. We're going to watch a video of the last night of the Proms," and Dan and I were singing There'll Always Be An England and Land Of Hope And Glory!'

Down at the start for the 3.40, a handicap for four-year-olds and upwards, in exchange for the stirrup leather Sir John hands over a bag of iced soft drinks sent down for the handlers by Guy Harwood's retained jockey, Ray Cochrane. 'When they're good they get iced lollies,' says the non-seq girl, who seems to be friendly with the handlers. Anyone without an immediate task to fulfil is sitting around in the sunshine and the temperature is now into the eighties. The horses are cantering slowly down the hill in front of the stands, and by the time they arrive at the stalls they are dripping with sweat. Willie Carson's film star suntan looks at odds with the other jockeys' pallid wasted faces. The grey horse Absolution is minded to romp round the course but pulls up just in time to circle around Sir John who is studying the draw, his red flag furled under his arm. The leader of the team of handlers, Peter Hickling, attempts to tighten a breast-girth on one of the runners, but Ted Jackson in regulation green jacket and hard hat elbows him out of the way.

'Against Union rules. No hat on.'

'Sorry mate!' says Hickling and stands back as Jackson, mindful of the rider's safety, adjusts a girth with some precision.

'Are you happy with that?' he asks jockey Nicky Carlisle.

Hickling's dread is an electrical or mechanical fault on the stalls. 'That's the worst thing,' he says. 'The horses are pretty good when they're walking round here; it's when they start to go in they get a bit stirred up. The ones that haven't run are normally a little bit more curious than the rest but, of course, when you come to these sprinters here, the older horses, they're all tightly wound up and ready for action – they're keyed up ready to go in one burst up to the end.' He stands beside the Starter's rostrum, arms folded patiently. 'We're one short at the moment . . .'

Our Freddie, one of the fourteen runners, has declined to accompany the others down the Rhododendron Walk and go out on to the course. He runs in a hood and blinkers because he is none too keen on knowing that other horses are near him, and he is also pretty choosy about the venue for his performances. 'Redcar, that's definitely his favourite,' say his connections. 'He's possibly the most laid-back horse in training,' says his vet. 'If I want a blood sample I can wander into his box, he'll give me one sideways glance and virtually present his jugular vein.' The horse's Epsom trainer, Walter Carter, was watching the race in a betting shop in Salisbury and when it was announced that one horse would not go down to the start he overheard a punter saying, 'I bet that's Our Freddie . . .'

One of the characteristics of the racing world is that no one (with the exception of Our Freddie) ever stays still, and this rule includes the handlers.

'Oh, we're travelling all the time!' laughs Hickling. 'It keeps the marriages happy – we're never at home long enough to fall out!' The winter break finds the team back at home in Newmarket. 'All the equipment goes back there for us to maintain; anything that moves on the stalls is taken off, renewed if it needs it, greased, painted and ready for action. And that's when you do the decorating,' he adds. 'And play the happy husband!'

'They're rather like sailors, you know,' chimes in a familiar voice. 'A girlfriend on every course. They turn up in droves!'

It is time to get the show on the road. The starting button on the end of a long wire connecting it to the stalls is fixed in place again on the rostrum and Sir John climbs up towards it, unravelling his flag. The stalls are rocking from the motion of the runners already in place. Frimley Parkson, a brown gelding, is awash with sweat and would be backing away from the proceedings altogether if there were not a fence blocking his exit.

'Three to go!' calls Judy Grange. 'Two to go! Last one coming in . . .'

'They're under Starter's orders! They're off!'

CHAPTER TWO

The Glory Hunters

It is the owner who pays the bills in racing. With this stark and painful fact staring him in the face, a new owner might be expected to take a long look at the racing game, investigate it thoroughly and seek the best possible advice before parting with his cash. This is not the case. Intent on his upward move to the elite Owners and Trainers enclosure in the grandstand with its superior view of the winning post, where he will take his place alongside the traditional owners from the shires and the Arab potentates whose wealth has restructured Flat racing, shifting some of the emphasis from the Turf's aristocratic old money, he hurtles into his new role with all the strategical foresight of a lemming.

To the outsider it is curious that men and women with sufficient acumen to achieve material success should be so very gullible when it comes to their leisure activity.

'But we see that so often in racing, I'm afraid,' says Toby Balding who has won some fifteen hundred races for his owners over thirty years of training. 'The people who are absolutely excellent in their businesses come and play the racing game, and get seriously turned over – probably with joy, by strange little men with straws in their mouths who make sure they talk a language the guv'nor can't understand, and go from there.'

Yorkshire trainer Charles Booth readily endorses this but delivers his judgement more from the hip.

'Businessmen are very very clever people; they obviously have to be clever otherwise they wouldn't be where they are. But in this business, they are led to slaughter – like *sheep*. And they haven't the brains to see it.'

Tearing up fifteen thousand pound notes each year – because that is what paying the training fees for an animal in a decent yard will involve – should be a powerful incentive to learn a few salient facts concerning horses and training.

'You'd want to know everything,' agrees Mike Burrell, a vet whose practice includes the top Newmarket and Epsom establishments. 'Unfortunately too many owners get taken for a ride because they're ignorant. All the principles which have led them to success elsewhere go out of the window. They entrust all this money to somebody, and I'm afraid in so many instances throughout racing history they have been ripped off. Eventually a lot of them tumble to it, and they never come back into training, which is a big shame.'

There is one school of thought amongst trainers which would have us believe that fleecing is no more than some owners deserve. A West Country trainer explains his theory. 'Ninety-five per cent of owners are in racing for the wrong reasons,' he says. 'They either want to show off, or they're in it to improve their betting chances, or they think they're going to make money. They think owning a racehorse will impress their friends, and that's sick . . . And the bastards end up getting fleeced.' A Yorkshire-man who turned in his licence still has vivid memories of his owners. 'I've 'ad some decent owners to work with,' he says, 'and I've 'ad some absolute rebels, rogues, renegades, crooks . . . Very few of them care what 'appens to their 'osses. When you get a bad 'un they make your life a misery. They want winners yesterday.'

Another trainer not blessed with the best of owners shakes his head in despair. 'The people that own horses are just not worth two bob. They're a funny breed . . . a bad breed,' and these views chime with the old saw which says owners should be treated like mushrooms – kept in the dark and fed plenty of shit.

A new owner who wishes to avoid conduct unbecoming to a racehorse trainer could do no better than heed the advice offered by Derby-winning trainer Luca Cumani, speaking in his Bedford House yard in Newmarket.

'What I would say to a prospective owner is – tell me how much you want to spend, and make sure that whatever that figure is, it is never ever too much for you. Then tell me what you want out of racing – do you want a trainer that has a lot of time for you, comes on holiday with you, spends weekends with you, or do you want a trainer that you have a good professional relationship with?'

From my conversations with owners and trainers it would appear that these are indeed the vital two questions to which a new owner should address himself in order to start off on the right foot. Luca Cumani continues with his cautionary tale. He came late to the English language and an Italian accent audibly influenced by a German nanny in boyhood Milan produces a most elegant cosmopolitan noise.

'An ideal owner can be many things,' he says. 'Ideally, obviously, a person who lets you get on with the job. What I always say is, if you are an owner and you go to a trainer, you should give him carte blanche. And give him your fullest confidence until such time as you have lost that confidence. When you lose your confidence in the man you're working with, then take your horses away from that man. Choose the right man and then give him your confidence because nothing performs worse than a trainer with no confidence, and unsure what he's doing. Training is all about making instant decisions every day, and you have to have the confidence of knowing that you *know* you're going to make mistakes, but you're going to learn from those mistakes. They're your mistakes, you're going to live with them, admit them to yourself and to your owners. But – you're going to try and improve on those mistakes.

'The moment you start feeling that you're basically not allowed to make a mistake you're going to feel at a disadvantage. Every time you say "I'd rather run in this race because I think we'll win this . . .", and then you get beaten and the guy says, "Well, I knew if we'd run in the other one . . .", you just feel next time I'm going to be confused. Next time I'll feel like saying, "Hey, if you want to run in that race, fine . . .", and then it gets beaten – then it's my turn to say "I told you . . ." But you won't say that . . . You don't say that.

'Then you come to the third time this happens and then you really don't know where you are – you're lost! And then the communication starts to break down, and then your rapport with the owner isn't as good as it should be, and that at the end of the day will reflect in your horses.'

Have you ever sacked an owner?

'Yes.' But he laughs and quickly qualifies this reply. 'Not many, not many . . . I'm very considerate!'

Guy Harwood, who trained the unforgettable Dancing Brave, offers characteristically brisk advice for a new owner.

'First of all buy an older horse – a horse in training. The first horse should always be a horse in training so that they can get plenty of runs out of it. The trouble is they buy a yearling and then they want action. I think the second bit of advice would be to keep himself in the best company and his horse in the worst until it proves it deserves otherwise and thirdly, let the trainer get on with it. Find a trainer you can trust and sit on your hands!' He laughs. 'Rev up your trainer by all means; keep him at his work – but let him treat the horses as his own.'

On another occasion I asked trainer Jim Old if there were such an animal as the perfect owner.

'Oh!' he cried. 'I've got one! He's a farmer and he's been with me for thirteen years. We have never had a cross word. He has never asked me *when* a horse would run. He has never complained about *anything – ever*. I trust him and he trusts me.' The encomium is recited like a chant. 'He pays – on the dot. I enjoy his company anyway. We share a brood mare and youngsters together. I am playing skittles on Monday evening with him. The whole relationship is incredibly easy. I'm not saying we were bosom buddies to start with, but it's grown over a long period of time. He would be a dead straight person and a bloody good sportsman. He takes victory and defeat just the same – but he's never asking when's it going to run and why isn't it. He doesn't even ask the question, therefore he isn't thinking, "What's the bloody 'erbert doing with my bloody horse? How long's it going to take?" And the curious thing is he had horses in training with two other trainers before me (both of whom are dead) and in twenty-five or thirty years of owning horses, only one horse in all that time didn't win. Which is incredible. I don't think it's because he's lucky – in fact, the best horse I ever had was his and was cast in its box and broke its fucking neck, and I don't call that very lucky. He's just good.'

Whatever his motives for trying his luck in the racing game, an owner will dream the same dream as every other owner. He dreams of glory. Against all the odds he dreams of owning a horse so remarkable it will find a place in the record books, a horse that will capture the public's imagination and win glory so great that some of it will accrue to himself. A horse that will be famous.

CHAPTER THREE

A Trick of the Light

'Fame is just a trick of the light,' says Richard Burridge, who has himself found fame because he owns a racehorse – a consequence he finds absurd. The race-horse is Desert Orchid, the most celebrated horse currently in training.

'Only in England really could you become famous for *owning* a horse!' he says. He looks as if he were born to success – tall, languid, very much at ease with himself – and yet he finds it all rather disconcerting. 'It's an odd thing because it's nothing to do with the way I earn my living, or with my own sense of identity. The presumption is that Desert Orchid has changed my life – but that's other people's presumption; it's because it's the only way they know me. I can see in some ways how it's changed my life, but I don't think in any major ways; I don't think I'd be doing anything different now if he hadn't come along. I'm very fond of him as I'm very fond of my dogs. I like animals. But I'm not sure I'd say I'm any *more* fond of him than I am of my dogs. When we sent David Elsworth the horse we weren't expecting that seven years later we'd have to run a fan club. We just weren't prepared for it: how could you be?'

Burridge writes film scripts and he travels between Los Angeles, Yorkshire, where he has a farm, and this flat in London's Notting Hill Gate where his is now trying to work, supervise redecoration and deal with the build-up to the 1991 Cheltenham Gold Cup. The telephone is a constant interruption.

'I've always been a film nut, and I was always crazy about riding. I started when I was about four; my grandfather used to play polo in the Indian Army and my Dad was a brilliant rider. In the school holidays we used to ride out every day, and I got spoilt by riding Thoroughbreds

16

really. I *liked* riding Thoroughbred horses – it was just so exciting. I was very much aware as I was growing up of the great horses: I was an enormous fan of Mill House, but they were all kind of much larger than life, something way beyond my range . . . I couldn't every have imagined . . . I knew all about the Duchess of Westminster and all these people, and then just to have a horse in training, just *that* gave me such a buzz.' Burridge speaks quietly and thoughtfully. 'When I realized we actually owned one of these horses, and we got a whiff of the invasion of privacy that was going to come, we realized that we could either share him with the public, or we could say, "Bugger off – he's our horse, don't be so annoying", and we made a conscious decision to share him. We thought the least we can do is share what we can because we're very lucky to have him.'

Arriving at Kempton Park at 10.30 a.m. on Boxing Day for the 1990 King George VI Rank Steeplechase could lead a punter to imagine that she might be first on the track; but the Desert Orchid Fan Club stall was already set up and offering mementoes. The rain was thrashing down, aided and abetted by a high wind.

'Awful day!' called Lord Oaksey with the brilliant smile of a man in his element, relishing the prospect of Desert Orchid's fourth victory in the race, and the privilege of watching the very best National Hunt horses competing for top-level honours. Wonder Man and Toby Tobias from Jenny Pitman's string; Remittance Man, the star of Nicky Henderson's yard; Tom Troubadour owned by Sam Musson; Morley Street; and The Fellow from France.

There was food and drink everywhere for the punters who had got into the swing of over-indulgence the day before, and by 10.45 they were tucking into overflowing plates of salmon washed down with magnums of Lanson Black Label, pausing only to complain of this year's £2 increase on a Members' Badge. There were many more mink coats warming their owners than might these days dare to edge down Bond Street: evidently they continue to be ideologically sound clothing on a National Hunt racecourse, but why anyone would wear one in the pouring rain is open to question. The true enthusiasts arrive sensibly rugged up, with hampers of provisions and golf umbrellas, unlike one girl in a skimpy velvet jacket, a mini and silk shoes; she was just six months too early for Royal Ascot. An elderly party followed by the bedraggled ostrich feather in her blue hat heralds the arrival of the Desert Orchid gang. This is Richard Burridge's mother and she leads her haunted tribe around like refugees until the horse is ready to go into the parade ring. They look as if racehorse ownership were the last thing in the world devoutly to be wished for.

The clamour about Desert Orchid was at its most uncomfortable for his owner in 1989.

'When he won the Gold Cup the whole thing did turn into a bit of a nightmare for about three months,' Burridge continues. 'It just never stopped, never stopped . . . and it did threaten to take over completely. I got two hundred letters, and David got two hundred letters, and quite frankly it was bad enough before that – I didn't get any work done for three weeks and there were just endless, endless people wanting this and that. When I went back to Yorkshire there were another two hundred letters! The addresses were wonderful: "Richard Burridge, Owner of Desert Orchid, Yorkshire", and it got there immediately! And a friend sent me a joke card from Australia saying "Richard Burridge, Desert Orchid, England", and it got here. And they all wanted photographs and photographs are expensive. David was being driven mad, my Dad was being driven mad and I said, "We've got to do something about this," and Midge, my stepmother, agreed to start a fan club. She took the thing by the scruff of the neck and said, "If we are going to do this, we *cannot* lose money: it's too absurd," so they began to market a few things. It was at a time when *everybody* was producing Desert Orchid stuff, and an awful lot of people who had nothing to do with the racing business were cashing in, which was faintly irritating. Some of it was so *bad*, and looked nothing like him. When you get into the basic mechanics of running a fan club, unless you have a certain amount of members you lose money; there was a break-even figure of about two thousand people, and I think Midge's got three or four thousand now.

'The thing has assumed a sort of logic of its own and I think we have mixed feelings about it. Everything about this horse has been so public. We don't get anything out of publicity; what *we* have is a wonderful racehorse, and the fun and pleasure and occasionally the pain of going racing. But that is a private thing – and it's all been taken over and the element of theatre involved in it makes us all pretty uncomfortable. We were just turning up and it was like showbiz – nothing to do with horse racing. National Hunt is a competitive thing, and the business of going into the parade ring with your horse, your trainer, your jockey – against *them*, that's where the adrenalin comes from, but certainly after the Gold Cup, the element of theatre in it was kind of overpowering.' A sense of wry amusement is never far away from Burridge's conversation. 'It was rather a relief when people started writing him off this year!

'I feel sorry for the press sometimes,' he says. 'They've all been on the bandwagon saying what a wonderful horse he is, and they all want to be first off the blocks to say this is really it – he really is through.'

More than most other owners, Burridge has had an opportunity to come to terms with what has been written about his animal. Practice makes perfect. 'It doesn't upset me. There is very little that is written that upsets me, but I think it used to, two or three years ago. Some of it was just such complete *crap*. I expected the tabloids would be the problem, but funnily enough the biggest villain of the piece is the *Guardian*. The *Guardian* has been *unbelievable*. I don't read that paper but I know people who do, and they ring me up and say, "What have you done to these people?" Well, I don't know what I've done to them!' He laughs and lights another Marlborough. 'All I can say is that isn't me, and if people think it is, what does it matter? People who know me know that it isn't.

'I am portrayed in the press as some sort of manic obsessive worrier, I know that. But National Hunt is about *emotion*.' He stresses the last word. 'If you don't get emotional, what's the bloody point of doing it?

'Any relationship with an animal to some extent can be represented as sentimental, and I get a lot of enjoyment out of Des, and I find him very entertaining. Even if he'd never won a race in his life people would notice him because he has that quality.'

Richard Dunwoody, Desert Orchid's current partner, reinforces Burridge's assertion.

'It's the charisma that makes him different,' he told me. 'That's one horse a lot of people will still be talking about when we've all been dead a long time. Superb horse to ride. He's very intelligent, and he's got so much scope and strength as well to go with it. It's a privilege to be part of the team and I get on with the Burridges very well.'

Richard Burridge's training as a scriptwriter assists him with this insubstantial thing called fame.

'As a writer you certainly have to have the confidence to accept your own perspective as being valid or you would never get started. I write 95 per cent of my stuff for America, and in the film business there is nothing precious about writing: it's very robust.' Reluctant student days at Cambridge had been followed by a pilgrimage to America, where Burridge made his way to Los Angeles; but rapidly realizing that he would not breeze into Hollywood by virtue of family connections or boyish charm, he returned to England and on the advice of Stephen Frears went to study at the National Film School.

'When I left Film School, before I started earning money, I was broke and I used to be a projectionist at night and a board man for Ladbrokes in the afternoon. That was great!' It was also part of what he calls his apprenticeship as an owner. 'I don't expect things to be perfect: I know something about horses and racing, and everything does not always go according to plan.'

When Burridge was ready for ownership, there was £1,500 in the kitty after purchase, and he made an informed choice of trainer.

'I was aware of David Elsworth's arrival on the training scene when he won the Sun Alliance and the Triumph Hurdle. There were several things I liked about him, and the first was that he came up the hard way; he wasn't born with a silver spoon in his mouth — what he'd done he'd achieved entirely by his own hard work, and I respected that, and liked that and trusted that. Secondly, he was obviously hungry: he hadn't got that many horses and it seemed to me when we still didn't know if Des was any good that he would give him a great deal of attention in the sense that he would try his best with him. If Des wasn't any good he would still try and win small races with him. At the same time he'd demonstrated that he was a good enough trainer to win the big races when he had the horse. Then there was the fact that he trained away from the main training centres which I personally liked because there's much more of a sense of community and less changing of lads. And also he agreed to take the horse! He might not have done.'

Since then, owner, trainer and horse have taken all before them.

'We've been through some unusual times together,' says Richard Burridge. Ownership and winning mean a great deal to him. 'It's unlike anything else and it's the *most* exciting thing. I don't know why . . .' His analysis falters. 'It is *incredibly* exciting to be standing there watching; it's completely overpowering. Maybe it's a reflection on our lives . . . It's extraordinary, and I don't know how to explain that . . .'

In his observation of the modern rich, Burridge has noted that winning means more than money.

'Rich people, in my experience, always have a problem. When they get very rich they don't really *feel* any different, and they want to feel different. They want to prove that they are different, they want to prove that they are successful — and yet they don't feel it. They feel this emptiness. And owning a wonderful, extremely expensive racehorse that is *theirs* and that other people would like to own — this is one of the ways of showing that they are somebody different. The same fate that dealt them the luck, the chance or the ruthlessness to make their millions has also dealt them this horse.'

How many people watch the King George VI 'Chase on Boxing Day?

The answer is as many who need to. The public needs its heroes, and today's hero happens to be equine.

While Jenny Pitman is pushing her owners forward into the winner's enclosure after their horse Wonder Man had so impressively defied top weight to record his third successive win, Desert Orchid is slouching round the pre-parade ring looking every minute of his eleven years. Champion jockey Peter Scudamore is elbowing his way through the crowds supported by a stick, a lingering reminder of his crashing fall from Black Humour. Mrs Pitman overtakes him, sprinting to the saddling boxes to deal with the brown gelding Toby Tobias whose fitness may have been in doubt, but never his ability. She had risked a fine of £700 with her threat to withdraw him if the rain did not come rather than risk his legs.

Desert Orchid is the last of all the runners to appear in the parade ring, and when he does cheers ring out from the crowd, some of whom are wearing orchids in their buttonholes so that there can be no mistaking their allegiance. With his besotted public in thrall, the horse instantly takes on his star persona.

'He's an absolute tart!' laughs Burridge. 'I find him a very entertaining animal. He seems to be able to sense the occasion.' The horse is cheered again as he canters to the start at the generous price of 9–4, and cheered yet again when the field passes the winning post first time round, at which stage he is in second place.

The moment of truth comes when the battle-hardened veteran Sabin du Loir and Mark Perrett hit the deck on the far side of the course, at the seventh fence from the finish. There is a moment's silence, and then a great roar from the crowd as they realize that Desert Orchid has side-stepped the faller and gone in front. Dunwoody gives him a breather in the strong headwind round the last bend. No one breathes as he clears the last, and then the cheering begins. Everybody cheers; cheers are torn from the most unlikely of throats and he sweeps past the post twelve lengths clear of Toby Tobias and The Fellow for a record-breaking fourth win in Kempton's big race, and his thirty-third win in all.

This was no trick of the light. 'If we're moved, or frightened, or even entertained,' wrote Ken Tynan, 'it is just a trick of the light,' but this performance deserved more than cynicism. The achievement was real, the emotion was real.

Mud-splattered and steaming, Desert Orchid walks into the winner's enclosure. Jenny Pitman moves forward to shake Richard Dunwoody's hand in congratulation, and to slap the grey on the rump before greeting her own runner, the second home.

'It'll be a different story at Cheltenham,' warns a punter.

'I don't think it's a coincidence that Des has retired two jockeys,' reflects Richard Burridge. 'They'd both got to the peak of what they could achieve. Simon Sherwood and Des suited each other perfectly; they both had that lazy, slightly arrogant, slightly snooty attitude. Simon trains one of Des's sisters now. He was terribly funny, Simon . . . there was an enormous amount of press interest because of that run he had, and as they got more and more excited, Simon used to wander into the parade ring yawning, slightly wondering "Who am I . . . ? Who am I supposed to be riding today . . . ? What are these colours – they look vaguely familiar . . . ? Oh! It's Desert Orchid!" He used to get up and nod and give a lop-sided smile while David gave him instructions – he just had complete confidence in the horse. But Des was a different horse in the beginning – he was a complete hooligan and Simon would never have suited him. One time he unseated Colin Brown at Ascot. He actually took off so far in front of the open ditch that he landed before it had started! He didn't fall, but he crashed through and Colin was round his neck until the horse behind clouted him and knocked him off.

'So that's two jockeys retired, and I think in a way he's retiring David out of jumping. After everything he's done with Des, all those incredible days that we've had, going back to Taunton and trying to win a novice hurdle doesn't quite appeal. And I think in a way it's probably had an effect on me as well in the same way. I don't go racing as much as I used to – I'm not as interested as I used to be.'

Richard Burridge has given fulsome public praise to his trainer, and privately he rounds out the image until it become three-dimensional.

'He is an *incredibly* sporting man – by far the most sporting man I have ever met. He never makes excuses. He's extremely charming and charismatic and of course he's a very stubborn man; he seldom changes his opinions. He can be completely and utterly infuriating to deal with! But I know how hard it is to do what he does; I know the pressures are intense, and I sympathize there. I've *learned* from David – definitely – and about much more than horses. There is a wonderful quality about him: the whole thing remains an adventure. And there can be no half measures in horse racing because we are not dealing with something that's real – we're dealing with a dream.'

CHAPTER FOUR

In All Weathers

Flat racing in the English midwinter is an unnatural practice if ever there were one and Kempton's Boxing Day razzmatazz is a world away from Lingfield Park on 28 December and a Flat meeting on the all-weather track, but it finds me – spirits plummeting – driving into the Members' car park where two elderly officials raise their hands to stop me and the day threatens to become yet more gloomy.

'Go along to the Owners and Trainers, madam,' says one of them. 'It's much nicer . . .' How very kind, I think; so far so good, and sweep into the next car park across a grassy slope which I assume to be well drained. The car comes to an unscheduled halt, stuck fast. I abandon it in disgust and as I gather up my glasses and hat along with my tattered dignity, I wish above all things I were not a woman driver at Lingfield's Christmas meeting. Help is promised for the end of the afternoon in the form of a tractor – which means staying for the whole card on a day when the wind could cut you down to a corpse in a second.

Across the road the small crowd of racegoers is short on festive cheer and long on a desperation to escape the enforced domesticity of Christmas. The punters' children have been dragged along too and every one of them is cold, and every one of them is crying. However, their little cherry-red hands and noses do add a touch of much-needed colour to the proceedings. Most men are wearing jeans; they must be icy, and since the management reserves the right to refuse admission to anyone inappropriately dressed it is a mystery how they got through the turnstiles. One woman sports a full-length black mink coat which scrapes the mud from the heels of her boots at every step, but this is no flamboyant gesture: this is someone failing to realize that even mink can be shortened. But who could blame her for wearing a full-length anything on a day like this when we are all risking the possibility of ending it up in a full-length coffin. The sole topic of conversation is the cold; each of the seven races on the card bears a name with a Crimean allusion, and the wind biting at fingers and toes could well be blasting over from that treacherous Sevastopol winter.

A cadre of young men with National Federation of Trainers badges swinging from their binocular cases to elevate them above the rest of the crowd all have shining pink faces, short haircuts, battered trilbys, covert coats and highly-polished brogues, and they stick resolutely together unhindered, it would appear, by any owners. Perhaps they should have joined the Army instead of getting a real job. Newmarket trainer Bill O'Gorman is clumping along in fetishistic cowboy boots with long pointed toes, and he does trail a little crew of anoraked owners to whom he is explaining the mechanics of racing culture.

The Ebor Bar is warm and steamy, and provides hot coffee and the temptation to watch the televised jumping from Kempton rather than the live action out on the track. The lads are in there too, clutching their charges' blankets and smoking cigarettes as if their very lives depended on it. 'It'll be cold at Newbury tomorrow,' says one of them. A punter with the merest time-lag in her conversation takes the last swig of her whisky and looks admiringly up at her escort. 'I don't know how you do it,' she says in amazement, apparently referring to his betting coups. A later outdoor sighting of her prompts the question, do knock knees keep one warmer?

Bravely outside to see the second race, won by Paul Cole and Richard Quinn; and from behind big dark glasses Mrs Susan Piggott oversees the return of her runner to second place in the winner's enclosure. Her girl claimer undoes the girth, and there is the squeaking noise of tack being unstuck from a horse's sweating back. Mrs Piggott never draws breath as she accompanies the tiny girl to the weighing room for all the world as if she were a Pony Club mum.

The winning owners in the third race, a two-mile handicap for three-year-olds and upwards, dash so speedily from the grandstand to greet Boulevard Girl that they arrive before the horse or, indeed, anyone else. Michelle Lyons in a black toque hat and a superb brown mink should surely be in a chic *quartier* in Paris, not here; she looks marvellous. Sasha, her husband, is momentarily defeated by the winners' enclosure – 'How do we get in?' he asks no one in particular. He holds his head high in triumph and greets the jockey wearing his red and green colours. 'Charlie will be pleased . . .,' he says reminding us of Charles Booth, the trainer, safe at home in Flaxton. Sasha hands his card to the photographer for a memento of this triumph and addresses the press, talking rather loudly as if he were a company chairman at the staff Christmas dinner. He is very proud that he bred the five-year-old Nicholas Bill mare and is now off to South Africa and Mauritius for a month's rest and to take in a little more racing.

Traipse back across the road to the car park like a dog returning to its vomit; but the car still refuses to co-operate and the resolution is made to carry sacks and a shovel in the boot until the end of time, or possibly longer. I wonder how it is men can get into a scrape like this without losing face, and begin to calculate the size of the tractor driver's drink.

Back once again to the track where the wind whistling through the corridors under the grandstand evokes unwelcome memories of school. The commentator is trying to inject some drama into the desultory proceedings by describing one runner as pulling its way to the front when a blind man could see it is being hard ridden. An owner (rich, Fulham) who had been intimidating an assistant trainer in a poisonous way in the bar and simply asking to be sent to bed with no supper suddenly finds that his horse is running extremely well. Equally suddenly, all his bullying bravado flies out of the window and he can't make a sound until the animal is all but past the post when a strangled cry of 'Don't stop!' bursts forth. He is struck dumb in the winner's enclosure too: no thanks or congratulations; evidently the reality of winning is more than he can handle. Finally he musters the courage to pose a question. 'How much have we won?'

There is only one place to be when things get as bad as this on the racecourse, and that is with the bookmakers. Never to bet, however, rather to find a sympathetic ear.

Racecourse bookmakers are far more sinned against than sinning. A boardman is despatched with a fifty pound note dealt from a flat bundle to buy me a restorative drink. 'Tell her the Australian story . . .,' suggests one of them who likes to see a shiksa smile.

'Many years ago' the story begins, 'there was a track in Brisbane called Kedron Park, long since closed down. It was the "bad old days" – it was sort of unlicensed, and there was a bookmaker . . . let's say his name was Art Garfunkel because his first name was Art, and he knew a few jockeys.

'One Friday night one of the jockeys phoned him up and said, "Art, I'm in terrible trouble and I'm riding the twos on chance tomorrow," he says. "How much to get beat?"' The Australian accent is convincing. 'So Art says, "Well, you've got to make doubly sure . . ." So the jockey said, "I'll make doubly sure – *it will not win*," he said, "you can lay it in the run – do what you like." So Art said, "Well, look – there'll be five thousand for you, all right? But if it wins, it's guns in your ears and all that business." "Don't worry," said the jockey. "It will not win." Art Garfunkel puts up evens, and they're coming out of holes in the ground; they mob 'im. Even two thousand, even four hundred. They come from everywhere to back it. He goes four to five on, and they're still coming. They're off and running – five-furlong race and the horse shoots five in front. So Art shouts out. "I'll lay evens the leader!" *They mob 'im* – even grand, even four hundred . . .

'It wins by two lengths. The jockey gets into the weighing room, sits on the scales, looks at the Clerk of the Scales and says, "Ow Jeezus! I've weighed in ten pound light!" he said. "I forgot to put the lead in me bag!" The Clerk of the Scales doesn't even look up. "Don't you worry son," he says. "*I* was on it!"'

It's not all jokes in the ring; the recession has hit hard.

'Bookmaking's only any good if you're changing dirty money – in other words, mafia money or drug money. Then it's a bloody good game being a bookmaker. Other than that – with your own money . . .' Hyperbole may have run away with this man because the overall total of money turned over in the ring – except at certain major meetings – precludes this possibility, and conduct in the ring is nothing like the old days when racecourse bookmakers were their own worst enemies with fights every day over pitches, and the business of getting horses stopped. It was all pretty unsavoury; but now, they tell me, there are never any disputes on the racecourse between bookmakers, and the standard of integrity is high in the betting ring.

Many people, however, might say that was merely honour among thieves.

'That's the sort of snide remark you have to put up with in this game. It's like some of the bloody stupid letters I see in the sporting press slagging bookmakers off all the time. The public wouldn't come racing if there weren't any bookmakers.'

No betting – no racing under Rules. Horse-racing is a medium for gambling and it is sheer sophistry to imagine otherwise. A breeder's endeavours, a trainer's endeavours, a veterinary surgeon's endeavours are all geared towards this one goal, to provide gambling machines for punters up and down the country. The two businesses of racing and bookmaking are separate but totally interdependent, and yet they rest side by side so very uneasily it can seem to the outsider that racing is run by lunatics hell-bent on self-destruction.

The bookies love the business. Ask any of them why they do it and to a man they will say – echoing the trainers – because it's a way of life. And there is generally only one way out. 'You go out in a wooden box,' agrees one man with an almost religious acceptance. 'But it's a dying business, bookmaking. Over the years though a high percentage of trainers finished up millionaires – started with nothing and they're millionaires, right? And jockeys an' all. The top echelon, they become millionaires. The middle rank get a very good living: they finish up with farms and studs and this, that and the other. But I don't know any bookmakers who've finished up with that. I don't know one. Do you know one? I'm talking about course bookmaking.'

Someone else wants his twopennyworth.

'I'm pretty sure that the majority of course bookmakers if they'd guide their talents to some other business, I'm sure they'd make a far greater success financially than they do making a book at the races. It's such a precarious game. You have a nice run for about three or four months, then all of a sudden in our vernacular, "the wheel falls off".'

'Another very important thing as far as the economics of the game are concerned,' says the pessimist, 'it is the last refuge of people with tax-free money – for the ones in a position to make use of it. The bookmaker is not; he's got to use his intelligence and see horses run and say, well, that wasn't quite what it should have been, you follow? And that goes on quite frequently. You'll see it here today. "Not today Josephine . . ."'

A clerk chips in with a jaded opinion.

'They all screams and cries to get into the game and yet 90 per cent of them don't even realize what it's all about, that's the funny thing. The owners these days . . .,' he shrugs dismissively, 'they're just glory hunters.'

'It's a very complicated game and most laymen . . . it's a foreign language to them. They don't understand the economics of it – nor do the people running it, unfortunately! There's more bookmakers go broke than all the trainers, owners and jockeys. They risk their own money, and a hell of a lot of them go wrong, right? They get caught in the middle of what I said, the tax-free game. A trainer might come up to me and say, "Get me five hundred quid out of my horse." It might be a 5–1 chance, so I offer six, so all of a sudden I lay it to lose £12,000. I give the trainer his five hundred and I put fifteen hundred in my pocket, don't I? Having said that, the day comes when the trainer says, "Get me money out of my horse,' and he says to another bookmaker, "Back it, will you?" You follow my meaning? Now this goes on quite a lot, and strictly speaking, it's dishonest, but who's going to prove it? I've always maintained I'm going to publish a book, and put all the excuses down in alphabetical order – I'm serious – so that the trainer doesn't have to think about it before he goes into the Stewards' room. He can look up . . .' He thumbs through imaginary pages. 'Oh, the going wasn't good, or it couldn't come round the bend, or it's a left-hand track and it wants a right-hand track, or the jockey lost his irons or it didn't get out of the gate very well. You follow?

'I've got a very low opinion of Stewards. As far as their mentality is concerned I don't think any of them should have anything to do with this game. They're probably very highly educated people but then they go into the Army and usually they're failures so they come out, but they look at his old school tie and think, "Oh we'll make him a Steward: he'll make a few bob at that." Right? They haven't got a clue. They get told things which the normal intelligent person would say – "Oh go and tell that to the bleeding fairies at the bottom of the garden," you follow?

'It's shocking, really. It wants a really big commercial firm to take racing over and get somebody with some brains in to really sort it all out and then . . . broom 'em all out. If a trainer's caught with a non-trier, don't fine him twenty-five or fifty pound – warn 'im off. Finished! They don't – they caution him. "Don't let it happen again, you naughty man,"' he minces. '"We saw that . . . we mustn't see it." Instead of saying, "Finished!" If I did anything dodgy making a book they'd quickly send *me* off.' His indignation is positively majestic. 'Marched off in quick time – that race! That immediate race! Off! But people with probably £50,000 involved . . . "Oh, we'll fine you £50."'

It is an exuberant send-off, and back in the car park it is immensely cheering to see the wheels of another BMW close to mine spinning impotently round and round. Get into the car and pray; but God is not a driving man, and allows no progress. Within seconds someone recommends second gear. He pushes; we fail. I leap out of the driving seat trying to disown this pathetic foreign car. 'You try,' I say. Then Paul Eddery comes running over. 'This happened to me here the other week . . .' I breathe again. 'He gets into the car with jockeys' agent Shippy Ellis and everybody else pushing. Success. Eddery does a lap of honour to a round of applause. His horse in the last race was Castcareaway, and he gave it his characteristic stylish and quiet ride to come in second; he drives a car in exactly the same way. Shippy Ellis is left dabbing at the mud on his trousers and Gary Carter grins. That's real racing people for you, I think with affection. They can redeem any situation – possibly because they have so much practice. In racing you can sort anything out: there's another race coming up, and there's tomorrow and then next week . . .

The next day dawns grey and very wet, but this is perfect weather for a National Hunt meeting at Fontwell, and no one dreams of complaining.

The figure-of-eight 'chase course looks like an hour glass with the obstacles, like the sand, at the bottom and all but invisible from the stands. Fog complicates the issue. But the atmosphere is urgent and a rumbustious crowd seethes in the Silver Ring. John Pegley, a kind man, is looking avuncular on the rails. The middle classes have cornered the market in style, dressed for rain and mud in ageing tweeds, well-worn Drizabones and an eclectic assortment of boots. Their children are less well protected but sharp prep school voices pipe up, 'I'm not cold,' as they shiver defiantly in royal blue nylon. Bars and restaurants are packed and doing brisk business in hot soup while the punters yell at the action on the television screens just as if they were outside in the stands.

Stocky but diminutive Brighton trainer Charlie Moore is about to saddle up a bay mare called Final Flutter who jibs at going into the box. 'Mind the filly,' he warns. 'She's wicked this one. She's a thief. She'd steal any race from you. The last owner wouldn't've sold her if she'd been any good for the paddocks.' The mare is encouraged into the box and lands an almighty kick on its rear wall. 'You can't get near her tail,' says her lad quietly. Her lower lip is flapping up and down to reveal dark brown teeth, her head is up like a pennant and all four legs are planted and shaking; evidently her enthusiasm for racing is limited. The lad whistles softly. There is going to be no happy ending for this horse.

'She's impeccably bred,' says Charlie before adding helpfully that he thinks Mr Akehurst will win this one. Charlie's daughter, Candy Morris, comes into the ring ready to ride, looking very trim in yellow with red stars. The horse is led to the start.

In the race Candy works hard to push Final Flutter up the field but concedes defeat after one circuit and pulls up. As the horse is unsaddled she gives the owner a concise and forceful reading of the race. 'I used up everything getting her up with them so there was nothing left for me to work on. Get her in a seller. A bad seller. Get her in soon and at a low price so that someone will buy her.' A punter holds his child up to the horse to pat it and we say as one, 'Watch out!' The horse kicks out. 'Get her away,' says Charlie, 'before anyone else tries that.' Ken Higson saunters up to mention he had £800 on the winner. 'That's nothing for him,' laughs Final Flutter's owner, Mike Culling, who trains animals to perform on film and television and takes defeat with total equanimity.

A trainer must be, almost by definition, an entertainer; some are forced to resort to artifice, but some are naturals and Charlie is a natural. He has no illusions about his profession, however, and his good humour can be eclipsed by his concern for the future.

'It's very hard for the small people,' he says. 'We get a horse for two thousand and we're supposed to win the Champion Hurdle whereas the top boys can buy one for fifty grand and it doesn't matter if it doesn't do a thing. I had one that cost half a million off Guy Harwood; we give seven thousand for it. He won £59 with it at Bath to be third. We did win at Plumpton with it . . .' He blows despairingly through pursed lips. 'I'll be quite frank. If I knew then what I know now I would never have come into the job. You're working harder than you should be for the return. You're underestimating your own brain to get up at 5 o'clock every day – then you get the owners . . . I've just been knocked for £6,400 on three horses. Well, that means to say I've worked all year for nothing. Oh, there's some trainers will lick the owners' shoes – that is not me, unfortunately. I won't. When a person comes to me and says will you train a horse, I say yes, and I'll do my utmost to produce it, but I will not (and I mean this) socialize. I'm not a miserable old so-and-so, but when I've finished, *I want to get home*. And there's so much work done in them bars . . . conniving to steal an owner from you – but it doesn't bother me. If an owner wants to go away because some *villain* is trying to thieve off of him, let him go.'

His mood lightens as he warms up to one of his favourite themes: trainers.

'Some of them . . . I call 'em actors. They are some of the best *actors* in the business – they wouldn't be out of place at the London Palladium. Some of these trainers couldn't even ride my bike, let alone . . . I had a couple of horses with a trainer once years ago, and he said to me, "Can you ride?" I said, "Yeah – I'll come up and ride me own horses out tomorrow morning." And I went up there and he started telling me to do this and do that. So I said, "Well, aren't you coming out?" He said, "I can't ride." He took my horse to Plumpton – a horse called Sandy Straight – and it won at 33–1, but I used to ride it out every morning and train it, and I never got the prize money. He knocked me for that, so that was the start of me getting a licence . . .'

An aproned jockeys' valet comes up with a message for Charlie's son, the jockey Gary Moore.

'I've got some boots for him,' he says.

'I'll tell him to come in,' says Charlie. 'They're not them Salvation Army boots, are they? Walk on your heel and save your sole.' Now he is on a roll. 'How many budgerigars can a Scotchman get up his kilt?'

'No idea, Charlie,' says the valet.

'Bloody common sense. Depends on the size of the perch.'

Back in the saddling boxes for the last race, Charlie's grey of almost 18 hands by Relkino will take his chance with nineteen others in a two-and-three-quarter-mile novice hurdle race. His owner, David Humphreys – a local estate agent – is very affable, but his fingers are brown with nicotine and anxiety. Silverino is more interested in the chestnut in the next box than anything else; Charlie reckons he needs a galloping track, but the owner wants it to run here, so run it will. Mr Humphreys' pretty blonde companion rides in Ashdown Forest on Sundays. 'I had my first ride ever last week,' he says. 'I thought I'd go with her. I was terrified!' He cringes in mock fear. 'I went to the loo at four o'clock in the morning, and it was pouring down with rain, and I thought, good, it'll be called off.' The rain buckets down at Fontwell as he tells the story and he smiles at the irony.

Jockey Gary Moore comes into the ring. He has the face of a boxer – cut eyes, broken nose and no front teeth – and Charlie gives him his instructions. 'If you're up with them, go for it – but don't give him a hard race. There's plenty of the season left.' He cocks an eye at Humphreys as he says this to invite the agreement which is readily given. Gary is legged up and the gang go off, but Charlie pauses for moment. There is a story he wants to finish, and it is about the time when another trainer put Candy up on a horse which got rid of her with dreadful consequences. It was less than he expected from a fellow trainer. 'Loyalty counts for a lot in this game,' he says. 'and we're a very tight community.

'This horse hadn't been properly schooled. It was at Newbury, and Johnnie Francome rang me up and said, "Charlie – Candy's had a terrible fall, and I'm going with her to hospital." She was out for days. My wife was crying to me all the way home when we went to see her, and saying she'd got to stop. Then Lorna Vincent rang up and said, "Charlie, she's come round and I'm with her. She's been transferred to the Royal Berkshire."'

We are alone in the ring at Fontwell; not a punter in sight. Charlie's horse is about to run. The rain is lashing down.

'I said to Lorna, "I'm getting in the car," and when I saw Candy I said, "Look, your mother wants you to give this up . . ." She said, "Dad, I don't want to." And here she is today, but . . .'

His implication is that if you break racing's unwritten rules you are courting disaster; life is hard enough without that in National Hunt racing. 'If you play straight with people in racing you generally find they're all right with you,' he concludes, and dives into the Silver Ring with a wad of notes.

Silverino moves steadily through the field and as Gary comes up the final straight in the lead, his father gives one yell of 'Come on, my son!' and then puts his glasses down before the last flight, quietly satisfied. The crowd in the grandstand clap him on the back, and he turns to one woman and says, 'I'm going to see Snowy after . . .', referring to Josh Gifford's travelling head lad who is in hospital having suffered a stroke.

Candy is in the winner's enclosure with David Humphreys waiting to see the horse she has done since he was a two-year-old, and she is whooping with pleasure as she rushes forward to congratulate him. Charlie holds court to a couple of press men. 'Would this be the best horse you've had, Mr Moore?' 'No,' he replies immediately. 'And I'm not going to be silly and say his next run will be at Cheltenham,' he adds. Humphreys is elated and hoping for a double with his other horse, Bendicks, in three days' time. We leave on this hopeful note, smiling and happy with a December day spent out in the wind and the rain.

CHAPTER FIVE

'Win on this if you can'

Jockeys' agent Shippy Ellis was still at sea as a navigator in the merchant navy when he was hijacked into racehorse ownership by one trainer's shameless chutzpah.

'Mick Ryan rang me up and said, "I've got you a horse." I said, "I can't afford a horse, I've just bought a new car." And he said, "But *everybody's* got a new car; not everybody's got a horse." And I fell for it.'

He named the horse after a captain's daughter – a memorably amorous lady – and Gilly Grope duly won at Yarmouth. To win at all was astonishing, to win with a moderate horse even more so, but the greatest surprise of all was the emotional force with which victory hit him. 'I knew I'd be very very pleased, but the actual feeling was quite something. I did actually write a poem about it . . .' He ducks down and searches under his desk to produce a small suitcase from which emerge the handwritten verses.

Now marooned in Newmarket, Shippy Ellis secures rides for his clients from an office in his front room. He sits in the window.

'Under a fluorescent sign . . .', he says.

Like the Reeperbahn?

'A bit like that!' he laughs.

He has visited racetracks all over the world on his travels in and out of racing, and over the years he has crystallized some trenchant theories which he is not averse to airing on how the game is played in England.

'Racecourses in this country treat owners like dirt,' he says, 'instead of getting the red carpet laid out. I think that any person who's got a horse in training should be welcomed into *any* racecourse in the country completely free of charge, irrespective of whether he's got a horse running at that particular meeting or not. And I think the admission charges are too high. In America you pay $4 to get into the best ring. You pay 50c for an informative racecard and you also get ten or twelve races. For $4. And a tote monopoly which ensures a true relation between the weight of money and the price returned – a much fairer way of dealing with things. Last year I went to Hong Kong and apart from being quite spectacular with sometimes seventy thousand people which is three times what you get at Cheltenham for the Festival, and you're in multi-storey grand-stands under floodlights for the evening meetings, and the atmosphere is electric . . . the courtesy, the service, the facilities are second to none. You really feel quite privileged to be there, and enjoy it immensely. At Newmarket, they don't take kindly to the general public going racing at all!

'I think racing has come to the situation where it needs to be run by commercial executives rather than the good old Jockey Club. Horse racing in this country is going to be around until the next world revolution takes place, and the problems of the industry should be looked upon in the long term and the government should purchase as many of the off-course outlets as possible, irrespective of the enormous expense, to facilitate a long-term handsome income from a Tote monopoly. The obvious problems preventing this progress are the bookmakers' strong lobby in Parliament, and members of the Jockey Club being permitted to owe their respective bookmakers money.'

Hong Kong also gets Shippy Ellis's vote when it comes to organizing the rules of racing. 'It is very very difficult to fault Hong Kong because first of all the trainers don't have to collect the money from owners because it's all done by the Jockey Club and the Jockey Club also pays the staff, they pay for the feed, the transport – everything. All the trainer does is train the horses. But he has to come up with results otherwise it's over. He's employed by the Jockey Club, and he's allowed so many horses, and if he's successful he gets presents, and it's quite a good life.

'Here the owners won't pay, so the trainers are in financial trouble all the time. Another strange situation is where some of the top trainers who can guarantee to fill a hundred and fifty boxes with decent horses . . . if I wanted a horse with one of them, I would probably have to agree before he would take it that my training fees would be deducted from my Weatherbys account, and that would be an automatic principle that I would have to agree to. The Jockey Club are prepared to do this for them – *but*, they won't do it for everybody. In my opinion, if they're going to do it for one they should do it for everybody.'

Aside from his pragmatic views on racing's executive inadequacies, Shippy Ellis's other platform is jockeys: the attribute they require above all else in order to excel is determination, he says. 'They have to work hard. It is glamorous, and there can be a lot of rewards, but in the summer a middle-of-the-range jockey would have to get up around five, go to one of the yards ready to ride out at a quarter to six, ride anything up to three or four pieces of work and as one trainer goes to breakfast, another trainer might be pulling out, and he'll zoom to the other side of town to catch him. Then he might have a cup of tea and a slice of toast, then get into the sauna, and around ten o'clock it's time to get into the car and go to the races. He will have maybe four or five races at an afternoon meeting, then zoom to an evening meeting somewhere like Windsor and not leave until 9.30 perhaps, stop for fish and chips and home about midnight.' For these exertions the jockey might expect to gross £50,000, but a handful can earn a good deal more.

'Last year the top ten flat jockeys won £15 million in prize money, but the alarming fact is,' says Shippy Ellis, 'that the top three jockeys won almost £8 million of that, and commandeered 2,421 rides between them. Don't get me wrong, I would be the first to concede what a supreme effort it is to ride that many horses and winners, but through the media the public is presented with the idea that to win races one must employ the best available, when we in the industry know that another dozen or so jockeys would be more than capable of winning on the same horses, given the opportunity. As Ray Cochrane said, and he's a very honest sort of guy, "Good horses make good jockeys." And what chance has the young lad coming through the ranks as an apprentice? Every time he gets lined up for a ride, one of the top jockeys says, "Oh, I wouldn't mind riding that . . .", so he calls the trainer, and the kid gets jocked off and bingo.

'The Jockey Club are the worst culprits because they want the best jockeys to ride their horses too, so they go along with the jocking-off process. In any other walk of life it wouldn't be acceptable.'

And *another* thing . . . ! Shippy Ellis in full flow is an impressive sight, and now he delivers his *coup de grâce*.

'In North America now, jockeys are subjected to drug and alcohol tests prior to riding. Should similar regulations be introduced here in the UK, it might be prudent to apply similar tests to the Stewards – especially at Ascot.'

The road into Newmarket had been empty of traffic except for my new, obedient and responsive motor, and with the assurance of *Vorsprung durch Technik*, I skated into a scene of astounding February beauty. Glittering powdery snow drifted back from the car, blanketing the great trees so that the road was enclosed in sublime white stillness.

Only woodpigeons, intent on survival, disturbed the perfection as they scrabbled for beechmast, and in the town thick dirty slush was a hazard; but there was barely time to close the car door on the brief journey between Shippy Ellis's office and Heath House, the training yard owned by Sir Mark Prescott.

Sir Mark Prescott, Bart., has a considerable appetite for success.

'Statistically, if you have a horse with me it is more likely to win a race than with anyone else in England. This is a fact.'

The remarkable strike rate Sir Mark conjures from his horses, some of which may doubt that speed is not of itself a mortal sin, is a tribute to his own prodigious industry and discipline which leave lesser men limping on the sidelines. 'If you can survive two years with him,' a former assistant has commented, 'you can survive anything.'

The trainer's cup of joy has not been overflowing today, and the weather has made things worse. Icicles hang feet long from the roof of Heath House and the Old English gamefowl peck belligerently at the snow around their tepees in the centre of the yard. A staff already depleted by illness and the head lad's holiday has been further reduced by one.

'Had a girl break her leg today. Got too close to the horse in front. Right through her shin bone. And she'd got leather boots on. To give her her due she didn't make a fuss. I had to ring her mother, but training is good practice for that because you're always ringing the owners up with bad news . . . "You know that horse I paid thirty thousand for? Well, I'm afraid it's useless."'

Prescott's schooldays at Harrow (where else?) and a brief career as a National Hunt jockey are best glossed over, and when a 'chaser called Pike's Fancy abandoned him under the rails at Wye Racecourse with a broken back, the future looked bleak. However, after a slow and painful recovery from paralysis, each new day has been something of a bonus. He took the privileged route into training, becoming assistant to Jack Waugh here at Heath House and grasping a once-in-a-lifetime opportunity to succeed him at the age of just twenty-one.

'Most people in the yard were older than me, and certainly every trainer in Newmarket was twice my age. Looking back, I haven't a clue how I did it,' he says. Arguably it was this early responsibility, coming after a long period of reflection in the Orthopaedic Hospital at Oswestry, which moulded him into what he is now.

'Which is what?' he asks.

The mind races. Another time; another book.

It was Mat Dawson who first had this yard. He was a trainer of very considerable distinction and it was to him that the long-legged eleven-year-old Fred Archer was apprenticed. Dawson did things on a grand scale – 'Damn the Blunt' was his motto – and although respected as a gardener and in true Newmarket fashion as a coursing man and a breeder of gamefowl it was always the horses which came first. All these traditions have been carried on by Sir Mark; and he further escapes the relentless predictability of the *Racing Calendar* with the brutal artistry of the bull-fight.

He disregards the tawdry, slovenly tourists' game and seeks out the real thing which is an integral part of Spanish culture and gets reported not, as he is keen to point out, on the sports pages of the newspapers but on the arts page. With its clever synthesis of sensuality and ritual this sport is just the thing for the Englishman still hankering to enlarge the emotional scale of life with the classical ideal of heroism and beauty for its own sake. He encapsulates the arguments for bull-fighting in a question: 'Would you rather be a bull in Seville or a veal calf in Hatfield Broad Oak?'

The relaxation provided by these extra-curricular activities enables him to maintain an enthusiasm for his profession.

'I always think in a very pressurized game I probably have as unpressurized a life as there is. I've got fifty boxes and I've always had fifty horses. I'll maybe run out one day, but I've been full up to now. I don't say for a moment that somebody can't train two hundred horses; all I *do* know is that the way *I* do it – fifty is plenty.

'In a stable like this, all the decisions are mine. In my opinion two things happen when you get over fifty horses. First of all, you start to have to delegate a good deal and secondly, from the financial point of view, you start needing two secretaries, two head lads . . . economically, you've got to get a hundred horses – I think it goes up roughly in fifties. In a set-up like mine I'm able to train for who I like, how I like and employ who I like.

'I train best for owners who understand the game and therefore I spend a lot of time with the newer owners – educating them so that they understand what I'm up to. One of the difficult things is if an owner is very busy. The helicopter comes in to the racecourse, he sees the horse run . . . the helicopter goes, and you can't get them to come round evening stables and see them all. Once somebody's looked at them, and they see the problems that all of them have got, they learn so much. The owner who gets most fun out of it is the owner who does study it.' Now he adds a caveat. 'The only time there's a danger is when a little knowledge is a dangerous thing. Once you get them through the "little knowledge" stage . . . And that depends entirely on how quick they are on the uptake! Some owners will own horses all their lives and still not understand.'

Sir Mark has a broad spectrum of owners which is one of the reasons why his yard is full. 'When they come to the yard,' he says, 'I make an effort to see they come on an interesting day when there's something going on; but if they simply pole up on a Wednesday, the horses'll all be trotting on the road in knee boots. One of the attractions of owning in this yard is that the staff and jockey and all those things stay the same, and for our older established owners, that is an integral part of it. They don't just follow me, they follow George Duffield: they don't want to see anybody else walk into the paddock to ride their horses. And the lad who looks after their horse will probably look after it for all the time it's here. If you have your horse with one of the top trainers, the Cecils and the other people, they have a very effective system which is the survival of the toughest. The good horse will get better and better under that regime, and the bad horse will get worse and worse. And if you have a very good horse, I'm afraid it will be better with Henry Cecil than it will be with Mark Prescott. If you have an ordinary horse it will probably be better with Mark Prescott than it will be with Henry Cecil.

'The most important thing in training,' he continues, 'is whether the animal has got any ability. If the horse is any good it takes a very bad trainer, a stupid owner and an extremely dilatory jockey to stop it winning races. But a clever man, and a conscientious man, and an astute man will do it relatively better.'

Barboured and booted, Prescott quits his tiny office to do evening stables, setting off in the dark and the snow with his assistant in attendance. As he pushes open each box door, a lad is at the horse's head, both of them standing to attention. The tuition begins, and a tendency to monologue is given free rein.

'Chicmond by Lomond,' he says of a two-year-old colt. 'Home-bred by Mr Goulandris. He is out of an unraced but well-bred mare called Chicobin and he's just clear now of ringworm. He's a bit weak. A horse with a lovely nature. Goes nicely. Wouldn't know how good he is because he just flicks along. I've never seen him get behind – I've never seen him go impressively. Nice horse I think. Very level. Very parrot-mouthed, not that that's ever stopped a horse yet.'

He thanks the lad and leaves the box, stooping to plunge his hands into a bucket of water after breaking its skin of ice, and moves on.

'Kanooz. Slipped through Paul Cole's fine mesh to come here. They paid eighty-eight thousand for him as a yearling. He's by Wassl out of a wonderfully tough mare called Countess Candy and two days after the sale when he was waiting to come over here, he fractured his hind pedal bone. He came to me in July; we gelded him and he's run three times. On the grass at STAND UP! WHAT ARE YOU DOING!' Kanooz is startled into immobility by a roar seismic with authority from the trainer who is running a hand down its hind legs. 'And he was eighth of ten at Leicester in the autumn, and then he was fourth in a *driving* finish at Lingfield on the all-weather. A very very bad race, and I said to George, "Go for your *life – do not miss it.*" And he didn't. Should've got life imprisonment. And he was in front with twenty yards to go and he got swamped and finished fourth. And I thought he'd never go again after that, but I ran him again on New Year's Day and he was second to a hot pot of Mr Elsworth's, and then he was off colour. He looks grand again now. He galloped this morning . . . badly. He didn't do a stroke.'

Next on the list is a three-year-old chestnut filly called River Chase: her trainer follows the identical routine of inspecting her closely while delivering a ruthless critique of her career and temperament. He runs a hand along her back.

'No guts but plenty of ability. Home-bred by Grahame Waters who owned Spindrifter, and he's a proper small owner – what a small owner should be. I've trained for him for about twelve years and he breeds them all out of Amboselli. I've won with them all: none of them have been any good. This one did a *little* bit of work this morning, third lot, and of course she hasn't eaten up. She works all right. I've just run her once and I said, "Win on this if you can, but don't be hard on her if you can't." He couldn't. She came home after the race and I saw her at evening stables; she was standing in exactly the same place as when they brought her home and rugged her up. The following morning she had not moved. Hadn't gone to her hay; hadn't gone to her water. Tick tick tick she was thinking, and when they're cowards there's nothing you can do for them. So, anyway, she had all this time off and shifted a little bit of work this morning – so little, and she cruised there, and she hasn't eaten a thing. She can read write and play the piano.'

Sir Mark has been issuing instructions along the way and when his tour of inspection is finally completed, he tramps across the snow to return to the office and more work. Each of the three horses which have been the subject of his caustic criticism will go on during the season repeatedly to win and be placed, with Chicmond giving his trainer a first Group race success in this country with a win at 16–1 in the Solario Stakes. Leaning on his cluttered desk, and inspecting the lighted end of another cigar, this tightly-corseted personality permits himself a venture into metaphysics.

'Logic tells me that if your system is so effective that more horses win here than anywhere else in Britain, there can't be anything wrong with the system. But logic also tells me that in twenty-two years, by accident – never mind by design – by accident the very good horse should have got here. No one can point at a horse that was a near miss. My greatest detractor cannot say, "Well . . . what about this horse?" because there hasn't been a near miss. I find that very interesting. And you have to say also that there are X number of trainers who, although they train not nearly enough winners, keep coming up with the odd good horse; most years, somewhere there's a good one. Why? Because their system is obviously not favouring most horses. Interesting. Interesting . . .'

But for the wind of change it could have been Mike Burrell intoning that famous line, 'I had a farm in Africa, in the Ngong Hills . . .' Not, however, in Kenya but lunching in the Epsom Club, he takes over the story from Meryl Streep. 'The indigenous gentlemen of the continent decided that they wanted our farm, so farming went out of the window and I thought the next best thing might be a vet!' Now his name is recognized throughout horse-racing for his development of the endoscopy technique.

Burrell's post-graduate research was funded by the Horserace Betting Levy Board, and he began by looking at pharyngeal lymphoid hyperplasia (sore throats in young horses) but changed direction as soon as he realized the blood and muck in horses' lungs were the more likely culprit when they were flopped at the races.

'I was at the Equine Research Station at Newmarket, and I said I wanted to put an endoscope down these horses every single month if not more often while they were in training. "No – can't be done," they all said. "Horses won't stand it – won't like it. Trainers won't stand it – won't like it . . ." But Peter Rossdale, bless his heart, said, "I know one trainer who might . . .", and that was Luca Cumani, and he duly did. Everybody uses the technique now, and if it wasn't for him, the whole thing wouldn't have happened. At that time he had sixty-six horses in training, and I'm very glad to see that he's now training two hundred and always in the top five in the table. Very forward-thinking man.'

Now in private practice (but by nature maybe still an academic) and dealing with all the yards in Epsom and some in Newmarket, Mike Burrell knows a thing or two about trainers. 'I used to go round trouble-shooting the yards with "the virus" – i.e. when they were running badly, so I've had a lot of contact with trainers round the country which was *very* interesting. There is the old school who have not yet embraced all this new technology and will go by what they can feel, what they can see and sniff and any other sense they've got to know whether a horse is right or wrong. Some are better at it than others. The good ones are pretty good, but the bad ones haven't a clue . . . Someone like Sir Mark Prescott, for example, knows his horses backwards, and even in the racing season he will get back from a meeting if he possibly can for evening stables; his attention to detail is marvellous, but even he uses endoscopy and blood sampling. Times are changing – it's a fast evolving game.

'Racehorses have to perform at their very best or they haven't a hope, and what people forget is that, on the Flat anyway, you're dealing with babies – you're racing adolescents, and like kids going off to school, they pick up every little bug and snotty nose going. So they're an incredibly unhealthy bunch of animals in the same way that primary school kids are unhealthy compared to a bunch of adults. And yet you're trying to have these things 100 per cent fit to go and win races. It's quite a challenge!

'It's a hell of a stressful job for the trainers, and quite a lot of that stress gets passed on to the vet too! The aggravation of a pushy owner with a sick horse that isn't getting any better – where do the frustrations get channelled? At the vet . . .' A wry laugh. Burrell's rational good humour is an excellent antidote to the carpet-biting which is not unknown in the racing world. 'It's a wonderful thing when things go right,' he continues, 'but they don't always go right and you feel for the trainers all the time; you understand the pressures and strains they're under, or just the frustration: you've got a good horse and you line it up for a race, and sod's law – two days before, it gets kicked.

'A lot of owners don't have a clue about the horse, do they? The level of ignorance of the general public on even their beloved dogs and cats – whether they're ill or not – is phenomenal. It's always worrying when an owner rings us direct; you're never quite sure what a trainer's told them! The other situation which is perfectly all right is when the trainer wants you to convince the owner there is a problem – there is a good reason why their blessed horse isn't running. Every day your racehorse is "off the road" it's costing money, and more often than not all we're trying to do is cure fairly minor ailments or injuries in as quick a time as possible. Surveys have been done about wastage in racehorses, and obviously lack of ability is the main one! But once you're down to veterinary reasons, leg problems are top of the list by quite a long way, followed by respiratory problems which keep it out of training but don't necessarily retire it.'

On rare occasions, disaster strikes.

When the portable telephone rings at lunch it is Burrell's partner with the results of a post mortem on a horse which had died unexpectedly after surgery.

Concerned that it could have been a particular favourite, Our Freddie say, I ask who it was.

'Some pikey's trotter!' comes the reply. 'But we treat them all the same . . . and he loved his horse very much.' Laughter returns again to kidnap sentiment. 'Now he's got a dead horse and quite a large bill. We're not stupid enough to only bill on results!'

CHAPTER SIX

Dreams Really Do Come True

Mrs Jenny Pitman can behave like the wrath of God. It is something she has learned to do over the years out of necessity.

'The thing is,' she explains in a measured way, 'I like training horses. That is my job. I actually like horses better than I like a lot of people.'

Training horses may indeed be her life, but ever since the day in 1983 when Corbiere won the Grand National and she became the first woman to train the winner of the world's most famous horse-race, things have been very different for Jenny Pitman.

'It was just such an unreal story to have happened to somebody like me,' she says. 'Some ragged-arsed little kid with the backside hanging out of its jeans ... You see, when I came into racing, for people from my background to turn up as trainers was totally out of order.'

Resourceful and extremely intelligent, she has developed a carapace to protect herself from the knocking and the half-truths which go hand in hand with the limelight. 'The only person who was more feared by reputation in Lambourn than myself was probably Fred Winter, but I think quite honestly it's unjustified. The trouble is that people who care about things and believe passionately in them have strong feelings, and I care about the job; I care about the welfare of my horses.'

Mrs Pitman is speaking in Weathercock House, her very comfortable Georgian home where she is always in sight of the horses. David Stait, her partner and assistant trainer, listens quietly and interjects an occasional comment to point up her theories and opinions.

When she is not breathing fire and smoke, this trainer is gurgling with laughter, and when she considers the compounding difficulties of being female, the laughter gets turned against herself.

'Most men think they can take advantage of a woman, right? Whether they are talking about the price of hay or whether you're going to buy a car, they think — "Uh huh, here comes a soft touch: we can have a few quid here." A few years ago when I rang up about buying a van out of the *Thames Valley Trader*, I told the feller that had the van for sale my name was Mrs Stait and first of all he asked me where I lived, and I said, "Down near Swindon," and he said, "I recognize your voice, don't I?" I said, "No, no . . ." Anyway, he did. "You're Jenny Pitman aren't you . . ." I actually held my hands up then, and we had a good laugh about it.' One thing leads to another in racing, and the story had another chapter. 'He sent me a little horse he had in training . . .' The man in the motor trade is called Gary Johnson, and now he has graduated to owning Royal Athlete, one of the stars in Mrs Pitman's string and leading novice 'chaser the season before last. 'He's just madly in love with racing,' she says, 'and it gives me so much pleasure to see ordinary people like him and his family with their enthusiasm and their love for their horses be successful.'

One of seven children, Jenny Pitman was born in Leicestershire and while some people in racing might use an upper-class accent to impress or intimidate, she tinkers with the Midlands inflection in her voice, fine-tuning it for dramatic effect when she deems it necessary in the same way that she lards her sentences with four-letter words: it is merely a question of emphasis. She has kept a firm grip on the traditional values she learned at home, and together with her tenacity and humour, they have seen her through a metamorphosis which took her from being a fifteen-year-old stable girl to the very top of the training profession.

Almost to the point of exclusion, horses and family are what matter to her. 'I was brought up on a farm,' she says, 'where my Dad worked with horses which, of course, were great big animals, and those horses we had, you know, we would never touch 'em until they were five. It just wasn't done in those days. I was not brought up in the type of world that the little Flat horses are brought up in; I would not get any pleasure out of racing two-year-olds and seeing them like you see them at the end of the year when they're like worn out little old people. If I go out and look at my horses — good, bad or indifferent, at least they're nice big horses, they're nice to look at, so even if they're not much cop you actually enjoy their company. And I actually like to have the horses for their career, like Corbiere who was the great love of my life. I actually live with them. It's a bit like getting married really — in fact I've got horses here that I've had longer than I *was* married!'

And given you more pleasure?

'Oh, they sure have,' she agrees readily. 'I went over to Ireland to see a horse that was in the care of a well-known dealer over there and he took me and Mark to his bungalow for some lunch and we were looking out of the window and a little ole fox comes trotting past in the distance and I said, "Hey up, there's one of your cousins over there!" So, anyway, he said to me, "Would you ever buy a horse without seeing it?" And I said, "No way!" "Oh," he said, "I send loads of horses up North" (to a particular guy) "and they've never set eyes on them." "Look at it this way," I said, "when you married your missus, would you ever've got married without seeing her?" And he looked a bit taken aback and he said, "What's that got to do with buying horses?" I said, "You've been married to your wife quite a few years and I think I was actually married for ten and a half years, and when I buy my horses," I said, "I'm literally getting married to 'em. And if I don't like 'em in the first place, I'd rather not be married to 'em."'

When Jenny Pitman took the Tote Cheltenham Gold Cup in 1991 with Garrison Savannah ridden by her son Mark, the horse had not run for ninety-two days prior to the race, but for everyone concerned with his victory, she proved that dreams really do come true.

The horse is owned by three men who combine to become Autofour Engineering and on the first working day after their victory, all they wanted to do was talk about owning a creature such as this. I asked Roger Voysey (the tall dark one) what was best about winning the race, and he answered without the slightest hesitation.

'The glory,' he said. 'That's the best bit. 'It's the thrill – the money doesn't come into it because in National Hunt, if you go into it thinking you're going to win money you can forget it. We've been very lucky and he's been a fairytale horse right from his first race.' His quiet voice and mellow Bath vowels hold the attention. 'It's a wonderful story if you take it from the very beginning.'

Mrs Pitman calls these owners 'The Autofour Gang', and they have a transparent and infectious enthusiasm for the racing game in general and owning in particular. Their factory is part of an industrial estate about a mile from Cheltenham's eighteenth-century elegance, and a stone's throw from Prestbury Park, the scene of their greatest triumph.

'One thing I will say about Roger, John and Malcolm,' says their trainer, 'is that they've never ever interfered. The biggest problem trainers have is not the owners – it's the owner's friends who are the mischief-making troublemakers. They wind the owners up and then they start questioning

45

what you do. And then, of course, you perhaps make decisions that you shouldn't be making. If a lot of owners had owned Garrison Savannah he wouldn't have won the Gold Cup, because they'd've got fed up with him by now. He has not been without his problems in the past,' she says, stating the obvious. 'He had a stress fracture of his cannon bone, and he had to be stopped; they never moaned, they never whinged. This year when he had the run at Haydock and damaged his shoulder on his first run . . . I mean, because Royal Athlete had gone wrong and Toby wasn't going to run at Cheltenham, I was bloody suicidal.

'My three horses were favourite in the Gold Cup and then when Gary got injured as well, I thought I just cannot believe this. I was thinking, God, how can you *do* this to me? Doing it to one of them is bad enough, to do it to two of 'em is serious, but to do it to the three of them . . .'

How did she deal with the frustration?

'Because I think He actually had it planned.'

Not only does Jenny Pitman have a religious faith, but she is also fascinated by the contingent factor in our lives, and so with both God and Fate on her side there is always an evens chance things will turn out right in the end.

'There are a lot of things that have happened with Garrison Savannah that are really uncanny,' she says.

She had first seen the horse in Ireland. 'He was led out of the ring unsold 'cos he didn't reach his reserve, and from that moment on, I guess, it was all meant to happen. I actually swore all the way from Holyhead to Lambourn, saying I should have bought that bloody horse – that was Saturday, and all day Sunday I'm still going on about it to the point where David said, "For Christ sake stop going on about that bloody horse. If you feel that strongly about it, ring up Willie O'Rourke and buy it." So I did just that.'

The Autofour Gang, meanwhile, had decided they needed to relax from the pressures of precision engineering and had settled on the idea of buying a racehorse. It was arranged that they should meet Jenny Pitman at Weathercock House.

'She had us in the lounge,' says Roger Voysey, 'and we could tell she was weighing us up.'

'I think Blue actually makes up my mind,' she says, referring to a dog which is snoring loudly beside me. 'She's very old and looks like a dog on wheels she's that scruffy and if she snaps at them when they put their hand down to stroke her, that is *not* a good sign!' she laughs, 'and she is such an old cow . . . I don't actually line 'em up on the settee, get them pissed and say "Sign 'ere . . . !" I actually like to deal with them when they're in sound mind!'

From the ordeal by Blue, she moved the Gang on to see the horses, but everything in the yard was sold, with the exception of one horse which was provisionally sold.

'He wasn't named at all,' recalls Voysey, 'but there was Gary as he's known in the yard, and next door (this is a great story), next door was Strong Gold owned by Terry Ramsden and in the next box was Pembroke Bay owned by Robert Hitchens and I thought, "I wish I could afford one of those . . ." Jenny Pitman told us, "I'm only giving them until 1 August to pay for this horse and after that I'm going to offer him to you if you're interested. How much do you want to spend?" I said, "Well, we're looking at perhaps £5,000 . . ."'

'Anyway, we left and I went on holiday to Barbados and I got a phone call from John, my partner. He said, "I've had Jenny Pitman on the phone – do we still want this horse?" We could have it for £7,000 and it was a little bit more than we wanted to pay, but I said, "Yes, we'll have it." And it was Fate, I suppose, but that day we went to a bit of a museum on a plantation, and on the wall was a picture of a horse winning the Barbados Gold Cup at the Garrison Savannah, and the name of the horse was Garrison Savannah. "What a great name for a horse," I thought, and when we got back I named him that. You couldn't buy him now for six figures. If an Arab walked in now and threw half a million pounds down there, I wouldn't sell him – no chance. Jenny always says, "You buggers, you robbed me with this horse! You're cheeky buggers – just like your horse!" He is cheeky; when he's had enough he'll bite you. He doesn't have a lot of patience, but he's a champion.'

On Gold Cup day, being rather superstitious, Roger Voysey was at the racecourse at 9.30 a.m. to be there when Mrs Pitman's box arrived and to greet the horse, thus replicating the events of the previous year when Gary had won the Sun Alliance 'Chase, but the build-up was terribly marred for him by the death of his father just the day before.

'I said to my partners, "I'm hoping he'll win," I said, "but I'm dreading it as well." Winning is *so* emotional. The first time he won and he came from last to first, I was crying – I couldn't help it – and the rest will tell you, I'm not soft. I couldn't handle it.'

His trainer takes up the story of the day's progress.

'My Mum's always gone to Cheltenham on Gold Cup day ever since I can remember,' she says, 'and for the last few years we've shared a table with my brother in one of the marquees down by the pre-parade ring. We had some lunch, but I don't eat much when I've got runners – God knows how I get so heavy: I'm fed intravenously through the night, I reckon . . . In 1990 when my Mum was at the Gold Cup, we actually thought that would be it, because at the Christmas they'd told us how poorly she was, so it was very much a bonus for her still to be there in 1991.'

In the parade ring, the horse looked magnificent. 'He looked like a fresh horse,' agrees Mrs Pitman. 'He'd still got meat over his backside and over the top of his loins whereas some of them had lost a bit of weight because of the runs they'd had through the season. As I was going to leg him on, Mark said to me, "How do you want me to ride this horse?" and that is really the first time we had discussed it. The year before when he rode Toby Tobias we set out to beat Dessie and along came Norton's Coin, and that knocks us off right on the line and I was that bloody despondent about this race because the bloody horse was lame four days before it ran, and I said, "Fuck it – that's it," and then I thought, 'No. I'll give it one more go."

'I said to him, "You're going to have to ride him the same as you rode Toby last year – in for a penny in for a pound. There's no point in coming here and not making a commitment," and so I legged him on and off he went.

'John came over to me and said, "What do you think?" And I'm thinking, "What do you *mean* – what do you think, for God's sake? We're bloody lucky to be here; if you'd seen your horse four days ago . . . God, what a thing to ask me!" It was such an unconventional way to get a horse prepared for the Gold Cup: it was *crazy*. I said the only thing I do know about him is – in his mind he is ready to rip the world apart and I actually think it's as important to have a horse's mind right as to have it physically fit. And Mark said to me that as he stepped on the racecourse, he said I promise you, the horse grew an inch and a half. He said, "I felt him rise up . . ." These things are very strange, you know . . .'

John Davies describes the last stage of the race. 'As near as I can put it into words . . . when I was watching them come down the hill I had to put my glasses down because I was shaking so much. I was *trembling*. I thought, "Whatever happens now, he's done us proud." And when he jumped to the front, he'd flown. When he jumped to the front three from home, *then* I was scared. Not for the horse, just scared. There was this gnawing feeling. And then he jumped the second last and I thought, "What's going on? This shouldn't be happening to us . . ."'

'Hell of a jump at the last,' says Voysey, 'and coming up the run-in I saw the Frenchman coming this side and I thought, "He looks to be going faster; Gary's going to get caught," and they were all cheering and I thought, "He's going to get caught, he's going to get caught . . .", but he didn't. That was it. We helped Jenny down, because she nearly fainted. She was in a state of shock. All she was saying, was, "We've been done again, we've been done again . . .", 'cos she was second last year, see?'

'I literally was dead standing up,' she recalls. 'I thought Gary was beaten and the one thing keeping me upright was the fact that we were crammed in there. I sort of got carried down the stands by people, and all I'm thinking is, "God, how am I going to get him through this?" thinking of Mark because he'd been second last year, and make no mistake about it, I know what the press people are like; they would've put him through a bloody garden shredder and he would've come out the other side mangled. Then, of course, you start thinking to yourself, "Why do you do this?"'

'Of course, when the announcement came over, "Number Six,"' says Voysey, 'she just filled up with tears, especially when it was Mark, see? That's what it was all about. So emotional. You can't believe it . . .'

Jenny Pitman tells her version.

'All I wanted to do when the horse came in and I'd put me arms round Mark and given him a cuddle . . . I wanted to clear off and go and hug me Mother . . . That's all I wanted to do. Terrible you know, but because of the way she was. Anyway, what happened was – I did my duty, then David and Mandy my sister and myself were walking back to the marquee and I said, "Innit fuckin' marvellous? It's just like a swansong for the old lady." Mandy started crying, and I burst into tears and we go back into this marquee and we are sat in there crying our eyes out, and because we are crying, Shirley, the wife of one of my other owners, Bill Robins, she started to cry!' She roars with laughter at the memory. 'She would not have known what Mandy and I were crying for! And Bill who owns Danny Harold who'd run so badly on the Tuesday, and Fifth Amendment who'd run badly on Wednesday, he said, "What're you lot crying for?" And I said, "Oh shurrup you! You were crying yesterday because your horse'd run so bad!" And Mandy and me were crying because we didn't expect Mum to be there in 1990 and I believe – and OK, people might think you're a bit eccentric for believing it – but I believe that's why Garrison Savannah was on my mind from when he was at the sales, and that all this was meant to happen. It couldn't've been for any other reason. Why was she still there?'

Mrs Mary Harvey died in August, four weeks before her daughter recounted this story.

'Through her life she had always been one of those people who had always been looking after somebody. It didn't matter if it was the seven kids she had, when they lived in Chapel Street it was the old lady next door, and then in her forties she went off and trained to be a nurse and took her exams . . . and I actually believe she was there when Corbiere won the National (and so was me Dad) and I actually believe her being there to see Mark ride the Gold Cup winner was her just reward. That's what I felt.

'We had an owners' party this summer because I wanted to thank them for supporting me and my family – but my family have supported the owners as well. My Mum, when she'd come down here, Stephen, my travelling head lad, used to come to her and say to her, "Mrs 'arvey . . . I've got one or two sets of colours that need repairing. Would you be able to do them for me?" And so she'd go through them, and if any of them were really bad, she'd say, "Couldn't this owner afford a new set of colours, Stephen?"' Mrs Pitman's laughter fills the room as she revels in the memory of a happy conspiracy to keep her mother chairbound. 'She'd bind *all* the seams, and I tell you what, she sat there for three days mending colours, and at least that was three days when she wasn't charging around, because she never gave up charging around.'

For Garrison Savannah's third owner, Malcolm Burdock, it had been a life's ambition to win the Gold Cup and be presented to HM Queen Elizabeth, the Queen Mother.

'We've had three runs and three wins at Cheltenham and we all live within three-quarters of a mile of the track. The Queen Mother was on about how close we lived to the track, and how special that was. I come from Prestbury itself, and she used to stop in the village every year. I hope I'm in that good nick when I'm ninety . . .'

'She's a very nice person,' agrees Roger Voysey, 'but although your ambition is to take the Gold Cup off her, when you got up there it was winning the race that was the achievement.'

While the Gold Cup made its way to his home in a bin liner in his daughter's car, he and his entourage were left without transport. 'We got the bus into town, and we walked round to the Pump and Optic which is one of the pubs we go down once a week and discuss the problems of the world, and racing mainly. And we stayed there until I couldn't stand up any more!'

Back at the course, the peaks and declivities of racing had been grotesquely exemplified for their trainer. God had snapped his fingers to extinguish the stars. After his shining victory in National Hunt's premier

50

race, Mark Pitman had adjourned to the sweat box to prepare for the last; had the jockey been other than her son, Mrs Pitman would have excused him the ride on Run To Form. Out on the course, the horse fell.

'I knew the horse had fallen and Mark hadn't got up,' says his mother, 'and by the time I got down to the spot where they are on the course, my brother was already there, and I could see by the way they'd got Mark tied up (he looked like a turkey that you're about to put in the oven at Christmas) that things ain't good but I don't want him to see how upset I am about it. They were telling him in loud voices what they were going to do . . . "Mark, we're going to put a stretcher underneath you . . ." and do you know what he did? He turned his head over, looked at my brother and tried to gesture to him to get me away. There are times when he infuriates me because he's so childish and there are times when he astounds me because he's so mature. My brother put his arm round my shoulders and didn't say anything, just turned me around and walked me off towards one of the 'chase fences, and I hear Mark yelling as they're putting this thing underneath him.

'By the time we were on our way to hospital, because of the quiet way they were working, I could tell it was serious and every time the ambulance bumped, Mark yelled, so I was getting a bit wound up with the driver. I said, "Go fucking steady, will you?" but those people, and the police that got him to hospital and everybody were just fabulous.

'When you see somebody there injured that's come off one of your horses – sometimes you actually ask some serious questions. I'm afraid this job is probably more dangerous than the boxing and it's often not how the accident happened, but how they're handled afterwards. But it's one of those situations you've got to accept because that's the job, and to be honest, although I would've preferred that Mark had done something else perhaps years ago, he never wanted to do anything but be a jockey.'

Malcolm Burdock says that when her boys were eighteen, Mrs Pitman gave each of them a copy of the poem 'If'. 'She said to us read "If," and Thursday was all that; one minute she was up there, and the next minute . . ." He points towards the floor. 'If you can cope with all that,' he says, 'then you're a real person. I rung Dave Stait up the following morning to see how Mark was, and he said, "All I'd like to say is, thank you so much you three for giving Jenny what she wanted."'

The import of that extraordinary day is summed up by John Davies. 'Malcolm, Roger and myself, we've worked damned hard to build up what we've got, and when we went into racing, it was just an interest for all three of us which made us go away from work for the day. And out of it has come such glory. It was done for fun. Real fun – not to win anything. I suppose that's why we've reaped the benefits. She's an absolutely magnificent person, Jenny is. She's very much a down-to-earth person and I appreciate that. I don't like being woven round people's little fingers, and she's got such smashing little stories she tells us about inside the game and because I'm the drinker of the three, I can pass them on in the pub! She's so warm. I mean, you go up there some days and she's so *distant*, and you think, "*God*, what've I done wrong?" You feel it. And then you walk away and realize she's so damn busy that she's not even seeing you. She's not even seeing you. Oh, I just love her to death. I was so chuffed for her, so chuffed.'

'It meant so much to her,' says Voysey, 'and all she kept doing was thanking us. If she doesn't get some sort of award as Trainer of the Year there's no justice in this world. That horse hadn't run since early December, and he comes out after three months and wins the Gold Cup. It was a training feat in a million.'

Owners, and winning owners in particular, can be more generous than fellow professionals, amongst whom the stench of envy can sometimes leave you breathless.

'You believe she's honest, do you?' asked another trainer, casting doubts on my judgement of Mrs Pitman. 'She portrays what she wants people to hear. She's full of deceit. But,' he added, going into battle with his visor up, 'you could say we're a load of jealous, chippy bastards . . .'

I could. And I rather think I shall.

Tethered by broken limbs, jockey Ray Goldstein watched the Gold Cup from his hospital bed when he should have been at the Cheltenham Festival to ride in the following race.

'I was rooting for Dessie because it was always going to be his last Gold Cup, but I shouted Garrison home basically to beat the foreign horse! I feel bad when they come over and nick our prize money! Mrs Pitman's a great trainer. A true professional. If she was a man she wouldn't be any different!' And praise for a woman comes no higher than that.

Goldstein has retirement staring him in the face with this latest injury. 'I've always worried that my life will end when I pack up riding. I've been at it since I was fifteen, and it hurts and it has its heartbreaks, but it's a great life. Every day is different.'

His career began with a week's trial in Peter Cazalet's yard. 'It was Aintree week and he had two in the Grand National, The Rip and Different Class which had a good chance of winning and was owned by

Gregory Peck. It was a different world from what I'd ever imagined and I can remember going around at six o'clock in the morning in the dark, and I hear, "Morning Raymond!" I turned round and said, "Eh . . ." It was him. "Cheeky little bastard! All you Londoners are the bloody same." I thought, "God, this is the Army . . ." I went out with the string on the gallops on a pony called Rhapsody, and this pony just *went*, and I'm flying round corners and thinking, "Where is everybody?" Then I saw them a couple of furlongs away walking in a big circle and he was in the middle. *Whoof!* I've gone again, and ended up in the middle with 'im. I was crying me eyeballs out. But it didn't put me off. God no. I thought I'd just met the only bastard in racing!'

He fared no better in his first public ride. 'It was at Ascot on a Saturday afternoon in a three-mile hurdle and there were eighteen runners. I'd never been to Ascot and everything was *big* and *posh* and God, scared me to death. When we passed the stands to go over the second circuit, David Nicholson who was riding shouted, "Lay over, kid!" so I've laid over and let him through. Nice, ain't I? You can intimidate kids – you roar at them which makes them wobble and you belt past, and that's what he did to me. Bastard. Then we started running down hill, and I'm poodling along till I look behind me, and I'm last! So I start flapping, and I came to the third last, and he ran out. He was an old shit anyway – he knew I couldn't bloody ride. He banged me up against the wing and from me toes to me face it was whoomph! and I'm straight off, flat on me back. I looked up and saw the St John Ambulance people were staring down and I thought, "I'm dead!"

'I'd like to train now,' he says by way of an afterthought. 'But that really does your head in.'

CHAPTER SEVEN

Putting On a Show

'Danger? Is the Grand National a dangerous race . . . ?'

Major Ivan Straker, Chairman of Seagram, the company which sponsors the race, is aghast. 'I simply don't understand that question. I'm not being facetious . . . I don't understand that question.' He is a noisy man (Harrow) and his voice, which is by Sandhurst out of Benson & Hedges, swoops and glides to hurl his amazement up and down a range of octaves which might be the envy of Pavarotti while the mobile face works equally hard properly to orchestrate his horror.

'If you want to change the National course, change the height of the fences, the character of the fences – what the HELL did my company pay Mr Davies £3.4 million for Aintree in 1983? We might as well have run the race at Haydock or at Wetherby or at Hexham! The answer is we saved the race because it is an integral part of our sporting heritage and it is the greatest steeplechase in the world. It has thirty hazards, if you like, which have got to be jumped, but they're inviting jumps. It is a tremendous challenge to both horse and jockey. But if you have fit horses, fit jockeys – in my opinion, the dangers are minimal. MINIMAL!'

The setting is the Cavalry Club in Piccadilly which looks out over Buckingham Palace but backs on to Mayfair's Shepherds Market where some of the elegant women are no better than they should be. Tall and pinstriped, Straker had marched into the Ladies' Drawing Room calling for a bottle of champagne, then chosen an armchair adjacent to the Bar.

It was a question about his company's decision to tie their name to an event which some perceive as dangerous that had provoked this accomplished performance. Seagram's sponsorship has succeeded brilliantly, both in saving Aintree and in promoting the company name.

'You can't measure the success,' says the Chairman. 'All I can tell you is that today there is a level of awareness of the company name "Seagram" which is considerable, and one had to build the awareness; one had to find a vehicle where you could get the name of Seagram over, and the National seemed an *obvious* vehicle. Very quickly my lords and masters in America realized it was a good vehicle and they were a very *willing* participant. I didn't have to use much persuasion – they saw the opportunity and they grabbed it.'

However, there are some in the winter game who regard the Grand National as a mere afterthought. 'It's a *handicap* . . .', said one, his disdain barely concealed. I mention the Gold Cup, and risk lighting the blue touch paper.

'No. No. No. The Cheltenham Gold Cup is not the greatest steeplechase in the world! I accept that it is the Blue Riband of 'chasing – I accept that. I accept that here you have the best 'chasers and hunters at level weights and the winner is, in theory anyway, the best three-mile steeplechaser in the country. No question about it. No question about it. Fabulous race, and to win the Gold Cup – great. But – I would rather win . . .', a laugh is perfectly concocted for effect, 'one National than ten Gold Cups! I would!' Now, as if by the turn of a switch, the volume dips and the tempo slows. 'To me . . . the National epitomizes . . . the very *best* . . . in British steeplechasing . . .

'I couldn't bear the thought of that race disappearing, and quite frankly – it would have disappeared unless Seagram had put up the money, and their motives were twofold – one the genuine desire to save an important bit of Britain's sporting heritage, but having done that, the Seagram shareholders, most of whom live the other side of the Atlantic, aren't going to say thank you for some of their investments being thrown away on some sentimental cause, and fun for me. There is a commercial side to it as well.'

Sir Donald Wolfit could not have declaimed the next speech any better than its author. Ivan Straker shifts forward to the edge of his seat, calls for more champagne, and the cadences sing out.

'I think that in staging a race like the Grand National there is no difference between that and putting on a show in London. To put on a show in London you need a stage, a theatre. To put on the Grand National you need a racecourse and it's Aintree. In London, for the show, you need the actors – and the actors are the horses and jockeys at Aintree. You need the star of the show – you have the star of the show in the winner. You need the impresario: at Aintree it is basically the Aintree management in conjunction with the BBC. The London show needs a backer – the backer is Seagram. The audience is the public – the punter at Aintree. There is no difference between staging a successful show in the West End of London and staging a successful meeting with the Grand National as a centrepiece at Aintree. There is no difference. If you work to this criterion it will be successful.'

We might all have leaped to our feet shouting Bravo!, but this is not the theatre, this is only the Cavalry Club and it is not yet lunchtime.

His passion for the sport is clear for all to see. He adores it.

'You can say that again. You can say that again . . . I just love racing. My father and mother were both totally racing fanatics so that it was inevitable that when I had time and when I had a little money I would also become involved in racing.'

As an owner, he came very near to winning his own race in 1987 with The Tsarevich.

'I was able to run him in the Grand National three times! Gave me *huge* pleasure – I can't measure the pleasure I got from him, and I think I was probably the proudest man in Britain in the year when I was second. Wonderful feeling to have a runner in the National, and if he finishes in the first three it exceeds all expectations. I don't know how I would cope with winning; it nearly killed me being second! It so happened that the man who won it that year was the great Jim Joel who was then ninety-two, and I can't remember the number of years he'd been trying to win and it would have been quite wrong, I think, for me to beat him anyway, and secondly he was a huge close friend of my father and he would have turned in his grave had I beaten Jim Joel. So proud. And for that I have to thank Nicky Henderson who trained The Tsarevich so spectacularly for me.

'Today,' he says, 'there are very few idiots like myself who own, in their own name, the odd horse to enjoy ourselves. Today, the old established owners can't afford the training bills. It costs you the thick end of ten thousand a year even in National Hunt racing to keep a horse in training, and nowadays you've got to win five, *five* ordinary races or 'chases in order to pay your training bills. Chances of winning five are pretty small; the chances of winning at all are not as great as all that.'

Ivan Straker knows where to lay the blame for The Tsarevich just failing to fill the coffers.

'He had terrible leg problems, and the only thing which stopped him winning the National – and not winning it once but I think probably all three times that he ran – was God. He hated the soft going – *hated* the soft going, and the first year we woke up to snow in the morning and that really ruined his chances; he finished sixth. Ran extremely well. The following year everything was right, but because of the implants in his legs the previous summer, Nicky had only had the chance to run him once before the National, so he went to the meeting short of a race, but finished second: great! And then the third year, yet again, having personally spoken to the BBC weather forecaster when he came to the course in the morning before the race . . . I ACTUALLY SPOKE TO THE MAN AND HE PROMISED ME . . . he said, "There is no way it can rain between now and the race tomorrow." We would have won it. No doubt about it. At five o'clock that evening it started to drizzle. By six it was bucketing. It turned Aintree into soft going – but even so the old man finished sixth. Had we had good ground in those three years he would certainly have won one; he could well have won two, and it was not impossible for him to have won all three and equal Red Rum's record. He was a very great horse. A cousin of mine is a Field Master of the Tyndale Hounds in Northumberland and she rides him as a hunter and I gather he's having a wonderful time. And he sent me a Christmas card!'

The Tsarevich's Lambourn trainer, Nicky Henderson, has looks which fill a void somewhere between Robert Redford and Tin Tin, and although there may sometimes be a noisy urgency behind his words, he is one of those civilized Eton boys. I asked him a straightforward question – what is training? – and I received a straightforward reply.

'Understanding your horses. They're all individuals. I think a psychiatrist would be a good word – you've got to understand the horse's head, and what *he's* thinking, what he wants to do and what he doesn't want to do and find out how we can make him do it better. Kid him – it is kidding. This is a very very different game to the Flat where they are only in action for two years; we've got to try and make these last six or seven. Now, you could go and burn that up in two years, and run the death out of them. Fine, they'll win a lot of races, but they won't last you very long. It's like a car: there's only so many miles on the clock and every now and then you have to put it into the garage and put some new tyres on, because that's the problem with jumping – wear and tear, and miles covered actually begin to clock up and that's when things like legs and tendons and joints start to go wrong. So you have to put the poor old thing into the garage, mend it . . . give it a bit of a rest and start again. They don't want to be thrown away because this is what they love doing, and if they aren't happy living here then goodness only knows where they will be. It's like staying in the Berkeley Hotel, isn't it? With the solarium and the pool – a beach and a rum punch is all they're missing. What else would you want?'

Possibly Henderson's best-known horse to benefit from the louche life on offer at Windsor House was See You Then. 'When he won his third Champion Hurdle it was a very special day. He was loony. One would love to say, "Wasn't he a sweet horse?" but he bloody well wasn't – he would eat you. He used to eat people. We had the most amazing love-hate relationship. Unfortunately he had terrible old front legs: he was quite tricky to train. He's over at Hungerford now, out in a field.'

Remittance Man, his current star, took the Arkle 'Chase at Cheltenham, and I wondered when he knew that this was a Cheltenham horse.

'I could tell you the day I bought him,' he says, 'but that would be a bit presumptuous! If you go to the sales and buy a horse, every single one you buy you must think, "Well, that'll definitely win the Gold Cup," and of course they can't all win the Gold Cup. It's not possible.'

I tapped his jockey, Richard Dunwoody, for his opinion of the horse.

'I've always said from the time I schooled him up in Lambourn he was one of the best novice 'chasers I have ridden. He was superb over an obstacle, and he gave me a very big thrill when he won the Arkle. Superb.'

'He is quite special,' says Henderson. 'He's just such a great athlete. He wouldn't be the prettiest horse I've ever seen in my life – but he could always move. And that's half the thing – they've got to be athletes, whatever they look like. That's terribly important. His temperament is terrible. His head is crazy; I don't know what goes on inside it except that he loves what he's doing. *Terrible* worrier – like me. We have a sheep with him, everything. For the first two years I didn't know what to do with him – he didn't have time to eat because he was so busy worrying. Oh, terrible . . . One had to go very very quietly with him. He only had the one run the first year – which he won, which slightly took the pressure off, but you've got to have very very patient people behind you to be able to do it. And in that way, I've been very lucky with our owners.

'I think a square deal is terribly important for the owners. You've got to do the best you can, as cheaply as you can, produce results *and* try and make it fun for them. With our owners, certainly, half the fun is people being involved with it: that is important, and one of the beauties of the game is that you get a complete cross-section of the world – out of those hundred people there's farmers, builders, brokers, bankers, doctors – you name it, we've got one. They've only got one thing in common at the moment – they're all skint!'

The economy being flat on its back has resulted in considerable changes in the lives of racehorse trainers, and Nicky Henderson is no exception.

'Three years ago you got up in the morning and went out and spent the day with the horses. The *only* thing I want to do in the office is the entries. I enjoy doing them; it's fun mucking around trying to place a horse, find the right race . . . It's hours of work in books, but the rest of the office, *I detest.*' The last two words are spat out with contempt. 'I hate bills, I hate cheque books, I *hate* accounts. *I* didn't know if the owners were paying or not; the business ticked along quietly and at the end of the year, there was a half-hour meeting with the accountant who said, "Well, you've lost this or you've made that." "Oh really?" I would say (he imitates his own energy), "Fine. Right, on we go. Thank you very much, I must get on." And that was *all* one understood about it. Now, we've got to be businessmen. And serious businessmen. All I wanted to do was play with the horses.'

At seven o'clock in the morning on 1991 Grand National Day we all want to play with the horses. The sky over Liverpool is pink and the runners will canter the course with the city's high-rise flats as a backdrop.

'Go For It Gary' reads the *Racing Post*'s banner headline, and Garrison Savannah's three owners arrive at the track to see him. A high link-fence reminiscent of Colditz greets them and since they do not have the necessary badges to gain entrance to the gallops and their horse, which is the favourite for the world's greatest steeplechase, the gates are slammed in their faces.

'They own Garrison Savannah.'

'I don't care who they are: they don't have a badge,' snaps Cerberus, denying them entry. The Autofour Gang look too apprehensive to defend themselves this morning, so a ringing middle-class voice comes to their aid. Not for the first time the ghastly noise of an Englishwoman in full cry achieves instant access to obedience.

'THEY ARE THE *OWNERS* OF GARRISON SAVANNAH!'

The gates are opened.

'Thank God you were here,' says Roger Voysey.

The runners have emerged from the racecourse stables to circle around where the start will be later in the day, and the proceedings are conducted in the Australian tones of the *Sunday Telegraph*'s racing correspondent J. A. McGrath, who stands on a Starter's rostrum with a tray of coffee and miniature Martell brandies at his feet for his interviewees. Straker appears briefly from the Atlantic Tower Hotel, supported by a shepherd's crook and a cigarette, and there is a quaint cross-party coupling of Tory MP Nicholas Soames (six foot three and a bulging sixteen stones) and wee

Robin Cook, Labour's Shadow Home Secretary who is so assiduously courted by the great and the good in racing with an eye to the future. They lean on the rails to confer. Mrs Pitman interrupts her royal progress around Aintree to impart publicly the news, 'Gary did a light canter.' A small crowd of owners and trainers is outnumbered by the press representatives who hang on her every word. She is wearing an unfamiliar uniform of headscarf and dark glasses, but the autograph hunters seek her out and she patiently signs her name for all and sundry.

Roger Voysey had said to me, 'She's quite an ordinary person, you know,' but Lester Piggott and Jenny Pitman are the two people in racing known to the general public by their Christian names, and ordinary is precisely what Jenny and Lester are not.

'I think the thing is actually,' she says, 'I don't try to be anyone else. I ain't clever enough; I really ain't got the time – I've got to think about my horses without trying to pretend to be something that I'm not, and I think that people can identify with that, and particularly the ordinary people like the Liverpudlians. When I go up to Aintree, it actually becomes a little wearing, because if you leave the weighing room to go to the loo or something, as soon as you sign somebody's autograph book, you've got loads of others to sign. And that's been going on since 1983.

'I do admit I find it difficult, but having said that,' she stresses, 'only because I've got an awful lot going on in my mind on Grand National day – it doesn't matter what price your horse is, just the fact that you've got a runner in the race, your mind is going over a million things. You're re-thinking how you've trained him, how you want him to run the race, what the ground's like . . .'

Nicky Henderson is bouncing about in a Tiggerish fashion.

'Nervous energy,' he says. 'I get like that. I think I hate the Grand National. You look forward to it all year – you think you've got the right article, but when the times comes, Jeezus . . .' He speaks quietly. 'The National is *totally* different from Cheltenham. It might not be your best horses . . . It's very big, it's got this special mystique to it, and all one says is, "Please God – let them come home." That's all we want. I hate it with a vengeance. We're masochists, aren't we! I mean, I love it dearly, but . . .

'Actually, it's the only time in the year when we go away – we go and stay up there with Bobbie McAlpine who's an owner of ours, and it's the only time in the season when we're ever not at home apart from when we go to Ireland looking for horses.'

Breakfast is served in a tent with a large fan whirling above the table – a nice irony, as the cold outside is becoming fairly serious. For those of us who rose at 4 a.m., the idea that excitement banishes hunger is a nonsense. 'I never see the racing,' says the waitress as she piles food into me, and I lace my coffee with brandy. 'Take as much as you want,' she encourages with true Scouse hospitality.

Lord Oaksey settles down with a bundle of newspapers, food relegated to second place as he ploughs through the newsprint; but since he is the second most popular quarry for the autograph hunters, he is continually interrupted. He wishes all of them a cheery 'Good Luck!' before his head sinks back into his hand as he studies the form. Out comes his pen and the scribbling begins, and then he reads to himself what he has written, mouthing the words, because he is writing his script for the cameras.

Back to the car park – the Jockey Club car park, no less, on the principle that one has to taste all life's available pleasures – to layer on more clothes. Mrs Tony Budge is being helped out of a Mercedes 560 and into mink-lined leather by her husband, and Peter O'Sullevan is looking quintessentially 1950s in mushroom sheepskin and an astrakhan hat. The first audible helicopter arrives at 10.20, and the rain is now driving down.

Police horses are sheltering under the geranium-filled hanging baskets fringing the winner's enclosure, and a 16.3 bay called Freshfields takes the eye. I should like to leap aboard and have a quick canter round to warm up. 'He's imposing but manageable,' says Sergeant George Jones. 'Just right for the job.' Already there are acres of people outside the weighing room transfixed by the sight of TV cameras, and they watch the preparations for broadcasting for all the world as if they were interesting, and in some confusion as to whether this is a horse race or a television show. Perhaps it no longer matters.

'This is holy ground,' says a right-thinking punter with a nod towards the number one spot. 'I didn't bloody come here to watch Desmond Lynham.'

More punters line up to photograph each other in front of Red Rum's statue which is buttressed by an excess of daffodils and tulips. Two small aeroplanes cavort in the sky and parachutists stream pink smoke through the rain. At 12.30 even Concorde soars over the course as racegoers in wide hats, high heels and polyester frocks pick their way through the rain to the glass-fronted corporate entertainment boxes which are packed with guests in shirt-sleeve order. The smell of roast chicken is all-pervading.

This is evidently very much a local festival.

'Where can we go?' asks a punter rhetorically.

'We can go anywhere!' replies one of his mates loudly but over-optimistically as he prepares to make nothing of petty distinctions while the security men have their concentration ruffled by small boys like minnows darting in and out of forbidden territory to cheat authority.

In the Seagram Suite, where the crème de la crème are downing champagne and realizing that the visibility of the jumps is not improved by chandeliers and swagged curtains, that most affable of men Terry Wogan is in hiding. Celebrity has driven him into the shadows – although it is less irksome here than at that other steeplechase.

'How could I, as an Irishman, go to Cheltenham?' he asks, and the familiar merry chuckle livens up a muted company.

Major Straker has an idea that the horse Seagram will do well. He had turned the horse down when trainer David Barons had offered it to him.

'I had to say no,' he says. 'But had he offered me a half-share I would have bought it immediately. David was only asking £20,000 for it, and I could have reached into my pocket and found ten, but I couldn't at the time have reached into my pocket and found twenty. He's a very economical jumper – he's just the sort of horse that might pop round the National. He's not a big horse, but a very *tidy* jumper . . .' His companion, Kay Clark, decides to plump for Seagram and places her bet with the Tote at the tiny counter in the corner of the room. She stands to win the princely sum of £76. 'I'll take him out for a drink!' she says with trans-Atlantic gusto. 'I asked Ivan last night how he would feel if it won, and he said he'd be very pleased for the horse but sad for himself, and of course, the publicity . . .'

Outside, the razzmatazz is going full bore, the noise is swelling and the cold is atrocious, but for one owner the atmosphere is going completely unnoticed.

Michael Jackson's chestnut gelding Morley Street is favourite for the Grade 1 Sandeman Aintree Hurdle and he looks dazed.

'Terrible pressure. Terrible pressure . . . merely waiting until the clock comes round to the starting time. Liverpool is a bonus really – the cake is Cheltenham, and the cherry on top of the icing is Liverpool. I've found that the further north that you go in this country, the more knowledgeable people are about racing. I think they love their racing more. If you go to Newcastle or anywhere like that, they are all form experts. They are more genuine about their love of horses and racing, and I think that shows in the way the courses are kept up here; I think the trainers demand better conditions of turf and ground from the Clerks of the Courses – the whole thing is immaculately turned out. I think they're sporting crowds up here in Liverpool and what I think is rather nice – and it reminds me of when I was a Chelsea supporter years ago – when the horses come round the first time, everybody claps. That's rather nice, isn't it? They're clapping the horses. That's rather good. Nobody's winning at that stage, it's just a horse race going on, but they're all trying.'

Morley Street wins the race as the 11–8 favourite, adding to the £252,751 prize money he has already totted up for Mr Jackson, and giving trainer Toby Balding a third victory in the race in four years. Jimmy Frost, the horse's regular pilot is delighted. 'He's very exciting, a supreme athlete,' he told me. 'A very exciting horse to ride – he's a dream. I always knew I was going to win.'

'Greatest jockey,' quips Jackson, 'let me shake your hand once more . . .', and he attempts to explain how he feels about winning. 'It's a feeling of tremendous elation. A feeling of security . . .'

Do you feel safe? I ask.

'Yes. *Absolutely* safe. I feel less threatened. I don't know what's threatening me! Life is a great problem of survival in a variety of ways; physically – and I've had five heart bypass operations, so I know a bit about *that* – and there are psychological pressures – inadequacy, lack of success . . . and winning makes a lot of those insecurities that we all have, and I have . . . go away.' His voice lightens on the last two words to levitate them into the inexplicable. 'It's a drug – it just smooths everything out. It does that to me . . .'

Seagram duly wins the National, beating Garrison Savannah who runs bravely and brilliantly to be second.

'Garrison Savannah has always been a natural jumper,' says Jenny Pitman. 'He jumps like a bunny and always has. I said to Roger when I watched him jump the fences, I said, "You're in precision engineering . . . and I saw Mark and that horse working together over those fences and it was running as smoothly and as finely as some of your engineering does, I expect." I like to watch that; I can look at a horse – the way it gallops, the way it jumps, to see the person on top of them riding them . . . I get as much pleasure out of that as somebody going to the ballet.'

CHAPTER EIGHT

From Headquarters to
God's Waiting Room

A trainer offers a piece of gratuitous advice.

'There are some serious bitches in Newmarket,' he says. Indeed – and some of them are women. The underlying theory is, we must suppose, that if you make enough noise about another man's life, your own will sneak past unnoticed.

The *mauvaise langues* twist and turn to pinpoint the illegitimate child, the redundant wife who trudges out to the gallops each morning to see 'our' horses, the owners' notorious ménage à trois with his trainer and their mistress, the selection process used to award some lady jockeys their race rides, the stolen wives and the battered wives. A proportion of the rumours will undoubtedly be true; but as the novelist cannot afford to live a life devoid of incident, so a number of trainers purposely design their lives as a source of anecdote and occasionally their zeal outruns their discretion.

'I wouldn't train in Newmarket if my life depended on it,' says Jenny Pitman. 'Bonking, booze and betting is all they think about. In which order I don't quite know!'

'You have to watch your tongue in Newmarket,' says a member of the Jockey Club. 'They're all related.'

'And if they're not related they're sleeping together,' confides another expert.

'We have had one or two divorces in the yard,' says a trainer, deflecting the attention towards his owners, but with a scintilla of chauvinism behind the admission.

Were you instrumental in these?

'Well, I think I was inasmuch as the wife probably wished that her husband was more like me. My philosophy of owners is you look after the wife and the wife will look after the husband. If you shit on the wife no matter how much the husband loves you, the horse will go. You have to keep the wife happy . . .'

What is your technique for this?

'I semi-flirt! But I always tell the truth. If anything goes wrong with the horses I tell the owner before anybody else does. It's a very small business this, and there's always somebody ready to stick a knife in your back.'

Confession now being the order of the day a second trainer chips in to agree.

'The women – the wives or whatever they are – they are the ones you have to keep happy. Never rub 'em up the wrong way or the next thing she'll say, "We'll have a yacht instead of a horse!" and you're in the wrong boat.'

A third man hints at more problems.

'I got a new owner the other day and I don't know whether I've got to give her one or not. I can't work it out yet . . .'

Do you work your way through your stable girls?

'No! I really don't fancy them . . .' He pauses and then delivers a gleeful qualification. 'Not while they're working for me!'

For one of the middle-class groupies who bob around the Newmarket trainers like talismans, this is the moment to assert herself and make sure her position in the social pecking order is understood.

'My grandmother is really cross because I'm going out with a trainer. She keeps banging on about, "He's only a *servant*, darling . . ."'

Plus ça change.

Newmarket has fifty-five trainers, nearly three thousand horses – and two thousand five hundred acres of Heath, on the ownership of which the authority of the Jockey Club is based. At the moment of writing, approximately thirty yards are said to be on the market.

'I'd hate to live and work there, to be perfectly honest,' says John Dunlop, who is the epitome of English style and trains in the shadow of Arundel Castle. 'The only attractive thing about Newmarket is its history, its traditions and the fact that it is Headquarters. There are so many horses there and it is perhaps over-utilized in some respects. And I think the feeling that everybody knows what you're planning must be disconcerting to say the least. I think it must affect what you do and how you operate.'

The lay public believes that the art of training racehorses pivots on

65

Newmarket and the name in consequence acts like a magnet for owners, particularly the newer ones.

But before questioning their assumption, it may be circumspect to consider if training racehorses is an art at all, or if it is merely a question of not screwing up the good ones.

'You've hit the nail plumb on the head,' says John Dunlop. 'I don't think it is an art in any way at all. It takes an awful lot to stop a good horse. Training is the avoidance of things going wrong.' He is speaking with the authority of a man who has trained the winners of fifteen English and Irish Classics. 'It's very easy for things to go wrong; you've got to have the right environment, the right staff, you've got to feed the horses properly, you've got to house them correctly and manage them correctly. I think you've got to be a manager, in a funny way, and with a great deal of common sense. And injuries are all-important in racing – these wretched things are so fragile. They have more problems than you could dream about. Basically, a trainer is only as good as the horse he's got to train. It's as simple as that, really.'

A brief twelve days after the National Hunt's jamboree at Aintree, Flat racing begins its frenzied quest for the season's Classic horses with the Craven Meeting at Newmarket. John Dunlop's colt Marju, having so very impressively won a minor event at York at the end of last season, is carrying the blue and white colours of Sheikh Hamdan Al-Maktoum and the prayers of a good many punters in the Craven Stakes. He had been working very lazily at home, but in the pre-parade ring his appearance denied any doubts, and some of us were certain he would win again today. The attention of the entire bloodstock world is focused on the contestants in such events as this Group 3 race, and for the trainers, this is horse racing at its most intense. The intensity this season is sharpened by the trainers' extreme concern for their continued existence in the profession.

'It's a very competitive business, racing,' says Dunlop. 'A lot of it might be in a very good-natured way, but underneath . . . it is very very competitive. It's all about winning, and particularly now and I don't know for how many years in the future, it is getting more and more competitive. Times are very hard for this industry nowadays, there's no doubt about it. It's a question of survival.' John Dunlop's habitual sang-froid barely masks his despair. When he began training at Castle House Stables, forty of his forty-five horses were owned by the Norfolk family, but this situation could no longer obtain some twenty-six years later.

'One's clientele has changed,' he says. 'The big trainers in the past trained basically for owner-breeders – the English aristocracy on the whole. Well, that breed has gone, which is sad, and now all the principal owners are Arabian. I had the first Maktoum horses. They are great enthusiasts; they want to win. They're always keen to compete successfully. The top horses – that's what they want. They're not in the least bit interested in owning moderate horses; they want the best performers.'

A while before the Craven Meeting, the Duke of Devonshire, whose ancestor the first Duke was a founder member of the Jockey Club, had spoken in the House of Lords of his conviction that racing should be fun. Some of his audience can go one better than owning a racehorse; several of them actually own racecourses. His Grace compared having a horse in training to owning a yacht and condemned those racehorse owners who bleat about the cost of their leisure activity.

Guy Harwood, another Classic-winning trainer, jibs at this comparison.

'I think what you have to remember is that we're not a participant sport. This is where all the politicians, all the newspapers and everybody get it wrong. They compare owning a racehorse to owning a yacht or going hunting, and what they forget is that when you play golf or sail a boat – *you* are actually doing it. You're driving the motor boat or putting the golf ball,' he says, his words heavy with emphasis. 'Owning a racehorse is like sending your kid to school – all you're doing is signing the cheques, so unless the owner's getting a real buzz out of it, or he's making money at it . . .'

The Duke of Devonshire believes, quite rightly, that if an owner cannot afford to pay his bills he should not be owning racehorses. To endorse his sentiment he borrows Truman's axiom: 'If you can't stand the heat', he says, 'get out of the kitchen.'

'I agree with him entirely,' says John Dunlop readily, but then he adumbrates his dilemma. 'But I'm in the secondary position; I'm like the man who builds the yachts, not the man who buys them, and if I go broke building yachts, nobody's going to subsidize me. There's a professional element if you like in both yachting and racing which has to work on a commercial basis . . .' His words trail away. 'Fun that it might be to cruise in the Aegean or race at Royal Ascot for the owners . . .'

'All that nonsense about "you shouldn't go into the kitchen . . .",' says Clive Brittain, the first Newmarket trainer to record one hundred horses in his yard: 'it's ridiculous. You need people to fund the industry. They call it a sport but so many people's lives depend on it that it's very much an industry. Unfortunately, the way the Levy's been drawn up, and the hold the bookmakers have over the money that's generated through the sport out of the punter's pocket, there's very little answer for the Jockey Club;

they can't do anything about it. I can only hope that we don't lose too many more people like the Aga Khan at the top end, and we've got to find some way of cushioning the owners at the bottom end.

'I've seen it coming,' he says. 'I'm surprised it's lasted as long as it has at the level that we're going at. It was growth, growth all the way through, but I knew it couldn't last because people are not getting any wealthier, and the average man in the street who was beginning to come into ownership certainly found that with the increase in costs, and very little chance of a return from prize money, he just couldn't cope with it. And with the escalation in the value of stallions, and you go to Keeneland and find that the Northern Dancer horses are going for ten million dollars, there's no way we could ever see that was sensible . . . We'd never be able to afford to buy those, and we are not at the bottom end of the ladder by any means. The business was over-pricing itself.'

The reasoning behind the notion that prize money either encourages people into ownership or binds them to the game once in it is, to my mind, somewhat flawed, so I asked Mr Dunlop how important prize money is to his owners.

'Funnily enough,' he says with a sniff and a small laugh, 'not as important as people pretend it is. The trouble is, too,' he adds, 'people say, "Oh, we must increase prize money . . .", but you've actually got to almost treble prize money to make it relevant. Treble it. Which means trebling the Levy and there's no way . . . Look at the comparison with other countries – South Africa has the best ratio between prize money and maintenance costs in the world. German prize money is so much better, and their costs are relatively low. French prize money is high, but their costs are high. The Arabs, too, are becoming more realistic about money; initially they couldn't care less about what it cost, but now they've got accountants who very much study the books, and they're making noises about the lack of prize money . . . Traditionally, I used to have quite a number of American owners: I've now got two, and I think for that particular reason. If they have a horse over here and it wins two or three races, they haven't paid their training bills for half a year.'

Guy Harwood draws the picture very sharply.

'In business, if you do a really good job, you make a profit. In racing, you can't make a profit. You're relying on your owners' ability to spend money, or their ability to lose money.'

To waste money?

'No, I think waste is too strong a word, because we're developing a product – we're developing a horse to make him into a good horse. We are doing something really creative. Anybody who owns a horse, they get great pleasure out of it. But what I think is unfair is that there is no *chance* for them to be profitable. And, therefore, we're selling a business which is very difficult to make profitable, which makes it vulnerable, very vulnerable indeed, and we are very vulnerable indeed at the moment. And we *shouldn't* be vulnerable because the betting industry here is a very big industry, and the success of that business is partly due to the product and the effort we put into it. And I think, therefore, that it's a crying shame that our industry has been so badly administered.'

Is the Jockey Club in any way up to it?

'There's no doubt that in the fifties and sixties when the opportunities were there to run racing and betting in harmony without any problem whatsoever, they weren't up to it. Why should they be up to it? Why should one hundred and twenty people doing something for nothing . . . There is no possible way that twelve amateurs can run racing.'

Now he adds another essential detail.

'I am not in favour of change for change's sake, and you've got to make sure what comes in its place is better than what went before. We need money very *badly*, so it has to be someone who has the ability to take on the bookmakers and the government head-on. It cannot be your existing Stewards or their executives. They're just not big enough to do it.'

I ask him if the government's awful disinterest in the horse-racing industry compounds the problems.

'Yes, terrible. The complete ignorance too. I can almost forgive them for fucking racing up – I can't forgive them for fucking up the economy because at least racing can survive if they run the country properly.'

As long as there is a leisure pound it will be spent on racing, I imagine?

'Yes. That's right. So long as they run the economy properly,' he reiterates. 'But I've seen six of my owners go broke, bust or skint in the last twelve months. I think they have made the most diabolical job of running the economy and what is so annoying is that they still don't seem to realize how serious it is. Of course racing should be fun, but a hundred odd thousand of us are totally reliant on it for a living.'

At Newmarket, on Craven day, Guy Harwood is suffering a further handicap aside from governmental incompetence. He has a leg in plaster and is making a halting but determined progress on crutches. 'I'm not really in any pain at all, fortunately, but running round the racecourse on crutches is hard work,' he reports in his idiosyncratically crisp, "Reach For The Sky" manner. He might well have crashed-landed his Spitfire on a dangerous mission over enemy territory rather than succumbing to a tennis injury.

'He is intensely accessible and a charming fellow,' recalls owner Christopher Bridge. 'He had all these owners who've won huge races and he treated me, I think, more than fairly. And he's got no horsey background at all. Absolutely none. I can remember seeing his daughter Amanda when she was tiny watching the string canter by, and she knew every single horse by sight and by name at the age of ten. I met him through a friend of mine in the Jockey Club. He's honest, hard-working and not spoilt. Honesty, I think, is what you require from a trainer. And I quite like to be told if there's a horse in the stable that's going to run quite well next Saturday. I don't mind a little touch. I'm not a big gambler. I like a punt. Very small. I learned in my Cambridge University days before the War that that was the one way of real ruin. I found myself with half a year's allowance on one race at Newmarket – and then losing!' His laugh is brittle and dismissive: his looks are of the enslaving kind, and the mind slips easily past what he is saying to a silk dressing gown, a long cigarette holder and 'very flat, Norfolk . . .' Ask him what winning is like, and he says, 'Indescribable. It's the most extraordinary sensation. Don't think there's anything comparable. And the smaller the margin of victory, the greater the joy.

'I always used to say when they won, "What's next?" but Guy was very good – he used to say, "You're not going to win any Classics with this horse." '

Hope, of course, springs more eternally in racing than anywhere else.

'But I don't know . . . this filly I've got now with John Dunlop is very well-bred . . . Guy Harwood bought me my first horse, and I called it Hollow Laughter. It was out of Wolver Hollow, and my friends thought that was rather good. It was quite cheap and it looked a total dud, but she went to Brighton and, my God, she won! We never expected it, and we cashed in smartly – sold her, and made a small profit. 100 per cent ownership is now too expensive, so I've gradually gone downhill and I'm only in a syndicate on a 10 per cent basis.'

Does that in any way equate with outright ownership?

'No. Course it doesn't. But I think Sue Abbott who runs this syndicate in John Dunlop's yard is full of energy, and she charges a very reasonable percentage on management. They made her a member of the Jockey Club. Quite right too. She's done nothing but good.'

Trapped these days by a wheelchair, Christopher Bridge is unable to go racing, and he must hope that the filly performs in a race which is good enough to be televised. 'My colours have been resuscitated because my name has come to the top of Sue's list, so I hope you'll see them this year; I think they're rather attractive. Eton blue cap, a red body and Eton blue and red stripes down the sleeves.' Eton, of course. 'I've never failed to win with a horse until this last one, which is astonishingly lucky. And my old friend William Douglas-Home, he . . .' (quick laugh) 'owned horses for twenty-one years before he had a winner. And when he eventually had a winner,' (slightly longer laugh) 'it was ridden by Lester Piggott. John Oaksey said he thought Willie was going to kiss' (smoker's cough) 'Lester Piggott on both cheeks! He's a changed man, Piggott, isn't he? I suppose a little bit of prison didn't do him any harm.'

One sentiment shared by Messrs Dunlop, Harwood and Bridge is that Australia is the country which runs its horse racing with greater efficiency than any other.

'I cannot see', says Harwood, 'how *any trainer* in England barring the number I can count on one hand has *any* chance of making a living outside of betting. I cannot see how they can possibly do it. And that doesn't bode well for the future.'

I yield to no one in my admiration for the top trainers; they should have wealth beyond the dreams of avarice heaped upon them for their bravery and fortitude. There is a nobility of purpose in preparing a horse for one big race – getting it right for that one big day so that it can run for its life in the great tradition of training and with the highest ideals and intentions. The win-a-week boys (or win-a-day) are number-crunching, and I should not care to over-estimate someone who gets to the top of the table by doing that. To run a horse which is sore to win a piddling little race may be better than putting a bullet in it, but it's not racing.

Beside the pre-parade ring at Newmarket, Grahame Waters is watching his fellow owner Sheikh Hamdan who in turn is watching his handsome colt, Marju. Waters decides that Marju is going to carry his money in the Craven, and makes off for the bookmakers. On the way he spots a fast food stall.

'Look at that, Glen,' he says, drawing his wife's attention to the goods on sale. '£1.50 for a baked potato. We're in the wrong business . . .'

Their business is a caravan park in Clacton-on-Sea, or 'God's Waiting Room', as he calls it, and the previous day I had driven into the bleakness of an out-of-season resort, past the greasy pewter sea to Sacketts Grove Holiday Park and Grahame Waters' views on Arab owners.

'I think it's them and us. There are two different leagues. Look at the runners declared for the big races: there's eight or ten owned by these guys. They're buying success and forcing people like myself out of the game. And there again, you go to the all-weather tracks, and they've paid half a million for something that hasn't made it in a Group race or a Listed race, and you suddenly find you're up against it. But that's their prerogative. It's an open market. But what chance does a little fellow like me have unless he gets an exceptionally good horse?'

An exceptionally good horse is precisely what Grahame Waters did get. Spindrifter won thirteen races for him as a two-year-old.

Mr Waters' entry into ownership was a touch unconventional. Bombed out of Lambeth as a child during the Blitz, he was sent to Cornwall where he remembers sitting on a pony and announcing he was going to win the Derby; but his first constructive move towards that goal did not come until 1978.

'I went to Newmarket races, and I'd never been to Tattersalls so I went there and this little filly came up. I thought she looked sweet so I bid thirteen hundred guineas and bought her.' He had launched himself into the unknown.

What did you think you were going to do with it?

'He didn't think,' says his wife, Glenda.

'I didn't think,' he agrees. 'If I do something, I do it. I didn't even know where I'd got to pay for it . . . and I phoned a neighbour up and told him I'd bought a horse. He said, "Where are you?" I said Tattersalls, and he said, "Naah . . . you haven't bought a horse there, have you?" "Yeah," I said, "a real *race*horse!" So excited, you know! He arrived with a horsebox about ten to nine. Everybody'd gone. He swore at me right left and centre, and then we tried to load it. And after being strangled with the rope ourselves, we eventually brought her home and I became "Master Trainer". I put her in the paddock at the back of the bungalow. I walked her three or four miles every day.'

Where?

'Up and down the streets. I'd had greyhounds for sixteen years and it was very similar.' To the ex-Guardsman, a 14.2 filly was toy-sized. 'Then she started getting a bit full of herself . . .'

'She started pulling him round and round the lampposts every few hundred yards, and he thought it was time for her to go somewhere else!' adds Glen, who is a ferocious giggler.

The filly was broken and he was advised to put her into training.

'Knowing absolutely nothing about trainers, I said, "Who do I put her with?" and I was told, "If you can stick one particular feller, go to him," and that was Sir Mark Prescott. She ran four times for us – twice being third and twice second – and then she was claimed by Jack Berry. Anyway, I told Mark I'd lost my Oaks winner, and he said, "Thank God for that. That horse will never win a bloody race." The following year, the first race she ran for Jack Berry at Thirsk, she won.'

Your trainer's reaction?

'Changed the subject. I was scolded by him never to buy another horse on my own, which was very wise. We went to Goffs with him and there was this little colt for sale which had a very nice stamp to him, but in my opinion the person selling him hadn't really done his job for a harvest – he was turned out poorly for a sale. Sir Mark had to go to ten thousand guineas for him, and Glen was sitting there saying, *"Ten thousand pounds ...?"* Sir Mark said, "Don't worry about it; if you don't want him, I'll have half with you." But I've never had partnerships with anybody, so I turned to Mark and said, "He's mine." And that was Spindrifter.'

In the middle of February, Sir Mark rang me up and said, "I think you have something very nice here." In April he ran his first race at Hamilton, and as we approached the course his words to me were that if he does not win, we'll carry on to John O'Groats. We won't be coming back to Newmarket ... So – out come every penny out of every pocket I had. Anyway, the horse won and then we went from race to race enjoying ourselves. After his sixth or seventh race, somebody said to me, "What do you get out of it?" and at the time, not knowing anything about racing really, I said, "It's the glory." That's how I felt – glory. Winning with him made me feel like a king. We're only run-of-the-mill people; we're not the Sangsters of this world. In those days, with Spinnie, it was glory ... But we lost him ...'

Can you talk about it?

'I can now. At the time I couldn't. I went to my office one morning and Mark phoned me at ten past eight. He said, "I've got some bad news for you. I've just had to put the horse down. He got kicked on the Heath and I had to shoot him." He could barely speak, and when he told me it was Spinnie, and not the other horse we had with him, I could not answer him. I left my office – it was about twenty past then – and Glen was walking over and the tears were coming down my face ...'

'I thought someone had died in the family,' she says.

'My tongue came up, double the size. I couldn't speak. After about thirty-five minutes I was back on the phone to Prescott – "I don't want him to go to the slaughterhouse! I want to bury him! I want to bury him!" I was in shock, if you like. The tears were coming down my face. Couldn't talk to anybody. The next morning I shot over to Newmarket in my car – we had this other horse and I feel if I hadn't gone, I'd've packed up there and then. We were on the Heath and Michael Stoute came across first on his hack, touched his cap, and said he was sorry about yesterday.

'He did go to the slaughterhouse. We had the shoes mounted and I gave Sir Mark one, I gave the lad who looked after him one, George Duffield one and kept one myself. Just as a memento.'

He had a good life, I venture. And I get the answer I deserve.

'He could've had a longer life, couldn't he? I took it on the chin. I didn't know what had happened, but obviously people tried to tell me . . . he got kicked . . . but you can't bring back the dead, can you? I never said to Mark it was anybody's fault and I think he appreciated that I didn't make a fuss. I don't think anyone could have a worse thing than losing a horse like Spinnie. His leg was too shattered . . .'

Grahame Waters quickly recovers his equilibrium.

'He made me feel like a king! Every winner's a Derby winner to me. Of course, you know I've got fifty horses, don't you? Every one in Sir Mark's yard is mine! I like to be among horses – I dream of having twenty acres with about six paddocks and four mares and swearing at anybody who drives fast down the drive. My wife won't let me: we live in Florida for about twenty weeks of the year and she won't forgo that – after thirty-four years we'd be getting a divorce!

'After the loss of Spindrifter, we still had his half-sister, Amboselli, but she broke her pelvis doing a light canter up the Heath and I thought I'd become a breeder! Ten years ago it wasn't too bad to be a breeder. I *love* the time with the foals being born; I'm like an expectant father! She's at the Rossmore Stud in Ireland. Her second foal wasn't very big, he was a little bit of a rabbit I think the term is – but we saved him. Sir Mark came across and saw him as a yearling – and thought "My God" – and when the horse came over to Newmarket in October, I know for a fact he said to people, "If I can get this to win it'll be a bloody miracle." He was that bad! But he turned out to be Nicky Dow, and he won a 21-horse race at Windsor as a two-year-old from the worst possible draw, and we gambled him from 12–1. And it was a claimer, and after the race I had this little carrier with money in. Prescott was chasing me round, "Quick, quick . . . give me four thousand – we're not going to lose him!" because somebody had put a claim in and we didn't have a cheque book between us and we had to put some money on the table.

'That was a new experience,' says Glen. 'Buying our own horse!'

Grahame and Glen Waters, having enjoyed racing's glittering prizes and endured its bitter disappointments, understand as well as anyone that the racehorse owner has no more right to look forward than a lover in the arms of his mistress.

'We're not in the racing world,' he says with outrageous modesty. 'We're just involved with Sir Mark, and if he packed up training, I'd go out of racing. He may have the upper crust in his yard, but we're the bread and butter. I don't like snobs. I'm not in the same class as some of them, but I enjoy my racing more I think than 90 per cent of them.'

Back at the Craven, Marju wins the races and is top-quoted at 7–2 for the Two Thousand Guineas – the first Classic race of the season for colts – and John Dunlop tells the press it was a very good run by a green horse who had not been pleasing at home. 'I wouldn't have been more surprised if he'd finished last rather than first,' he says. 'Training is not a black and white matter.'

In the very next race, yet again, everything turned up trumps. Mrs Julie Cecil saddled her very first winner since taking out a licence the previous November and establishing herself in Newmarket's Hamilton Road at Southgate Stables. It was ridden by Lester Piggott, who had met her when she was ten and he was the eighteen-year-old jockey to her father, Noel Murless. He kissed her as he dismounted, and the whole of the racing world joined in with their congratulations: she was kissed by every trainer one had ever heard of, with the exception of her ex-husband who shook her hand.

'Owned by Lord Howard de Walden, ridden by Lester and here at Newmarket . . . wasn't it wonderful!' enthused a member of the Jockey Club. 'Marvellous!' said another. 'Bloody cheeky race as well . . . The Craven Stakes has gone into the background after that . . .', and everyone was content.

CHAPTER NINE

'Shout? I don't know that I shout . . .'

Driving down the High Street of Yorkshire's great training centre of Malton with Flat race trainer Charles Benjamin Brodie Booth is not without its dangers. The sword of Damocles threatens to fall.

'We've just got to get past Barclays Bank now without being seen,' he warns, and in a defiant sentence spells out the perils of his profession.

'They're all whingeing in Newmarket now because there's all these yards for sale. I'm *so* sorry for them!' he mocks, the voice booming. 'I've been chasing my arse since I left school! I shall be chasing my backside when I die! I've struggled since the day I left school – with nothing – and I've got nothing now. This lot is just learning what struggle means. We've been struggling for bloody years in the north – nothing's new!'

But Charles ('Shout? I don't know that I shout . . .') Booth is one of the last Romantics for whom the worst of all possible solutions is compromise, and he squares up to the challenge of training until and beyond the last moment of financial disaster for the very best of all possible reasons: that come hell or high water, this is what he wants to do.

He trains the animals in his care as if they were all Classic contenders. 'But that's what I would call training racehorses,' he says. 'I train my horses as if they were all nice horses; that's how I was brought up. There are a lot of people with trainer's licences; there are very few trainers. I don't think it's their fault; it's a sign of the times. Some people hate their bloody horses – they're just a means to an end. I *love* horses. We don't have many runners and we don't have many winners. I don't see the point of running horses for the hell of it; when they're ready, the buggers'll run. One of my owners rang me up the other day and he said, "Charles! Henry

Cecil has got a four-year-old maiden. There's somebody else like you!"'

One of Charles Booth's more frequent insults is unique. 'It's not their bloody fault they're English,' he says sardonically. 'Good luck to them!' and he derives an inordinate satisfaction from the fact that the bottom line of his pedigree is Italian. But while the *brio* is unquestionably Mediterranean, it is difficult for the naked eye to discern any Latin influence. Admittedly he does favour tinted spectacles and a cigarette is never far from his lips, but the crumpled check shirt, the baggy cords, the flat cap and the brogues – the brogues which are about to give up the unequal struggle ('Jeezus Christ, more expense . . .') are the standard camouflage of the Englishman. So was the public-school education. 'Uppingham,' he thunders. 'A very very good school for racehorse trainers. Robert Armstrong and I were in the same house together.

'I made a lot of money out of punting when I was a boy. I used to bet with William Hill in those days. I got caught. I had a very big win and it went round the school like wildfire. The old man said, "If you want to train racehorses you don't need a bloody university education,' so I wrote to hundreds of trainers for a job, and they all said I was too big and too heavy. Then Bill Elsey took me on as a pupil when I was seventeen, and I've been involved ever since.

'It's a wonderful life. It *is* a wonderful life. As long as you can sort out the good guys from the prats, and any trainer who tells you he works hard is telling you bloody lies.

'I love getting hold of a racehorse and training it; getting a raw recruit and making it into a racehorse – seeing it improve. I was born and bred in the hunting field, but I've always loved the Flat. I'm not a snob, but I basically couldn't walk out into the yard and look at a load of great big heavyweight hunters. Anything can win a jumping race – if it was bred by The Mucksack out of the Feedpot – but if you buy The Mucksack out of Feedpot on the Flat, you're going to be very lucky to win a contest. If somebody said to me tomorrow, "You can go out and buy fifty yearlings, Charlie, and you can spend what you like," I could go out and buy a nice horse or two. But when you come up to *my* end of the market . . . I'd make a bloody sight better job of it than these star turns that the Sheikhs employ. Most of these guys buy pedigrees and you go to the races and you think, "What the *hell* did you buy that bloody thing for?" But it's like everything else, if you're buying two hundred you haven't got to be very bright to buy a good horse. It's very difficult when you only buy seven or eight a year, but every year I've had a nice horse. Every year without fail. Mademoiselle Chloe, she cost me ten grand and was beaten three lengths in the Cheveley Park.'

Mademoiselle Chloe created a singular dilemma for Charles Booth, and one which an outsider could find very perverse.

'Life runs so sweetly if you don't train any winners,' he says. 'As soon as you start training winners, all the other owners want to know why their horse isn't bloody winning.'

You can't win?

'You can't win. No way. You cannot win. When I trained Chloe, there was more aggravation with Chloe than if it'd been a selling plater. If it'd been a selling plater there would have been no worries. But Chloe became the property of the North of England, and everybody wanted to know what she was doing . . . *and* she was being trained in half the golf clubs in north London. I love training fillies. I love them. They try harder . . . Until two years ago and Chloe I'd always dreamt of having a yard full of machines. A yard full of Cecil horses, or Cumani horses, and then two years ago I got a machine which would hold her own with any of them. I was spellbound watching her work. Absolutely spellbound. I *long* for another Chloe . . .'

Gravel Pit Farm where Charles Booth train lies north of the city of York in the Howardian Hills with the Palladian magnificence of Castle Howard just across the fields. In the summer, hollyhocks colonize the garden along with lupins and lavender, red hot pokers and golden rod, and roses clamber all over the apple trees; but now we must content ourselves with the bright yellow forsythia. The trainer leans on the stone wall and looks towards the more distant hills on the skyline beyond Malton.

'Yorkshire is probably my ruination. I shouldn't be up here. If I trained in Newmarket there is no doubt in my mind that I would have a hundred horses: I couldn't train a hundred horses – but I would definitely have fifty horses. The trouble is, I can't stand Newmarket. And of course half the buggers in Newmarket shouldn't be training horses anyway. I did leave Malton for a while and I couldn't wait to get back. If I didn't train in Yorkshire, I'd train in Berkshire – that's my kind of country. There's clowns there too . . . There are very few racehorse *trainers* as such today and that is because owners won't *let* them train. The type of people who own racehorses these days don't bloody understand racehorses. Thirty years ago when I was at Bill Elsey's, everybody understood horses. They knew that you don't just get on them and switch on. I got a horse the other day and I'd only had it three minutes before the man wanted to know when it was going to *run!*

'During the big York meeting we have P. Walwyn and J. Dunlop standing on the Langton gallops here and saying, "I didn't know you had these sort of facilities here!"' He mimics Peter Walwyn with pinpoint accuracy, and then says, 'Christ Almighty! Some of the best horses that have ever looked through a bridle have been trained in Malton. And racehorse trainers in those days *were* racehorse trainers – not like us today. The bloody horses had to work for a living. The art of training racehorses is you don't gallop them to get them fit – you get them fit to gallop. That is the art. The modern-day man thinks all he's got to do is go like lickety-split from A to bloody B and his horse will get fit. I'm afraid the modern-day lad is a bit the same. They don't understand that a horse wants to be on the bridle and *pull* you to the top of the bloody gallops. If a Newmarket jockey came here and rode work, by the time his horse was halfway up the hill it would *walk* because he would go too fast. I remember the famous day when I was standing at the top of the hill up there and there was a horse of Peter Easterby's going round the mile and a half. Now Peter Easterby's gallops are as flat as a board, and by the time this horse had got seven furlongs, it was walking. And it was Sea Pigeon. A week later he won the Champion Hurdle, and going round here he couldn't put one leg in front of the other because they'd gone too fast. I go up to those gallops most Sunday mornings, and there's nothing *nicer* than being there with six horses and watching them work against that backcloth – there's nothing like it. And a little bit of a crack with the other trainers . . .'

The tune of music hall is always audible in Charles Booth's performances. There are echoes of Max Miller in the timing and repetition – 'Now here's a funny thing . . .' he might say as he beckons down the limelight and the better horses that would go with it.

'There was a horse on the gallops the other day,' he begins, 'and the trainer was trying to get a pair of blinkers on it. Now . . . I suppose it's because of my size, but there isn't a horse born that I'm frightened of. I suppose it's because they don't look so awesome to me. I'm bigger than them. Well, this trainer couldn't get near it, so I said, "What's the matter with you?" "Oh, watch 'im! Watch 'im!" he said. I said, "Watch him? The bloody thing isn't big enough to hurt you. Come here . . ." and I grabbed hold of it and put the blinkers on, and the trainer stood back and said, "Fookin' 'ell. I couldn't't've done that. 'e would've 'ad me . . ."'

He walks into his yard, and the horses gaze after him.

'They're my best friends. Happy as Larry.' He pauses at the open door to one box. 'This is a horse very similar to me: his best performance is at the feed trough.' The girl grooming the animal giggles.

'He's a fat horse . . .' she says.

'He's called Milton Rooms,' continues the trainer, 'because he's by Where To Dance and I used to do all my boogying in the Milton Rooms in Malton. He's going to be ridden by one of the stars of Emmerdale in the morning. A female. We only have females here.' He walks out of the box and lowers his voice to an uncharacteristic whisper so that the Fates cannot eavesdrop. 'Happy horses, happy staff, theoretically should win races . . .' The volume returns to normal. 'This is a lovely yearling by Midian. We bought her at the December sales and she's a little bit hot. You'll have to learn to settle down, won't you?' Right on cue, it fly-bucks across the box and the trainer's voice erupts with disapproval. 'YOU ARE A BAD-TEMPERED LITTLE BUGGER!'

A round-faced blonde girl is grooming a cheerless brown gelding in the next box.

'Trish has had her hair permed and she knows I don't like it . . .', he announces. 'She's been here fourteen years,' he adds, as if to excuse the personal remarks. 'This horse has just come to me from one of the most successful trainers in the country, and he was so wrong in his back that he was unable to gallop. He just couldn't. He looks a lot happier than he did. I think we'll quarter-mark him in the end.' He takes a stable rubber and tries. 'Nearly . . . He's not there yet, but he's not far off. In those big yards they don't get the attention they ought to get.'

The kitchen is so near to the boxes that the horses' wickering mingles with the loud ticking of the wall clock. An elderly dalmatian with brown spots and rheumy eyes grins at her master. There is a headcollar on the doorknob and a motto on the wall which reads, 'When there are horses to train and race, women and wine take second place.'

'It's not true,' reflects the trainer. 'I think women would possibly still . . . Well, it's very close. Very close.' He brews up more tea and describes his current owners. 'Not all those horses out there will win,' he says by way of introduction, 'but providing the owners are happy, I'm happy. I get a hell of a buzz when I get a winner, a hell of a buzz. I've been close to tears when I've had a winner. But winning isn't everything because basically my job is to keep my owners happy. As long as they're happy I'm happy because I want them to reinvest. There are very few trainers who enjoy their owners going to the yard. I *love* them to come: it's party time, providing they come when I say come. When the horses win – my owners are very generous. They are very generous,' he reiterates. 'In fact, to a man, if I was in big trouble, they would bail me out. To a man. They work hard, and they play hard and when they come up they treat us very well. Whenever they have a winner, they give the lad a hundred quid. Every time, they get a note. Sasha sends them *a note*.' He emphasizes his appreciation. 'And they write back and thank him for it because I make sure they do. The other day he had a winner and he wanted to give the jockey money. I said, "No, bugger the bloody jockey. He's had plenty out of it as it is. The buggers get over-paid as it is." Course, he's never been used to that. He'd always been in a yard where it was on his bill.

'I've been very lucky as a trainer – most of the owners that I've had have been reasonable, but I have had a few star turns.

'I had a man that nearly bankrupt me. I had to go out and buy three yearlings for him and of course once you buy a yearling, it's devalued. The whole yard nearly had to go. I'd had the man in the yard five years – never reneged on his bills or anything; I thought I knew the guy. But he owed me a lot of money on those yearlings. We also had a guy who went to gaol for fraud, and I sold his horse, for a lot of money. I told him to come up for the cheque and he came with his heavies. I'd got the readies for the horse even though it hadn't gone – I'd moved it into a box in Malton. "I've come up for the seventy five grand, mate," he said. "I'll get the cheque cashed – make sure it goes through, then I'll bung you what I owe you." I said, "Yes – fair enough," and then presented him with a cheque for thirteen grand. "Where's the rest of it?" I said, "You owe me the rest of it . . ." "I'm going to stop the sale!" "You can't. The horse is halfway across the Atlantic. It's been paid for, the passport's gone and the horse's gone." So one of his henchmen walked out of the house and I sniggered to myself, and he came back in and said, " 'es not 'ere, guv . . ." And he left with his tail between his legs. About a month later the police arrived on the place. He'd been lent a million pounds on false number plates to buy fictitious vehicles, and he'd told them I had two of them here. Ended up in gaol for three years. Oh, he was a star. We've learned by our mistakes.'

Nevertheless, an owner may still surprise a trainer to the point where he begins to wonder if there is anything at all behind ownership other than a desire to make mischief. Charles Booth lights another cigarette and pushes his spectacles up his nose.

'I lost a horse the other day . . . you wouldn't believe this – well, you might believe this, I've heard of it happening before, but it's never happened to me . . . I had two winners at Ayr the other day, and a man took his horse away because I didn't ring him up and tell him to back them! I never do. It was a new owner, he'd been on the yard about three months, and he probably thought I should ring up. Christ Almighty! I've got enough to do without ringing them up and telling them to back a horse. And I've always felt that people don't mind paying training fees, but as soon as you start punting for them, and they start losing . . . that's when they move on.'

Sasha Lyons is a dapper city slicker who started betting at school when he was evacuated from central London to Somerset at the beginning of the War. 'In those days, gambling was rather a funny affair – totally illegal, and the bookie operated from a shed in a garden and that's where one placed one's sixpenny bets!' he says. Now, with companies in London, Frankfurt and Brussels, his racing interest centres on ownership, and he chooses to have his horses trained in Yorkshire to offset the lack of prize money on offer in this country. 'It costs me only about 60 per cent to train up in the north compared with Newmarket so therefore one can win fewer races because you've got to win at least five races a season to cover your costs. In France, two races will do the trick. In South Africa, *one* race will do the trick.'

Finance notwithstanding, Sasha Lyons' enthusiasm for racing knows no bounds.

'I remember when we first started and we went out on the gallops the horses were just four-legged animals galloping round; I didn't even know which were mine. Now I can tell mine a mile off, and I can give *my* ten pence worth at the sales. I was at Chantilly on Tuesday looking at a horse I've bought in France. I thought we were just going to see it in the yard but the trainer had obviously decided to give us the full treatment and wanted us to see it on the gallops. I'm not really a country boy. We weren't dressed for it. We had to traipse through mud. I told him afterwards, "I'm going to deduct the cost of a new pair of shoes from your training bill!" I did think of more involvement with my brood mares when I retire, but I can't see myself running around in Wellingtons.'

He values a hands-on approach to training, thrilling to a frisson of excitement derived from a pursuit the businessman in him regards as dicey to say the least.

'For people like the smaller trainers, it's a vocation rather than a job. I tell you what amazes me so . . .', he confides, 'I find trainers are very uncommercial. I suppose some of the Newmarket boys make money. Must do. They all drive flashy cars; they wear good clothes; they go off to Barbados in the winter . . . The top boys don't do badly out of it at all. There's their cut of the prize money, there are presents from grateful owners, some of them bet as well – but it's hard work.'

As a promotional exercise for Innovative Marketing International, one of his companies, Sasha Lyons sponsors a race day each year in May at York, which is a favourite course. A charter train leaves Kings Cross (for a mere £8,000) carrying his sixty or so personal guests and enough champagne to float the Titanic. Michelle Lyons, his wife and business partner, is in a fetching pale pink Chanel number and iced with covetable diamonds, and she always makes sure there is a prize for 'the best dressed horse.' Sasha's son is intrigued to see that Bobby Charlton is responsible for the training of one of today's runners: he has seen the name R. Charlton beside Sky Prospect in the 4.40, and the remainder of the company still capable of speech falls to a discussion of the relative merits of Sevruga and Oscietra caviar.

Poured out of the train and into boxes in the grandstand, there is lunch followed pell-mell by a sumptuous tea, and when I gamely totter out to enjoy several of the races I hear – through a haze of pleasure – a protesting voice. 'You *what?*' it says. 'Jockeys? Bloody jockeys – they're a liability. Over-rated, over-paid, one remove from stable lads and if they had any brains they wouldn't've gone into racing. *They* don't know. They don't bloody know. They're only like vets; they only guess.' Charles Benjamin Brodie Booth has stumbled across one of his favourite targets for abuse and is enjoying himself no end.

Delusions of Grandeur

Reality so quickly becomes a memory in racing, but Mystiko's dazzling front-running victory in the General Accident Two Thousand Guineas was a reality which both vindicated trainer Clive Brittain's policy of cock-eyed optimism, and proved a turning-point in his long career which already boasted a string of international successes and two previous Classic triumphs.

The $150,000 grey Secreto colt, owned by the 82-year-old Dowager Lady Beaverbrook, had already shown a tremendous turn of foot on the Rowley Mile when taking the European Free Handicap a few weeks before, but now it is May and the mutterings around the pre-parade ring are devaluing the colt's ability. His stamina, they say, is in doubt, and he certainly has no right to claim favouritism. The stuffed shirts in racing cannot sometimes disguise a gut feeling that anyone – and Clive Brittain is one such – who began their racing career as a stable lad is suffering from delusions of grandeur when he takes to training. They blame it all on the Sixties and the modern type of owner who wanted to be impressed not by the crusty old men steeped in the great traditions of training racehorses, but by the grassroots boys. Clive Brittain, however, never troubles himself with his stake in the status quo. He is too busy enjoying himself.

'The boss is as sound as a pound,' says his travelling head lad, John Spouse, who has worked in racing all around the world. 'You couldn't wish for a better man. He's always laughing!'

Guarded by Burglar, the Jack Russell which looks as if it knows far too much for its own good, Mr Brittain sinks into a leather armchair in his immaculate Newmarket home in the Bury Road, and tells his story.

'I'm one of thirteen children; I was about seventh, I think. The clothes got handed down, but luckily there was a nearly equal number of girls and boys so we got round that one all right! My father worked in Harris's bacon factory in Calne, Wiltshire, and my brother and sisters all followed him there, but I was always interested in horses.

'I used to steal rides when I was about six on the ponies belonging to a livery yard. No tack – just a rope headcollar, and ride them round the fields till I got caught, and the owner gave me a job after kicking me up the backside! I started to break in ponies when I was about eight years old. We got the ponies semi-broke before we ever put the tack on them by just jumping on and off, and I got away with it for about three years before I broke my collar bone. My parents weren't very happy because they never used to see me, but at least my mother knew where I was! He only had one field, this chap I used to work for, but depending on the sales, he could have anything up to twenty horses, so my job last thing at night was to open somebody's gate wide enough for the horses, herd them in, and leave the gate just ajar. I had to get up early in the morning to get them out again before the farmers came down!'

His first racing job was in a flapping yard in Bristol, but he had got himself known in Noel Murless's Beckhampton yard by walking the six miles over the Downs to see his string out at exercise during his school holidays, and in 1949 he started a five-year apprenticeship there. Thus began his association with top-class horses.

'I had a lot of fun,' he says, 'but I never got a ride while I was serving my time, partly because it being a big yard, there was very few opportunities, and I suppose I wasn't good enough, anyway! At sixteen I was five and a half stone, and I boxed in the Stable Lads' Championships at Marlborough two years.' With his present head lad, with whom he served his time, Brittain moved to Newmarket with his guv'nor, and then went into the Army. He was one of the 'poor bloody infantry', but even that failed to stem the exuberance. 'There was good days and bad days,' he recalls, 'but if you don't enjoy yourself, nobody's going to do it for you.' Another of the Brittain aphorisms which make light of any situation.

'I never did get to head lad; I was one of the senior staff, but like me now, his staff were with him for years so there was no chance of promotion. I don't take too many apprentices because I don't think it's fair, either to the horses, or on the apprentices themselves. There's very few of them going to make jockeys anyway: that's a certainty. Mainly it's the very ambitious ones that gets the rides because they put extra into the riding, and I don't reward lazy people, so if they're not putting 100 per cent into their work, then I don't give them 100 per cent of my time. I sometimes think it's better if they come in green, and they're schooled in *how* to ride and any bad habits, you stamp on straight away. They're not worked all that hard to start with; they skivvy for the other lads, but they're not taken advantage of; having been through it myself, I don't want anyone to be unhappy. If they are going to go, they usually go in the first week or ten days. They get homesick, and the door bell goes at about 9.30 in the evening, and you can see a little tear-stained face, "I wanna go home . . ."'

'I did twenty-three years with Sir Noel, and when he was beginning to talk about retirement, it suddenly dawned on me, who the hell am I going to work for now? I've never really worried about what's going to happen next year before this year's over – I'm not that sort, and the idea of training didn't really appeal to me that much.'

Eventually, however, he was persuaded by the promise of horses to train that he should give it a go, and he and his wife Maureen, who had been secretary to Sir Noel, began to look for training premises.

'All the stables in Newmarket were handed down from father to son, and trainer to assistant, so there was very little chance of taking over an established yard, but there was just this one yard that came on the market, so I took a three-year lease on it, and spent a year doing it up. I couldn't afford to take a year off to do it; I'd had one or two tidy little bets through the years, and got a nice few quid behind me, but really I couldn't afford to put everything into the yard, and I had to make it pay from the very first day I opened it up as a stable. I was going in there in the afternoons and evenings, and all weekends. The lofts had been used as chicken sheds so we had to get all the manure out and scrub it down, and when I say "we" – there was a site foreman building some houses on the other side of Pegasus, and his daughter had got two little ponies and he didn't know what to do with them and I didn't know much about laying concrete, so we brought the ponies into the yard while he did the concreting. We had thirty-eight horses to start with, and at one stage there was one lad and me to look after them.'

There is one maxim he has learned over the years which he holds more sacred than any other.

'Training is full-time PR,' says Clive Brittain. 'This is the entertainment business.

'You have to keep in touch with owners and let them know they're needed. If all they're getting out of it is bills and the odd day at the races, it's not enough. We have owners down for breakfast and lunch, and it's all

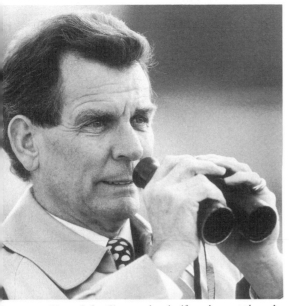

Above left: 'You can't win if you're not there,' says super-optimist Clive Brittain

Above right: 'A trainer is only as good as the horse he's got to train,' says John Dunlop. 'It's as simple as that'

Below: 'The tougher the times the more the owners need looking after!' says Guy Harwood at Coombelands

Right: 'The choice is a simple one between progress and stagnation.' The Senior Steward sums up the dilemma facing the Sport of Kings

Far right: Would you accept membership of the Jockey Club? 'Good God, yes!' exclaims the Baroness Trumpington. 'I love my racing'

Below left: 'Racing must speak with one voice,' says owner and Jockey Club member Tony Budge

Below right: 'I always look a worried man on a racing day, but I love every minute of it!' says Nick Cheyne, Clerk of the Course at Sandown

Opposite: A great racehorse: Generous, winner of the 1991 Epsom Derby

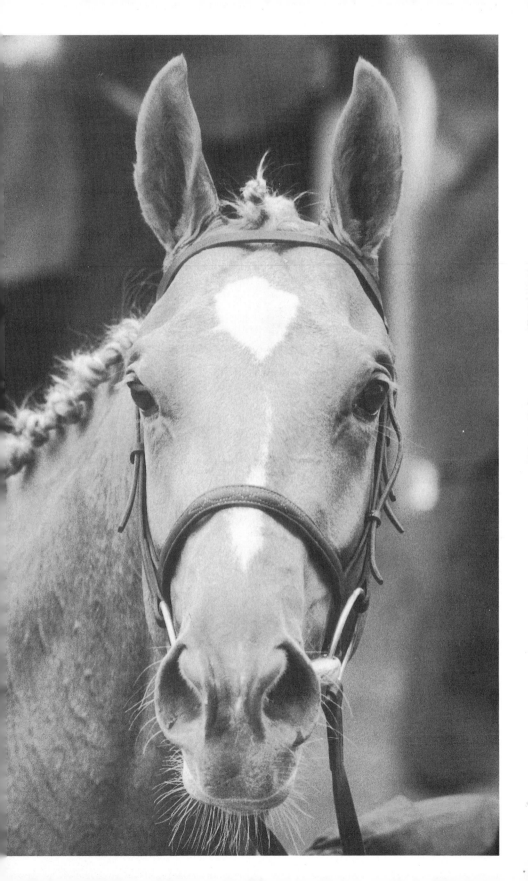

Opposite above left: *'The amateur spirit is still alive and kicking,' says one of National Hunt's most devoted fans, Lord Oaksey*

Opposite above right: *'I like owners who let me run the horses where I want; but you've got to please 'em — they're paying the bills,' says John Spearing*

Opposite below: *Desert Orchid and Richard Dunwoody jumping to victory in the King George VI Chase at Kempton, 1990, for Richard Burridge and his partners*

Above: *'Just because the Flat jocks get paid very well, don't let anyone tell you it's an easy job,' says Geoff Lewis, here with Paul Eddery*

Below: *Morley Street, trained by Toby Balding and ridden by Jimmy Frost, winning the 1991 Champion Hurdle for Michael Jackson*

Above left: *'I never believe there is much point in finishing fifth at Ascot when you can win at Carlisle,' says Luca Cumani*

Above right: *'Racing is a funny business but life's too goddamned short to be arguing with people,' says Liam Codd*

Below: *'Training's a bloody young man's game!' says Nicky Henderson. 'I'm knackered at the end of the year – and I mean knackered'*

Opposite above: *John Dunlop trains Marju to win the 1991 Craven Stakes for Hamdan Al-Maktoum*

Opposite below: *Clive Brittain trains Mystiko to win the 1991 2000 Guineas for Lady Beaverbrook*

Right: *The Queen at Royal Ascot, 1991. 'My philosophy about racing is simple. I enjoy breeding a horse that is faster than other people's'*

Below: *'You have the glory,' says Peter Chapple-Hyam, master of Manton, here with Dr Devious, 'but you also have the defeats!'*

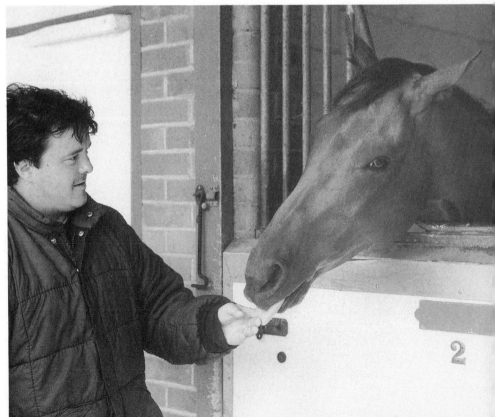

part of the working day. It's no different for me than having to get into a car and go to London and sit in an office, and deal with people: to my way of thinking, it's my office and it's my job. We have privacy when we want it. In most cases, the owners are very good friends of ours. For some of them the side of it they really enjoy is to watch their horses working, and Captain Lemos, Bill Gredley and John Hislop would come out nearly every work morning, and then we'd get back and have a coffee and talk to the jockeys, so they have total involvement – and in the afternoon, we go to the races. It's as much part of their life as it is of mine.'

Willie Carson and his then wife, Carol – old friends of the Brittains – were instrumental in getting them owners in the early days, introducing them to the Khans and also the Gulrajanis who sent the new trainer seventeen horses in one go.

'The next break,' he says, 'was my horse called Averof that Bernard van Cutsem had trained. Funnily enough, again Willie was involved. Captain Lemos who owned it didn't think Willie suited the horse, and Bernard van Cutsem said, "Willie's champion jockey and stable jockey, and it's very difficult for me not to put him on," and so the horse was sent over to me. So Willie and me were pals – he was riding all my horses – and suddenly I get a horse he couldn't ride! We got beat a short head the first time I ran him in a handicap at Newmarket, then I ran him again and won, and then I won the Dee Stakes at Chester with him, the Diamond Stakes and the St James's Palace Stakes. So that was about the second year, and that really set me off.'

Years of doubt, hesitation and pain were hardly likely to feature in Clive Brittain's scheme of things yet there was, none the less, a con-siderable surprise in store for the debutant trainer.

'I didn't realize how little I knew about training until I started,' he says. 'It was a tremendous grounding I'd had because I dealt with so many top-class horses – pedigrees and temperaments which are still with me now, and the accumulation of riding the horses and knowing them over that period of time was certainly a big help. But as far as helping me with the actual training . . . no, it didn't help! You are your own man; you've got your own way of doing things, and you can't take somebody else's head with you.

'I was always confident we were going to do well. We didn't soar right to the top but we did extremely well when we got good horses, and I honestly felt well, I've done as well with these as anyone could have done. I can't say I did better, but certainly as well. I haven't trained a Derby winner, but I haven't missed that because I've had Pebbles and won the Breeders'

Cup, and Jupiter Island won the Japan Cup and came close to winning the Kentucky Derby.

'Every year you get through I think is a great satisfaction. Every season. Without being at the top we've never hit the bottom. Basically, I go for training the type of horse that is exciting – that can excite people, and you're always looking for the really good horse. And every year we've come up with a very good horse. Touch wood it carries on!'

Lady Beaverbrook's greys, Mystiko and Terimon, were certainly two such horses for 1991, while Luchiroverte and Sikeston cleaned up abroad. Clive Brittain will end the season fourth in the trainer's table with his desire to do the impossible thoroughly accomplished, and still laughing.

The hype behind Mystiko's bid for the Derby was remarkable, and the Classic horses, the great horses, stake out their claim in racing's long memory.

'We had a great horse called Flying Childers in the eighteenth century and we had to wait another two hundred and fifty years before we got another!'

The 11th Duke of Devonshire pours champagne in his London house, on the front door of which is a brass plate bearing the legend 'This is a private residence', and remembers his great mare, Park Top. His antique Whig vowels carry echoes of an age when to be well-bred was an end in itself.

'It's all got a bit of romance about it,' he says. 'The first Duke was a founder member of the Jockey Club and my straw colours are the oldest registered colours on the Turf. All pale yellow is simply lovely, but not so lovely when they're running badly – they're very conspicuous . . .'

By his own account, the Duke is a very rich man; why, I wonder, does he not run a string of some considerable size?

'Expense.' He utters the word quietly and with the greatest possible speed to dismiss a flawed proposition. 'I suppose I could afford more horses, but I've had too many bad horses, and too many good horses that wouldn't try to know that it is not worthwhile putting the money in – I mean it is pouring money down the drain . . . One tends to think one's more unlucky than others, indeed, I was quoted at one time as the unluckiest owner there was; my bad luck was quite conspicuous as well.'

Experience has taught His Grace to be intensely practical when it comes to the business of racing horses.

'Buying a racehorse is a hell of a gamble. And the thing about it *is* – I've often thought about it – there's absolutely no point in going into owning horses unless you *care*. Why one should care, I don't know; but one *does* care. One's heart's in it. You've got to ... you've got to love it.

'The fatal thing is to be lucky to begin with: you could think, "Oh, this is easy." Damn well isn't.

'The odd thing about racing is that you cry when you win, not when you lose. It's very emotional. When you lose you're disappointed – just disappointed. And there's nothing to say, there it is. And of course there are far more disappointments and defeats than triumphs, but the triumphs *wouldn't* be so triumphant if it wasn't for the disappointments. A sense of proportion ... The thing I liked best about George Lambton's book, *Men and Horses I Have Known*, is when he says that there is nothing in the world that can make such a fool of a man as a horse.'

The Duke remembers as a child attending his first meeting. 'I think it was 1933 – it was Cameronian's Guineas – and my mother, her sister my aunt and my first cousins who were also mad about racing (and they lived not so very far from Newmarket), and our good mothers took us off to the Silver Ring to see Cameronian win the Guineas. And I can note the place on the Cambridge to Newmarket road, just four miles this side of Newmarket, where we had our picnic. It's etched into my mind.

'When I came back from the War, my father knew I was mad about racing, and though *he* didn't like racing he was perfectly happy to buy me a horse. It was trained by Reg Hobbs and ran first at Ludlow, and I couldn't *go*.' All the necessary background information is rattled off as quickly as possible in a monotone, and then the important words are enunciated slowly and clearly, and sometimes with a deal of emphasis so that, after a short while, it is like listening to a piece of music. And what is more, a piece of music conducted by Sir Georg Solti.

'And I *suspect* – it may not be true – I *suspect* they thought we don't want to win today with the owner not here, so it wasn't too busy. Then it ran at one of the early autumn meetings at Cheltenham and broke down – badly: never ran again, and it was twenty years before I had a winner. And I've always thought that was my punishment for perhaps my first runner being a non-trier!' Self-deprecating laughter. 'My first winner was in a modest little race at Lincoln. And then it all came good.'

There is nothing glib in the Duke of Devonshire's conversation, and in an effort to present an accurate view of what he feels, the delivery can verge on the falsetto as he tortures the right words into place.

'When I started out on the Flat, I went to Marcus Marsh and I brought nothing but *terrible* misfortune to poor Marcus – when I went to him he had ninety horses, two of which were mine, and when he retired, he had thirteen horses, seven of which were mine. So I didn't do Marcus any good!'

By this time he had become a great friend of the Newmarket trainer Bernard van Cutsem, and it was to him the horses were next sent.

'We just missed each other at Cambridge, but he was a great friend of my elder brother's – they were contemporaries – and we became friends in '38. Saw a bit of each other during the War. We were not particularly similar characters, but we got on very well. He had a reputation for being rather "hot" which was *quite* unfounded. He was a man of scrupulous honour. He may have given his horses the odd easy race, but what trainer doesn't? I think it's not par*ti*cularly difficult to be an *ade*quate trainer . . . but to train a Group 1 horse – to produce your horse right on Derby Day is much more difficult than run-of-the-mill training. To get him with the right number of gallops in, and not over the top so that he doesn't have a candle-light when he's pulled out, I think that is a great skill. I think it helps enormously if you've got that extra sense which makes them a better trainer. I think that people like Henry Cecil and Fulke Walwyn have *got* that instinct, and you can say to them why did you work that horse over seven furlongs rather than a mile today, and I don't think they'd be able to explain, they just . . . understand animals.

'Bernard rang me up in this house – I remember it so clearly – he'd bought this filly for five hundred quid, would I take her?' This was the beginning of a story he told in *Park Top – a romance of the Turf*, a book he dedicated to the memory of Bernard van Cutsem. 'If ever there was a labour of love, that was it,' he says. 'The object behind it was to try and show people who weren't in racing it wasn't a completely philistine pursuit.'

Like Spindrifter, Park Top won thirteen races in her career, but in her case over a period of five years, and at the age of twenty-one she died of old age.

'She was an absolute freak. She pulled out a little lame every morning. I've got a set of her racing plates framed, and both of her forefeet are deformed, the off fore very much so. As a two-year-old she was a bit backward, and then got a cough – *badly* – and so never raced which possibly was lucky because she was going to have a very hard racing career. We ran her in the last race at an evening meeting at Windsor – I was frightfully lucky there – and she started at 6–1 and won very easily. At Newbury next, she first showed her astonishing speed coming from last to first in the time it took the commentator to say she was bringing up the rear, and the jockey was quick with his advice. "She's a very very good filly and she'll win the Ribblesdale for you." So we took her to Ascot.

'It was unbe*liev*able – the first runner I'd ever had at Royal Ascot. She came past the form horse like that . . .' A slender hand mimes lightening speed. 'And then I betrayed her. I always swore that once I had a good horse I would never miss it running. I had promised to go and stay in Venice, and I went. The horse won the Brighton Cup really well in my absence, but then things went wrong. She was steered on the big three-year-old fillies' race at Longchamp, the Vermeille, and she ran one of her few bad races.'

You felt responsible for that?

'I did, yes. I said I'd always see it that I'd deserted my great heroine and she got beat. Her four-year-old career was a bit mixed – she wasn't very *easy* to ride, but she won her last race so I decided to keep her in training, and then her five-year-old career was her great year. Of course, in a way she was more famous for what she didn't win to what she did. She certainly should've won the Arc, and her last Coronation Cup in 1970, but Lester rode an ill-judged race; I think he'd be the first to admit it. He apologized to me after the race. But as a friend said to me the next day, he said, "Well, I'm sorry about yesterday, but you're pretty intolerable as it is, and you would have been quite intolerable if you had won, so . . . !"'

Another disappointment was the Eclipse Stakes at Sandown. The jockey remembers it well.

'It was the day I wished the earth would open up and swallow me,' Geoff Lewis told me. 'That would have been the most embarrassing day of my life. It's a long walk back at Sandown to the second place in the winner's enclosure, and to see him standing there – a big tall man he was to me . . . He took it – but I suppose he was too much of a gentleman to say what he thought. I rode a pretty awful type of race, and came unstuck completely.'

Park Top ran her last race at Longchamp, and to her doting owner's desperate anguish, she was booed as the beaten favourite by the French crowd.

'Horrible people – punters; they talk through their pockets!' he says. His Grace turned on the crowd and gave them the famous Harvey Smith gesture, and in his book he wrote, 'I have always been slightly jealous of him for getting the credit for bringing this singularly expressive gesture into the public eye. I feel the credit should go to me.'

Over his racing career the Duke of Devonshire seems to have suffered more anguish than triumph and I wonder if it is the extreme difficulty of achieving success wherein lies the attraction of the game for him. Is it the challenge . . . ?

'Yes it is. That's the word. The *challenge*.'

His body language is by now as expressive as his words as he redoubles his efforts to tell the truth. His innate elegance is confounded by the contortions; a little more straw sock is revealed above the black suede shoes, and his lapels point skywards as he winds himself around his chair and frowns at the floor for inspiration.

'You're going to lose money, and you're going to have bitter disappointments, so when my luck changed and I started having winners, it *did* seem almost unbelievable. And I realized that I was never going to have the like of Park Top again – ever. That was certain.'

Geoff Lewis rode his first winner at Epsom in 1953 at the age of seventeen, and in 1971 he completed the great treble of Mill Reef in the Derby, Lupe in the Coronation Cup and Altesse Royale in the Oaks.

'It was the greatest week in my life,' he says. 'It'd never been done before – but I didn't realize I'd done it at the time. Noel Murless was the first one to tell me, when I came in. He said, "Well done on the treble," and I thought this is the only ride I've had today; I don't know what he's talking about. I thought the old man had been on the champagne.'

His first job was as a page boy at the Waldorf Hotel in the West End. Born in Wales but brought up in Shepherds Bush along with twelve brothers and sisters, he reckons he was so small he could have ridden the dogs up the road at White City when he went there every Thursday and Saturday with his father, a painter and decorator. When he was fifteen and a half, Ron Smyth gave him a job at Epsom, and his first ride on a horse. He loved it from day one.

'Oh God, yes. When you're one of thirteen children, there's one dog in the house, and it belongs to everyone. All of a sudden I got a whole horse to look after! The life was great – just to go back to the country. The guv'nor don't like fools too often – won't stand for them, and he does like a day's work for a day's wages.'

Few jockeys, so they tell me, make good trainers, but Lewis is an exception. He took over Staff Ingham's Thirty Acre Barn yard in 1980 and since then has helped Espom to revive its reputation as a training centre – but the transition from riding to training was not all roses.

'The transition's easier for the jump jockeys because they ride out from the yard every day and they're handling horses, but with the Flat jocks they haven't got the time to think about the welfare of the horse. I was fortunate because of the six years' apprenticeship I had; that stood by me, but I still didn't know anything. Handling the staff is the big thing to kick off with. You can't believe sometimes what happens, and you do your pieces and I do have a sharp temper . . . Jekyll and Hyde my family call me. The mistakes I made, and I made plenty, were overlooked by my owners because they were friends of mine apart from two or three. The first year I had only five winners with forty-four horses, and that makes you realize that you're doing something very drastically wrong. You're apt to work the horses too easy when you first kick off; you're too soft with them, and you don't give them enough work and there's nothing worse than a fat horse who can't win; and their mind goes wrong – they don't get dedicated enough. They're not professionals.'

Geoff Lewis's flat delivery almost defeats a stammer, and his voice is coloured by Wales, London and an Australian intonation borrowed from his wife. Numerous trips to Australia and Hong Kong have left him jealous of the conduct of racing in those countries, in particular the way in which the small punter has the chance to win a fortune with a minimal stake. 'In 1961 when we were the Sport of Kings, they thought, "Let 'em have the betting shops – what difference does it make?" Racing was never a business then; it was just fun for the people who could afford it, and now we're in trouble.'

Something else bothers this trainer.

'We're so underestimated here at Epsom. Our facilities are so good for the number of horses we've got, and what makes me a bit hurt is that every owner in England strives for the day when he can win that one race at Epsom. They'd bend over backwards, sell their wife, their dog, their cat to buy a horse they thought was good enough to win the Derby. Yet there isn't any of the people who can afford to buy the horses that are good enough to win the Derby helping subsidize Epsom by putting horses here. I feel they think a handicap centre is all we are, and the Sheikhs rely on their managers who've been brought up with the people who're training in Newmarket and Lambourn and they think they are the only places to train horses . . .'

On Derby day, he has a runner in the Diomed Stakes, a Group 3 race, and punters are making their way on to the track impeded by whirlwinds of grey concrete dust from the building work in progress to update Epsom's period charm.

'I want to see Epsom closed down,' says John Dunlop, who won the Derby in 1978 with Shirley Heights. 'Never seen such a waste of money in my life. The amount of money that's being pumped into it for literally one profitable day a year . . .'

The punters are more forthright.

'Christ! It's a hell of a bloody scrum! What a bloody mess!' Morning dress is filmed in dust, and gypsies in the grip of some frenzy push white heather into everyone's clothing. I take the risk of sidestepping them only to discover that most of their relatives are ensconced in the Epsom Club Bar, but wearing more expensive clothes.

'You ain't got your Porsche?' asks the lady wearing the yellow hat which cost an arm and a leg.

'No,' replies her companion. 'They're gradually taking it all away. I did have two; one never got wet. It cost me fifty-four and I sold if for fifty-two . . .'

He leaves his character behind when he makes a brief exit.

''e 'ad a Lamborghini. It was red . . . 'e 'ad a mistress – and a wife. 'ad a mistress for years. This was when we 'ad the Post Office.'

The companion returns.

''ere,' he says. 'Them old toilets are medieval, ain't they?'

There is a tremendous air of expectancy in the bar, and it is not induced by the race card alone. Dress the English in their best on a weekday morning, put them in unfamiliar surroundings, and they are soon on the verge of hysteria – with or without champagne.

The thousands of faces behind the winning post on the Downs would drive a pointillist clear out of his mind, and up at Tattenham Corner there is a carnival atmosphere.

Mick Smith, a part-time bookmaker and publican, is on Pitch 131.

'Some people play golf – I go bookmaking. It's a hobby. I'm just here for Derby day – the other two days are no good, and from the minute you get here, it's one big party.'

Loudspeakers are belting out 'Memory', and Mick is sitting in a deck chair on his pitch with half a lager and a Lanzarote sun-tan, watching the men who graft for him. One is wearing high laced Doc Marten's, his shaved head partly covered by a track-suit hood.

'He's Sween.' Mick makes the cheerful introductions. 'He's an accountant for a hospital in Rugby. And Div . . . Martin Divine – he works for Fords, and this is Terry the driver. Basically, we've all got one thing in common, we love racing.' They would all prefer full-time work on the racecourse, but the problem lies, apparently, with the pitch applications. 'You fill dead men's shoes, basically. It doesn't cost anything but you have to apply to each course individually, and I applied to Cheltenham fourteen years ago and I'm still eighty-nine on the waiting list, and that's in the cheap enclosure. Unfortunately, that is the one thing in racing I do despise because the pitch application is still . . . crooked. It is. There's a lot of bookmakers who had prime pitches who've gone bust in one way or another, but they still actually hold the pitch, and it's some Jack the Lad behind who gives them a wage to keep him his pitch but takes all the profits, and it's him the punter is dealing with. I was down at Newmarket for the Craven Meeting, and you could see them looking over their shoulder to ask, "Shall I take this . . . ?" It's as obvious as that. But proving it is the hard thing. If a bookmaker has failed, he should be off and let everyone else move up the line.'

Mick Smith's sunny personality never dwells too long on the downside of life and having made his point, the mood changes in double quick time.

'My parents didn't know which end of a horse was it's head. *'Now* . . . my father, I can't keep him away from the game! He has a bet every day which is something I don't do.' And Mr Smith Senior now has one to follow which is close to home. 'I'm a small-time owner,' says Mick. 'I've got a racehorse purely as a fun thing – to *go* racing. I left one trainer, but I was honest with him. I said, "Look John, you're too big for me. I'm not big enough for you . . .", and now I'm with Liam Codd at Evesham, and win or lose, we go out to have a party, and it all stems from Liam. Maybe Liam's got it wrong; maybe that's why he's struggling. We don't know. But at least he's enjoying what he's doing. Racing *is* a social event.

'Ever since I was a kid I've always thought . . . a racehorse owner – I'd love to be one! And when I'm in that parade ring with my owner's badge on, rubbing shoulders with the Sheikhs, my chest's out there. The adrenalin runs in me more than the horse! You take last year when my wife's horse ran up in Ayr. It finished third to Lord Bolton's horse. We was in the winner's enclosure and Lord Bolton invited us up to his suite afterwards for a drink. You know – a couple of years ago who would've thought that Lord Bolton would've invited me up to his private suite for a drink? But it's a great leveller – me and Lord Bolton, all the same level.'

A punter approaches Mick's oppos with a wad of £10 notes. 'What was that on?' he calls to them. 'It's terrible when there's a great long queue and you've got to give it back to them, and more! The ideal thing is to make a 12½ per cent profit – everything *should* be running for you. It'll start getting busy when the Queen goes by. About one o'clock. "I now declare the Derby open . . . !" Another peal of laughter and he pulls on an anorak against the cold wind.

Her Majesty is looking very frisky when she disembarks from her car and walks across the winner's enclosure towards the Royal Box followed by red-waistcoated flunkies carrying a collection of zip-up bags, silk scarves, wooden boxes and a plaid rug. They, in turn, are followed by Lord Carnarvon, the royal racing manager, Sir Michael Oswald, the royal stud manager and a clutch of women who are to fashion what making money is to Lloyd's.

The loyal crowds settle back to the business of the day. Lord Derby looks forbidding in black, and Brough Scott blows into his hands, the tails of his coat peeping out from beneath a raincoat. Clive Brittain is clustered about by Arabs. There is a cabal of racing worthies on the balcony above the weighing room.

'We'll have to duck and dive and peek, Caroline!' says one to her chum.

'Yah! Soon get the hang of it!' comes the plucky reply.

'I think it's snowing . . .', complains a less brave fellow as he pulls on kid gloves that were meant for show. His woman takes off for the Tote to place his bet. 'And bring back the change . . . !' he calls, giving her grounds for divorce.

Just one short week before Derby day I had posed the ultimate question to Guy Harwood at Coombelands, his training complex at Pulborough which is rated by many as the very best in Europe.

Are you going to win the Derby?

'I've got a great chance. I'm going to try very hard.'

He then invited me to meet Cruachan, on whom his hopes were pinned, and it says a very great deal for racing that such an invitation was ever issued.

There are many kind people in the game who both tolerated my ignorance of the sport and tried their best to diminish it, and I owe a particular debt of gratitude to the ones who continued with the kindness past that dizzy moment when my outsider's objectivity went out of the window, and I became as partial and opinionated as hell.

As Guy Harwood walked me to Cruachan's box I said what a pleasure it always is to look at any Harwood horse.

'A lot of them are Delahooke's,' he explained, mentioning the blood-stock agent with whom he has been associated down the years. 'What happens is we end up having to buy all the big ones usually because they're the only ones we can afford!' He laughs, and goes into Cruachan's box which is as smart as paint. A lad is already in there.

'This is Phil, and he just looks after this horse in the *hope* that if there's any infection about, he won't get it.'

The animal looks stupendous; he looks powerful enough to take on the world, his coat is like satin and he has a hard eye. Tell me what's special about him for you, I ask.

'Well . . .' Harwood ponders his answer for about five seconds and then the words bark out. 'He stands over a nice piece of ground – the most important thing is you've got to have the scope for it. I would suspect that this horse is a little bit longer than he is tall, and he's a tall horse. The depth of arse is very important, and your hip to hock measurement is very important. I wouldn't say hip to hock he is *that* long but for a big horse he's got quite a long forearm.' He indicates the focus of his attention with the end of a crutch. 'You've got lots of muscle and power there, and you don't want *too* long a cannon bone. He's *slightly* behind . . .' The catalogue of delights continues until the star begins to show what he thinks about being used as a blackboard. 'All right Phil, don't annoy him!' The trainer turns to leave the box. 'And he's got an incredibly good constitution – look at the coat on him. I know he's been well looked after, and he's in magnificent shape . . .' His voice dips as it wanders into the realms of the unknown. 'You never know if they can cope with Epsom until you race there, but if he's going well enough, he'll cope. Keep your fingers crossed . . . We have a week . . .'

The next day the horse was injured in training and pulled out of the Derby.

The second race on the Derby day card is the Diomed Stakes, a Group 3 race offering a prize of £17,243 to the winning owner, and Eddy and Sylvia Grimstead are making their way from the Members' Bar to the parade ring to inspect their runner, Sylva Honda, which is trained by Clive Brittain. Eddy runs his horses under the name of his chain of Essex Garages for publicity purposes but without any support from Honda, whose motor-racing team colours of red and black he has adopted as his own for the horses.

'Your hands are cold!' he admonishes, happy to stop and chat even at a moment like this. Everything about this 57-year-old reminds me (happily) of Tommy Cooper. His wife is petite, blonde and a star.

'We got the winner of the first!' thrills Sylvia, and give or take a mishap or two, she now expects to be lucky on the racecourse. Lady Luck certainly favours her. 'I put my money on what some little old man sitting on a bench by the winner's circle told me to – we were sitting there talking, just a complete stranger, and I said to him, "You don't happen to know my uncle, do you?" and we was chatting and he knew my uncle and auntie . . .'

'Ted Greeno,' says Eddy, supplying the essential detail. 'He wrote a book on crime on the track. He helped to smash the racetrack gangs.'

The two of them make off for the parade ring. Her Majesty is already there, accompanied by one of the Stewards, Captain Macdonald-Buchanan, who always looks as if he's forgotten to slip his teeth in. Eddy and Sylvia wait almost deferentially outside, and then accompany their trainer into the ring. The atmosphere at this end of the proceedings some distance from the grandstand is professional, soothing and peaceful despite the occasional whooping as the punters inside the eau-de-nil striped corporate entertainment tents pop champagne corks and strike back at puritanism, but they are masked from the ring by yellow laburnum, chestnuts and cherry trees. Having cast an expert eye over her runner Enharmonic – her best horse this season – Her Majesty hoofs it back up the course to the Royal Box and is applauded by those lining the rails. A surge of top-hatted punters follow her, eager to place their bets now they have assessed the runners.

'Can't you speak English?' despairs a policeman trying to hold them back.

'That's not a happy copper,' loudly declares a hooray type. 'If you can't take a joke you shouldn't've joined.'

Eddy and Sylvia return to the Members' Bar to stand on the steps and watch the race. Clive Brittain is slightly in front of them studying the action through his glasses. Sylva Honda and jockey Alan Munro make it to the front of the field by the final furlong and they hold this clear advantage to come home at 20–1, two lengths ahead of the second.

It was Eddy's colours which held the eye as they took the lead and stayed there; it was as if we were open-mouthed children watching an incredible and glorious conjuring trick – it seemed hardly real, and the emotions were not quite as tightly held together as might have been hoped. Clive Brittain was smiling fit to burst. We rush down the steps and on to the course to greet Sylva Honda, and Sylvia leads him into the winner's circle. The trainer cuffs the horse's Japanese lad in complicity and pride before being submerged in press men cocking an ear towards him, hunched over their notebooks. Clive refuses to be surprised by the victory even though it was in no one's script but his own; Sylva Honda specializes in unexpected victories at Epsom, taking the Woodcote Stakes last year as a 7–1 chance. He rushes off to supervise Mystiko's appearance in the big race, but with Eddy charging ahead we return to his champagne in the bar. He pulls a tiny globe out of his pocket.

'A gypsy gave this to me on my way in. You can't ignore them.'

What did you give her?

'I put my hand in my pocket to feel for the smallest note!' He guffaws slowly. 'We sell them generators from the garages, you know. We have to be ever so careful when we send a service engineer out to them. They put a curse on you!'

Sylvia looks terribly expensive.

'You like it? Now where did I get it . . . ? Oh, Shirley Lucas, in Chigwell. Don't tell no one – I've had it about four years! But everyone kept saying black and white would be "in", so . . . ! We are lucky,' she giggles. 'We are lucky.'

Having seen the horse run disappointingly at Newbury – obviously he finds that course as depressing as I do – I have to admit to astonishment that without the help of jet propulsion he made it to the winner's circle today.

'That was a bad day, wasn't it?' agrees Eddy.

'I said to Eddy that day, "He won't win, you know, 'cos I'm not there." ' Sylvia had been busy with a golf tournament. She sips more Krug. 'I think winning on Sylva Honda is very good for that new jockey. What's his name . . . ?'

'I heard Clive speaking to Alan Munro giving instructions to him,' says Eddy, 'because he'd never *ridden* that horse before – not even gone out and done any work on him. But Clive said he's ridden all sorts; it doesn't really matter.'

The next race was the Derby. Alan Munro won on Generous.

Marju, John Dunlop's contender, ran brilliantly to be second: as Lord Oaksey so eloquently put it, he would have won by seven lengths if Generous had not been there.

Trainers disagree as to the merits of the Derby course.

'I go along with the old school,' one told me. 'It's a good test of a horse to go up hill, down dale and round corners. The horse that can only run in straight lines should stay at Newmarket!'

John Dunlop is adamant in his opposition to this opinion.

'Well, it's wonderful if they can deal with it, but it's really not a very fair track. *I* don't like it, and it's not a track people like running horses on. It's a bloody awful place, and it's also frightfully unlucky.' With beguiling modesty he concludes his pungent thoughts on Epsom and its stellar race. 'Oddly enough, the Derby result is usually proved a true result – a correct result!' He smiles at the irony.

And this year too?

'Undoubtedly.'

CHAPTER ELEVEN

On and Off the Rails

Four days later some of us are back at Epsom. Two miniature Union Jacks flutter above bookmaker Charles James's board.

'On the Oaks, folks! On the ladies, on the gels . . . !' The noise of the ring starts up. A sign on the board announces, 'Betting without Shadayid', which is John Dunlop's hot favourite for the fillies' Classic, the Gold Seal Oaks. '5–2 the field!'

Mist hangs over the Downs and there is a cold breeze. Only silence comes over the loudspeakers, and an air of fatigue suggests there has been too much hard work and too much partying since Generous proved himself to be a real racehorse. There is a whiff of seedy, post-war utility about the place; the rusting girders and the blue paint of the Club Stand turn it into a municipal swimming pool on the point of closure due to lack of public demand. Subtract from Epsom the intoxicating and highly enjoyable Derby day atmosphere, and the crowds, and little is left. Newmarket trainer and punter Barney Curley is deep in conversation on the rails; he reminds me of Alec Guiness in *Bridge Over the River Kwai*, and the men he engages in conversation repeatedly flash him subservient smiles.

The racegoers today are subtly different from the Derby crowd, and it is all too apparent that the normal flows of cash through the economy have dried up. The women have lifted eyebrows and pert smiles, and wear short skirts regardless of the age and condition of their legs. Men wear camel-hair coats and carry handbags, and one of them has about him the febrile jocularity of the almost defeated.

'I'm thinking of going into Ford,' he says, referring to the open prison and not the Dagenham motor works. 'It's near to you, isn't it?' he asks his friends. 'You'd come and see me . . . ? You can smuggle Bob Hope in like it was going out of fashion. And you can guarantee somebody's making a book . . .'

'Yes!' laughs a sympathizer. 'Probably you!'

A man with an MCC ribbon on his panama and an Old Harrovian tie is as thoroughly labelled as a pot of Womens' Institute jam, while his wife bears out a private theory that the more an Englishwoman dresses up, the worse she looks. A generalization, but none the less true for that.

Making his customary late entrance, rails bookmaker John Pegley strides suddenly on to the scene. He is a tall man and you don't get many of those to the pound in racing. He delivers his opening line.

'Who says it's not going to stay? It won at Longchamp as a two-year-old!'

His suit is a triumph of classy elegance; thank God someone on the track knows how to dress.

'My tailor made it for me in, oh . . . about 1983. A very nice man called Fred Harding. He has a little office in Manchester Square, but he has been lacking my business for some years because the readies have been a bit short!' Rueful laughter. Pegley, it must be said, had been taught the meaning of life long before he ever hit the racecourse. 'In 1957,' he begins, reciting a story too painful to be tricked out with emotion, 'my two sisters and myself had something approaching five million pounds in trust for us, and in 1957 that was quite a substantial chunk.' Before they could grasp their good fortune, however, it evaporated. 'Unfortunately,' he says in a level voice, 'it went. I don't laugh about that too often . . .'

Some ten years later when he was looking for sites for laundrettes, an enterprising estate agent sold him a betting shop instead.

'A betting shop with a licence,' says Pegley. 'I opened that shop on a Wednesday afternoon, and I had fluked a very good pitch. From memory, I think I put two hundred quid in the till to serve as a float, which was probably about the same as two grand now, and on Saturday afternoon when we finished trading, there was thirteen hundred pounds left in the till, and I thought, "My God . . ."' The emphasis falls on the first word; it is a proprietorial statement. 'My God had heard my prayers and sent me money to pay the instalment on the car, pay the rents, pay the electricity, get the housekeeping up to date and it can't possibly happen again. Anyway – the end of the next week, another fifteen hundred quid, and when it happened the third and the fourth week, I suddenly realized it wasn't just a fluke. This was before betting tax started and bookmakers that were located in good situations were enormous money earners, *enormous* money earners, and I made a fatal mistake. I thought to myself, "How quickly can I have a hundred of these?"'

In no time at all he was back at square one, and on the racecourse.

'In those days I was more interested in laying a horse I didn't fancy than in backing a horse I did fancy – only in a very small way: take fifty quid out of a horse, say, which of course is contrary to the bookmakers' pitch rules. Nothing that I did would have any influence on the market at that time because it was only for very small sums of money, but there were two bookmakers coming racing – John Banks and Dougie Goldstein – and they were taking very large sums out of horses, and distorting the racecourse market, so the BPA decided they were going to stop it, and they introduced a rule saying that nobody could lay a bet on the racecourse unless they were a pitch-holder on the racecourse. I got rowed into that net and told that if I didn't stop laying horses, I wouldn't be allowed to come racing. They allocated me pitches on the Members' rails which had been suicide alley for the previous few years. Everybody who'd bet on the rails had succeeded in going broke, and they obviously thought that if they put us up there we would go broke as well. It's taken about seventeen years . . . it's getting nearer!'

When he is describing his own melancholy tale John Pegley's expression remains impassive, but when he moves on to the arguments against the present conduct of the racing game, it collapses instantaneously into a mask of despair.

'There is alleged to be an enormous shortage of money available for the owners of racehorses to win races with which to pay the trainers, but the people who go into racing surely don't go into it expecting to make it pay? Any person who has sufficient money to enter into a leisure pursuit, whatever it may be, can hardly expect to make a profit out of that pursuit. I am aware that the prize money levels in this country don't compare with those abroad, but I think that the money that is being ploughed back into racing – the yield from the Levy, it's not *that* inadequate, and it's a subsidy directly to the owners.

'What worries me is that far too small an amount from the Levy actually finds its way back into prize money. If you wound up the Levy Board for a start, and allowed the racecourses to negotiate directly with the bookmakers using the SIS service on which to hang the commercial transaction, you would arrive at a far more efficient way of financing racing.'

Here Barney Curley offers me a little advice.

'There is no common ground between the Jockey Club and the bookies,' he says and smiles faintly before gliding off around the ring. John Pegley is more polemical.

'The problem is that the Establishment people who *run* the game – the landed gentry and the retired soldiers – none of them have a thorough working knowledge of betting, of bookmaking.'

Historically the rails bookmakers, such as Pegley, were there to cater discreetly for just such men who could whisper their commission in the ear of their own private bookmaker. The rails were as close as the supposed ruthlessness and dishonesty of the Ring were allowed to the Members' Enclosure.

'The Jockey Club submission that claims £100 million from an increase in the Levy and a reduction in betting tax is ludicrous,' says John Pegley. 'And it's a good illustration of what's wrong with racing that the people who run it are responsible for that submission, and obviously believe that it is reasonable and workable. It patently isn't. The Establishment people think that betting and the people involved in it are beneath their contempt; they want the money out of betting, but they don't want to understand the operation of the betting business.'

It seems to me that I have encountered vaguely similar sentiments before but applied to a pastime even older than racing under rules. Prostitution, perhaps?

'I think that is an excellent metaphor,' he says. 'That is *exactly* how I would see it.'

'Elizabeth! Do you see the absolutely *vile* company that you are keeping . . . ?' The spluttered accusation comes from another racecourse bookmaker in mockery of the reaction which sometimes prevails in Members if I admit to the merest penchant for the company of racecourse bookmakers. He is ready with another Australian joke for fear that the tearing cold and a fast-disappearing voice may be sapping my enjoyment.

'Kevin Langley rode a horse for one of the titled press magnates that they have out there. I won't mention his name: it was Kerry Packer's father. It crossed the line a fast-finishing third after being virtually tailed off at the 600 metre mark, so Packer said to him, "Jeezus," he said. "I thought you'd be closer up to them early on . . ." And Langley said, "I'd like to've been – but somebody had to stay back there with your horse!"'

Rocky joins in with the laughter. He is one of the south's two public tic-tac men; he wears an orange jacket and white gloves, and he stands on a wooden box.

'The wavin' of the arms about is the easy part,' he confesses. 'Doin' the accounts up in the evenin' is the hard part.'

He has an enviable serenity about him which is so rare now that stress has become fashionable, but Rocky is a happy man. Something like thirty or forty thousand pounds pass through his hands each week in settlement of bets between bookmakers.

'And there's never any mistakes,' he says in a lugubrious voice which makes you want to smile. He relays the prices that are available on the rails to the bookmakers on the boards.

'It's never like goin' out to do a day's work,' he says. 'When you get up in the mornin' you look forward to comin' to the races. Definitely. I love it. If you get a long lay-off during the winter you do miss it. I don't do the all-weather – it's not good enough. I fink the all-weather's run mainly for the bettin' shops more than actual racecourse people. My two favourite racecourses are the July course and the Rowley Mile; I fink it's a great atmosphere there at Newmarket. I like gettin' up there early in the mornin', havin' breakfast up there . . . even to the point of goin' into the butcher's shop and gettin' the sausages . . . yeah, it's all part of Newmarket.'

'What you have to remember about racing,' John Pegley reminds me, 'is that it is like a little goldfish bowl, and the people who have full-time involvement – either professional or not – think that the world ends on the edge of the horse-racing business . . . and one of the problems with the whole business, and certainly the aspect of it in which I'm involved, is that it becomes a way of life – and a rather pleasant way of life when you're succeeding. But outside the racing fraternity, it is *irrelevant*. Irrelevant.'

Is racing any more reprehensible than any other endeavour? I ask him. Some people take the view that you need a long spoon to sup with anyone in the game.

'Corruption is actually limited to a very small number of people,' he says.

If you steal the integrity out of racing, does it have any value at all?

'It has enormous value to the people who go into the world's betting shops,' he replies with some urgency. 'They neither know nor care about the integrity of racing. They say, "Oh, Lester's riding the second favourite – we better have a few quid on that." And they don't care whether they take 6–1 or 7–2. And they don't care whether they pay tax on it – it doesn't make any difference. But horse racing isn't the be all and end all that the people who run horse-racing would like to make out it is. Don't let anybody run away with the idea that you couldn't have betting without horse-racing because you jolly well could. If the off-course bookmakers were denied access to horse-racing tomorrow, it would be an enormous blow to them, but the people who frequent betting shops would still want to have a bet – and they'd bet on dog racing, cricket, golf, anything.'

Are there only fools in racing, or are there knaves as well?

'Me, personally – and you see the halo here above my head . . .', he smiles, 'I don't condone anything that either breaks the law or breaks the rules. The top Flat jockeys are all millionaires and it astonishes me that they are even interested in doing anything wrong. But most of it isn't tax-free and the advantages of doing something wrong is that they can get the money in their hand. As far as the National Hunt jockeys are concerned, that's very different. The prize money in National Hunt is very much lower than in Flat racing so their percentage of the winning prize money is nominal, and I think if I was a National Hunt jockey risking breaking my neck six times in an afternoon riding horses that can't jump round tricky little courses like Plumpton, where if I actually win I might get 10 per cent of eleven hundred quid, there's obviously a temptation if somebody comes along and says, "Here's ten grand in readies *not* to win." I'm not justifying it, but it is understandable. And it has to be the people who have the opportunity. So why do the Stewards of the Jockey Club, as they apparently do, believe that nothing goes on?'

I was reminded of an anecdote Jenny Pitman recounted to me that highlights the same dilemma.

'I went to Stratford races one day a long time ago, and I was in the weighing room waiting for the tack and somebody came up to me and said, "Do you want to do any business?" I did wonder if they thought I was a hooker or what . . . and the only reason I knew there were two kinds of hookers is because one of my kids used to play rugby, and he came home one day and told me he was a hooker and I thought, *'Christ!'* Anyway, they said, "Do you want to do any business?" And I said, "What are you talking about?" "You *know* . . . do you want to do any business?" I said, "What's it worth?" And they said, "Five hundred quid." I said, "Go and tell them to fuck theirselves."

'What happened was,' she continued, smiling at the memory, 'my horse was running in a race that was worth 340 quid, so my percentage was going to be thirty-four pounds if he'd won it, and what was funny was (I could never work this out actually) it comes to the last a long way clear – from here to that bloody feed house clear, and fell. And I promise you, it must've been lying on the ground for five minutes before the others got to it, and I could never understand the justice in that because I could've been handed five hundred quid for the horse to have got beaten when my percentage was going to be thirty-four quid, and I decided that I would sooner stick with my percentage because that's the way I was! And then the horse that's going to win it ends up on the deck . . . I could never work that one out!' Even an expert on natural justice can be confounded by its mysterious ways.

Back at the Oaks, John Pegley is working up steam for some radical moves. This is not reform; this is revolution.

'I'd wind up the Tote board, and allow each racecourse to run its own Tote as the dog tracks do. At the present moment the Tote revenue is squandered.' Furthermore, he wants racecourse admission to be free, and amen to that. 'Racecourse attendances have fallen off *tremendously* in the last eighteen months. I don't *care* what the official figures are: I must go by what my field book says, and there are no people coming racing to have a bet – in the context of three or four years ago. It's too expensive. By the time a family has parked the car and got in, and they all want a lousy racecourse sandwich and a rotten cup of coffee in a paper cup which is disgusting, they've done sixty or seventy quid before they even look round.'

It was virtually impossible to find anyone willing to defend the Tote, and its chairman, Woodrow Wyatt.

'Woodrow Wyatt obviously amused Mrs Thatcher,' said a member of the Jockey Club.

'He was her Jimmy Savile,' remarked another considerable insider.

'Her great friend,' continued the original complainant. 'And there's no doubt he's a man of great wit and style, and he wanted the job. Badly. The Tote's a great moribund giant, but it could be everybody's pal and as big as the football pools. But . . . under this leadership? I don't think so. We'll never get rid of the bookmakers, so we'll have to live with them, but the Tote has something like 5 per cent of the betting turnover; it should have 50 per cent.'

Another man of some distinction in racing added a footnote.

'I'm afraid, in my opinion, Wyatt is a terrible liability,' he said.

John Pegley says racing missed a golden opportunity to make money when television in betting shops was legalized. It was thrown away like a withered branch.

'It's probably too late now, but each betting office should be charged a percentage of turnover for that service which would have to be recovered from the punters. At the present moment, the punters pay nothing – nothing whatever for the television coverage that they get from the racecourse. And the justification for that from the powers that be is, "Oh, it increases their contribution to the Levy." I think that's nonsense. Absolute nonsense.

'And Sunday racing is probably irrelevant. It would improve racecourse attendances for a bit, but only if they dropped the entrance charges. But how is it going to improve the finances of racing? You won't be able to open betting shops on Sundays. And the people who are advocating it aren't doing it for the right reasons; they're only doing it – going back to your principles of prostitution – because the prostitutes might be able to earn more on a Sunday than on a weekday. Can we get a bigger slice of the action?'

John Pegley turns his attention towards the fifteen runners in the Oaks, ten of which are Arab-owned.

Sheikh Hamdan Al-Maktoum accompanies his trainer John Dunlop into the parade ring with the favourite Shadayid who had emulated her stablemate Salsabil with a dazzling victory in the One Thousand Guineas at Newmarket, only troubling herself to get into gear in the last two hundred yards of the race, when she trounced the opposition. She looks very settled today; nothing like the time when she had been led out with a lad aboard to parade in front of great crowds of admirers at Dunlop's Castle Stables open day and had bucketed up and down like a rocking horse.

'We're on a bit of a knife-edge here,' John Dunlop had announced to the assembled company as the big, hyperactive filly danced around. 'It's always a bit of a worry,' he said, projecting his voice as if he were addressing the troops before battle commenced. 'This is good practice for her, for the parade. I'm glad you've had a chance to see her. Keep all your fingers crossed for us, for three weeks' time!'

Now it is her trainer who looks anything but relaxed, and he stays resolutely tense as Hamdan chats to him with more animation than we are accustomed to seeing from the Arab owners.

'Hamdan is mad about his home-breds,' Dunlop had vouchsafed. 'He's more enthusiastic about his home-breds than he is about the ones he might buy, which is rather nice actually . . .'

'I think the Arabs are wonderful,' the Duke of Devonshire had commented before. 'They don't cheat, they don't bet and they're extremely generous; I think they're wholly admirable. And where would racing in this country be without them? In a sad and parlous state.'

Guy Harwood concurs with this view. 'They have done an incredible amount of good,' he says. 'I take great note of good stallions – the ones that are really successful; the ones that continually produce good Group horses. Not so long ago the Americans were all-powerful, and they bought every decent horse we had – we were exporting all the bloodstock. Now, through the Arabs, we are all-powerful. The best young horses are at stud here now; all the past Derby winners are here – by courtesy of the Arabs.'

The race is run and three Arab owners end up in the winner's circle. Maktoum Al-Maktoum with the first, Jet Ski Lady, Sheikh Mohammed with Shamshir in second place and Hamdan with Shadayid whom he went to greet out on the course every bit as keenly as if she had won.

'They take their reverses well,' says Dunlop. 'In my experience anyway.' He smiles: 'Or to me they do . . . they might go home and kick the wall! Outwardly, they're very good losers, actually. Always have been.'

Owner and City man Christopher Bridge injects a note of realism.

'Why didn't they all go to France or America where the money's much better? Luckily they've *got* so much money. Look at their figures – their profit and loss. They must be losing a fortune. They love their bloodstock *per se*, isn't that right? And Sheikh Mohammed loves the glory of it, isn't that so?'

Luca Cumani, who was responsible for the training of the second horse, Shamshir, throws some light on another facet of the trainer's game. He looks very pleased after the race, but he takes both victory and defeat very graciously.

They tell me you are very ambitious, I had said to him previously.

'That's what people always say. I've always had great difficulty with defining ambition. I've always believed that if you do something, you might as well do it well. I would also say if you train racehorses, the aim is to win races and therefore I am in it to try and win races.'

Some owners have suggested to me that they simply want to take part; winning, *tout court*, is not the object of the exercise. Mr Cumani replies very swiftly to this one.

'On the Flat, if an owner tells you he's not in it to win races, he's lying.'

Emboldened by the straight talking, I ran another theory past him, and his rejoinder this time is equally swift.

You are destined, so they say, to be champion trainer.

'I doubt it – the way things are going.

'The reason people say I will be champion trainer is because I've had a very good steady rise through the ranks. It wasn't instant success. I was lucky in that nearly every year I had a good horse and, as you can imagine, it's not really easy if you are a foreigner and not knowing everybody in racing when you start. It takes quite a while to build up.'

Although Cumani's father was champion trainer in Italy, he had encouraged his son to take a different direction.

'He was pushing me to go to university to become a doctor – in Italy, as you know, everyone has to become a doctor of some description! I did three years, and after the third year I said to my father, "I'm not really cut out for all this: I want to be something else." So my father said, "For a start, why don't you learn to speak English?", which I didn't speak at the time. Not a word.

'I was always involved with training because of being with my father during the holidays, so I knew all there was to know at that stage, so I thought, "I'll go and see what happens abroad," and came here to Newmarket, and at the same time to learn to speak English – and I've been struggling with *that* ever since!'

He spent three months in 1972 with John Winter, and loved it.

'The following summer I was back here again, and I had met Henry Cecil before, and one day in passing at the sales he said to me, "I'm looking for a pupil assistant." Just in passing – he didn't offer me the job. I went back to Italy and one morning I just woke up and I knew I must ring him. So I rang up and said, "How about me? Will you have me?" and he said yes, and I've been here ever since.'

Some of the smaller trainers hold to the idea that life is easier at the top; is that so?

'I know the feeling. I used to think much the same when I was at the bottom. I used to look round and see the successful ones, the people who were at the top at the time, and think, "Wouldn't it be wonderful one day to get there – they look so happy, easy and relaxed. It must be wonderful! They get wonderful horses and this and that and the other."

'But it's harder. It's harder because the higher you get, the more you want. The less satisfied you always are. You're always striving for more, or for better. Once you get that high, you – or at least *I* am – are very very scared of going back down again. It can happen. Look at Peter Walwyn . . . in the seventies he was number one. It's been a constant slide for him. He's an example, and one is enough!

'Over the last five years I'm always thereabouts in the first four or five in the tables. So it's possible that one day I will get there. The reason why I'm slightly pessimistic about it now is because we've lost the Aga Khan, and I will probably suffer a little bit more than my colleagues in this contraction in racing because I am less Arab-strong than they are – and the Arabs are recession-proof, contraction-proof and everything! Whereas all the other people involved in racing are not. So in the next four of five years I'll be suffering more than most.

'Like everything else in life, success as a trainer can only be measured by results, and if you look at the top trainers operating at this moment –

Michael Stoute came from Barbados with no connections, Barry Hills was a stable lad, I came from Italy with no connections, so there's only Henry Cecil who was handed over something, and if he'd made a mess of it, he wouldn't be where he is today.'

Are Classic victories the ultimate aim?

'Let's not put it that way,' he says, with studied restraint. Another cigarette is lit and the legs are re-crossed. 'My aim is to carry on a successful operation, be happy with myself, have a happy and contented staff working for me, and a happy relationship with my owners. That's the aim. It sounds awfully idyllic, but that's the aim.

'In order to do that, you also need to win the races because if you start having bad years, your staff isn't very happy, the owners aren't very happy – so you can't have that. So when one says, "I want to win another Derby" or something like that, it's all *part* of the big picture. Not necessarily another Derby, but certainly it's necessary to win the *big* races from time to time in order to keep the whole thing together.'

CHAPTER TWELVE

Privilege

What passes for privilege in English racing is admission to the Royal Enclosure during the week of Royal Ascot.

Picture this.

It is the second day of the meeting. Sylvia Grimstead has a horse running in the first race, the Jersey Stakes. It cost almost £500 to enter the horse for this Group 3 race. Sylvia, wearing an owner's badge, attempts to cross the boundary into the Royal Enclosure from the paddock to exchange a few words with a friend, but she is refused entry by an official with words that have me reaching for my revolver.

'All you are is just an owner, madam.'

Sylvia smiles, apologizes and retreats.

Just an owner . . . And where exactly would racing be without the owner? I admit I am no egalitarian; I hold nothing against entrenched authority and privilege (particularly when I happen to be on the right side), providing it works. The moment it ceases to function for the greater good, then it's on your Marx, get set, and 'broom 'em all out'.

This is the Queen's own racecourse and time was when entry to the Royal Enclosure was refused to anyone stained by divorce, but since that ruling would now exclude half Her Majesty's own entourage, it has been abandoned. What does remain, however, is a system of allocating badges which can confound the unwary.

Captain Mark Smyly, an exceptionally wise man who gave up training and sold his yard (albeit with profound regret) before the recession could bite, recalls an illustration.

'One of my owners who had horses with me all the way through who is

Jewish, and lives in London, a rich man, extremely nice – again, people one would never have met but for training racehorses – and he made a mistake by signing his and his wife's name on the application form. His wife should have signed her own name. OK, he was stupid; he made a mistake . . . but he got told he couldn't have his badge. I wrote to Piers Bengough and apologized, and I got my owner to write a nice letter and apologize, but they still wouldn't give him a badge again this year. To be snobby, he's not a gent and all the rest of it – but he's got horses in training, and he's at least as good as a lot of other people in the Royal Enclosure, but he's down at the bottom of the list and may have to wait I don't know how many years for a badge. That to me is wrong.'

Two other owners who are passionately involved with the game describe the paradox of Ascot.

'To me', says one, 'this is "the" racecourse – except for this week. I'm an owner's guest this week, but what would really infuriate me would be to come as an owner to Royal Ascot and to find that to get to that end of the racecourse' (he indicates Tattersalls and the Silver Ring) 'I've got to be funnelled down that tunnel or down that alleyway. I'm a Royalist – but this, to me, is complete . . .', and he spreads his hands, palms down. The people who make racing are the owners, and they should get a little bit more than they do here.'

'And the punters . . .' adds his fellow owner.

'And the punters,' agrees the first, 'but they expect to be treated like this.'

The best four days' racing in England takes place during this week; the Thoroughbreds are spectacular, and this season they happen to be exceptional. The privilege lies in being present when they race.

There is one ineluctable fact about racing which apparently escapes a good many of the people who are here today: racing is about horses, and not about social cachet. However, as Sir David Money-Coutts will endorse, even the people who don't need cachet still like it.

Wrapped in the bunting of affluence, full of illusions, full of nonsense and full of drink, they clamour for each other's attention. Ascot has the fashion victim foisted on it in large numbers: women who choose to wear what might be best described as evening dress – backless and strapless, chiffon and lace – for a cold day at the races. And these women are allowed to vote, and drive cars. A breed that is on the rise, buoyed up by money and gentrifying itself with the Thoroughbred horse. Good taste is rarer than energy, and reality is only the terrifying silence hidden beneath that energy. Meanwhile, quite unsullied by the counterfeit charms of junkets like this, the English class system is alive and well, and doing very nicely.

'Every since we come into this racing it's been really bad weather . . .'

So it's your fault then?

'I know,' says Sylvia Grimstead. 'I blame myself. I've got this lovely new white outfit, but in the cold weather . . . and Di wore white yesterday, didn't she?'

Did she?

'She had white with black accessories. Then I thought cerise with black accessories, but the hat's too big . . .'

Sylvia's final choice of outfit is very chic. A lilac suit topped by a wide-brimmed cream hat, baroque pearls at her ears and throat and a golden Marbella sun-tan. We are in the Owners' Bar – the best bar in the place, and sited behind the Owners' and Trainers' Stand which has a better view of the proceedings than the Royal Box. Eddy Grimstead is generously anaesthetizing my croaking throat with gin. The approach to this first-floor redoubt is guarded by the BBC's mournful commentator, Julian Wilson and his cameras, and he looks almost affronted by the crowds. He shuffles into position to talk to the waiting millions sporting a pink net daffodil in his buttonhole. Channel Four's clowning behemoth, John McCririck, fits in rather well here. Each of the broadcasters was at Harrow: I rest my case.

'There are an awful lot of yobs here,' complains a fastidious trainer. 'But they're in, and what reason have we got for kicking them out?'

None whatsoever is the answer to that. A punter who has paid for a badge and is enjoying himself has a perfect right to be here; liberty is what mattered most to the revolutionaries, who espoused equality and fraternity as afterthoughts. But it is high time the shreds of pretence disappeared and the Royal Enclosure was transformed into a straightforward Members' Enclosure. Anyone professing something less than a total passion for racehorses should, however, be encouraged to go to Henley or the Chelsea Flower Show or almost anywhere that is not Ascot this week.

It is possible to gauge the success or otherwise of a hat at Ascot by whether the photographers snap you crossing the tarmac beneath the press balcony. Gossip supremo Nigel Dempster is celebrity-spotting down there: he bags Lord Suffolk, throws an arm around his shoulders and calls up to the waiting paparazzi.

'Lord Suffolk!' he shouts, indicating the peer with his free hand. 'Duke of Leeds!' he shouts again, this time pointing at himself and gilding the lily somewhat. 'Me better than him!'

In the press room, the hacks are seated at wooden desks like school-children doing their prep and Peter O'Sullevan in waistcoat and shirt-sleeves is studying the pages cut from his race card, mounted and amended with notes and colours.

Back in the Owners' Bar, Eddy is bemoaning the state of the motor trade.

'This year, we've got to be very very very competitive, so you've got to reduce the prices, over-allow the customers' old cars, give big discounts, but deep down in their hearts the public think you're still rookin' 'em. They talk about car dealers being bent: they're not. You shake a hand and have a deal with a car dealer, and you *have* a deal. That's it. The public are the ones you have to be more careful about. It's the general public. Four parts of the members of the public, they'll go away and stop their cheque or whatever; they think the car dealer's fair game. They've just got this preconceived idea that you make a fortune out of selling a car. We lose money sometimes, selling cars! One of the reasons I'm into horses is that all the fun has gone out of selling the cars. Selling cars used to be fun: a challenge. Now it's too clinical, too commonplace. What do you come here for? You come to win!' He gives a slow guffaw, and then considers the realities which underpin his enthusiasm. 'It does cost a lot of money doing racing,' he says, 'which dulls it a bit. But I'm in front – for the moment. I'm not counting the four two-year-olds in that. I mean, they're still in training, aren't they? In other words it would be unfair at the moment to consider those, wouldn't it? But I'm very lucky; Clive says I've been lucky . . .' With that, he rushes off to the saddling boxes to be there waiting when Sylva Honda arrives in the pre-parade ring. Sylvia smiles indulgently.

'He's here, he's there, he's everywhere . . . Story of my life.'

Down in the Troy Bar, another 'Di', Di Smith, is shepherding thirty-three girlfriends who have come racing in a charabanc from the Midlands to enjoy themselves. One of the gang got caught by the three card trick on the way in.

'The man before me won £100,' she protests.

'But they all work *together*!' the others chorus. She is unconvinced.

Di is an owner, but her horse Colorfayre would be embarrassed by the company he would find here.

'Ooh . . . ,' she gasps, 'to have a horse running here . . . crikey. But you never know – after Colorfayre there'll be something else I suppose. You just live in hope. I never ever would've dreamt I would own a horse. Not in a million years did I ever dream it.'

Di encountered her horse at a friend's livery yard; it had been sent there to be broken by the trainer Liam Codd.

'I thought how nice she was, and they introduced me to Liam, and that's how it goes! And then to actually have a winner, crikey! That's absolutely something else.'

Di's winner ran at Kempton.

'I was going, "What a horse! What a trainer!" That's all I kept saying, till I got to the winner's enclosure, and then I was speechless. I was jumping up and down in the air; people were looking. I hadn't got my binoculars with me, so I'd been looking at it on the big screen, and I thought he'd won when he'd still got another fence to go. I thought, "Oh no . . . !", but he jumped that . . . ! I threw my arms around Liam. Your stomach's fallen down and your heart's going nineteen to the dozen, and I was shaking like a leaf! I couldn't speak. And then I was interviewed by Derek Thompson on Channel Four and all I could say was, "I'm speechless. I'm speechless." I've played that video loads of times, and I think, "Oh crikey, no!"'

Di Smith is married to Mick Smith, the publican with a pitch at the Derby, and his horse is better bred than hers.

'We're fortunate, I suppose,' she reflects, 'because we both love racing. The pub's covered in pictures of racehorses.' Di is a good-looking woman. She has flame-coloured hair and a Lanzarote sun-tan disappearing down the decolleté of her svelte navy and white cotton frock. Her cook from the pub has come along for the day out. Siobhan, a.k.a. 'Shifty', is a very pretty girl in a pink and cream wrap-over dress and a sailor hat. She is showing cleavage from here to next week.

'Cover yourself up, Shifty!' Di tries ticking her off, but Shifty is not one of nature's shrinking violets, and she wears an advanced pregnancy like a fashion accessory.

Di is cold.

'I'm not going to think about it,' she says stoically.

'Why don't you put that on?' asks Shifty, pulling at the white cardigan slung over Di's shoulder-bag.

'When I put this on I shall hide up by the bookies.'

'There's nothing wrong with it.'

'There's everything wrong with it.'

'Just 'cos you got it in the market . . .' Shifty has the last word.

For Di, racing is about horses, not clothes – and she knows her horses. She will win a thousand pounds today, and immediately reinvest it in racing, handing it over to her trainer. She gets very exercised about

115

racegoers who sit and drink through a meeting and stir perhaps once, to put a bet on.

'A pound each way, and what good does that do racing?' she asks indignantly with the slight gasp of the committed smoker lying behind each word. 'I like the atmosphere of Ascot,' she says, putting the emphasis on the second syllable, 'but I prefer ordinary Ascot.' And don't we all.

Eddy Grimstead is at the saddling boxes.

'I get a bit pumped up, but I don't get nervous. I just try and make sure we do everything we can as an owner – I don't want to interfere, I just want to *be* here. Talk to the staff. After all, it is my horse. I think this is the best track for me. It's gorgeous. We came off the M4, through Windsor, past Eton College. Marvellous. Beautiful . . .' he is holding on to the globe the gypsies flogged him at Epsom. 'It's worth about 5p that, but to me it's worth a lot more!'

Sylva Honda arrives in the ring with his Japanese lad, Taka.

'Here he is! Here he is!' But Eddy's excitement at seeing his horse evaporates instantly. 'He's been plaited. It's not really natural; it interferes with him . . .' He strides over to Clive Brittain's travelling head lad, John Spouse. 'I'd much rather he'd not been plaited . . .'

'I like him plaited,' says Sylvia.

'Spin a coin . . . ?' suggests John Spouse, ever the diplomat.

Eddy is in the saddling box with the horse as the quarter marks are touched up, and then Clive Brittain walks towards us, throwing open his raincoat as he does so.

'I've got my flasher mac on!' he says, and everyone laughs. He greets each member of the party individually.

'You plaited him . . .', says Eddy.

'*I* didn't do it!' says Clive merrily. 'They do these things behind my back!' It is clear who sets the standards of diplomacy in that yard. Plaiting is forgotten.

Sylvia's lipstick has transferred itself to Clive's cheek and she scrubs at it with a lace handkerchief.

'The old Aga Khan'll be spinning in his grave!' he says.

'He'll come back, the Aga Khan. To race . . .', Eddy says.

'Oh, he must do,' agrees Clive. 'The horse looks a picture . . . the only unfortunate thing is I think the penalty's a big savage . . . You meet the horses that fall just short of a mile, and there's a lot of good horses like that. Still . . . you'll have Taka with his lucky suit on!'

Sylvia now produces a packet of Polo mints.

'Am I allowed to . . . ?' She gestures towards the horse.

116

'Oh no,' says Clive quickly. 'But you can give one to the trainer.' He tucks an extra mint into his waistcoat pocket. 'This'll get 'em talking!'

'He's so full of fun which makes it nice,' Sylvia confides. 'One day we were in the parade ring and it was all quiet and Clive said, "Sylvia, have you seen Sylva Honda yet?" So I said no. So he said, "Look." As I turned round . . .' She lowers her voice to a whisper, 'his private was showing! And I'd never seen a horse's private! And I've gone, "My God! It's a boy!" So Eddy's turned round and said, "Sylvia, will you shut up?" So I've gone, "What do you mean, shut up?" So he's gone, "You're giving me an inferiority complex!" And then Clive's going, " 'Course, you know, Sylvia, when the Queen's at the races . . ." We stood in that middle at Epsom, and we laughed and laughed so much it was unbelievable. I was so shocked – and that was genuine . . . huge! I said, "He's got five legs!" Clive said, "Sylvia, I think it might be that hat you're wearing . . ." You know what he's like! I'll never forget that. The tears were rolling . . .'

The trainer leads everyone into the parade ring and the element of entertainment is so strong it would occasion no surprise at all if he suddenly said, 'OK kids! Let's do the show *here*!' and we all tap-danced across the Royal turf and over the rainbow.

The horse is jig-jogging and snorting.

'He's having a blow,' says Eddy. 'I don't want him to get too excited.' He looks at the horse's rug. 'We were talking about having our own done, but I like Clive's blanket. He's the trainer, isn't he – he's doing all the work.'

Sylvia has her binoculars trained on the packed crowds on the rails who are, in turn, observing her.

'I'm looking at the warts on their noses,' she reports.

'It's going to be a tough race because of the extra weight he's got to give, but having said that . . .' Clive Brittain always leaves hope open-ended. 'There's the Sheikh, Sylvia . . .'

A flock of Arabs sweeps into the ring, and Sylvia gives us a few bars of 'The Sheikh of Araby.'

'It was lovely, that champagne, wasn't it?' says Eddy's sister. 'And we haven't eaten anything because we thought we wouldn't have the time . . .'

'Which one's the Sheikh?' whispers Sylvia, redirecting her glasses.

Jockey Michael Roberts appears to join in with the jollity and for some abstruse reason is teased about his maize and potato farm back in his native South Africa. By now we are in the mood to laugh at anything, but Roberts also manages to confirm that the horse has a hard task ahead of him.

117

'I tell you what,' says Eddy, undaunted. 'If he wins this race today, this horse is going for a real big race. Goes right to the top then.'

'The place to take him then,' advises Clive, 'is Arlington. They're sponsoring horses to go out there; it costs you nearly nothing, and you'd be racing for two or three hundred thousand dollars.'

'Where's that, Clive?' asks Eddy.

'Arlington. In America.'

'We'd have to charter a Jumbo!'

Never were an owner and trainer more suited to each other than Eddy Grimstead and Clive Brittain. This is a marriage made in heaven.

The bell rings for the jockeys to mount and Eddy shoots off with Clive and Michael, shouting 'Good luck, Michael!'

Finally, our little party walks out of the ring and up the shute along with half the names which count in racing, then up to the Owners' Stand to rub shoulders with Lord Howard de Walden, who won the Derby with a home-bred and is now, sadly, one of England's very last great owner-breeders. This remarkably civilized stand with the best company in racing is a reminder that however marvellous horse-racing looks from a spectator's point of view, it looks infinitely and incalculably better from the inside. Being a member of the public is a waste of a life.

The Sheikh's horse wins: Satin Flower.

The moment the race is over Eddy makes for the door and follows his horse from the ring to the wash-down boxes where John Spouse takes off his blazer, rolls up his sleeves and gets down to work. Sylva Honda stretches his neck and lifts his feet, revelling in the cold shower. Taka makes soothing Japanese noises to him. Eddy taps anyone and everyone for their opinion of the race until the horse is led away in the direction of the stables, when he stuffs notes into Taka's pocket.

Sylvia is keeping everyone's spirits up in the Owners' Bar. She was playing boomps-a-daisy with someone until she discovered it wasn't Clive.

'Eddy gets all excited,' she says. 'But that's lovely, isn't it? He said to me, "Have you put your money on the horse?" So I said, "No, darlin' . . . I really don't feel it this time." Isn't it funny? I'm a bit like that – I go by what I feel . . . like some old witch! And I won a thousand pounds last time, at Epsom. I bought myself a suit, a hat and a pair of shoes. Where does it go? Then by the time I've treated the grandchildren . . . But that's part of the fun, isn't it? That's what racing's all about.'

CHAPTER THIRTEEN

Thank God for the
Irish at the Races

On his last Royal Ascot as Her Majesty's Head Coachman, Arthur Showell looks up at the lead horse drawing the first carriage.

'Look at Iceland,' he says, glowing with pride. 'He'd win any of them races out there.'

This is an arcane spectacle: a gloomy barn across the road from the racecourse filled with sweating horses and the Ascot landaus which have just delivered the Royal party to the winner's enclosure at the races. The round journey from Windsor Castle is sixteen miles; the men mounted at noon and will return at around five o'clock, and while briefly resting the horses here, they tuck into packed lunches sent down from the Castle kitchens. Stephen Matthews, Mr Showell's successor elect, is riding Iceland postilion, which involves riding one horse and leading another alongside. Both horses are attached to the wheel horses behind and they, in turn, are attached to the carriage; riding postilion has riding racehorses knocked into a cocked hat when it comes to hard work.

Matthews lights up a cigarette and removes his scarlet jacket heavy with gold braid; his shirt is soaked with sweat.

'People sit at home and watch us on the telly,' he says, 'and they think all we do is trot these horses round the block. They don't realize what we're putting them through. Every horse has got to do so much; it's got to be a good riding horse, plus the fact that they've got to go in any and every position in a team, or posting. And daily – not once in a while, but daily they've got to pass bands and traffic.'

'It's so quiet here at Ascot,' says David Pope, one of the Senior Liveried Servants (Royal-speak for riders) who is on Mulgrave Danty. 'The silence

119

is what you notice until you go through those golden gates. Then there's a crescendo of noise as you go along the course, and it starts to get very noisy with the two bands and the crowds cheering just before you turn into the enclosure.' The crowds had noticed HRH Princess Margaret alight from her accompanying limousine to wave a hankie at the passing carriages and shout her encouragement, which must have been an additional surprise for the horses on their long journey.

Pope and Nigel Day, who is riding Clarence on the same carriage, are sharing their strawberries and cream with me while Nigel's father Joe attacks a pork pie – no mean feat since his teeth, one by one, have vanished over the years as the result of various equine endeavours.

What these five men don't know about horses isn't worth knowing. Their charges are normally stabled in the Royal mews at Buckingham Palace where all the hard graft takes place which goes into making and breaking the harness horses to produce the familiar pomp and glitter. In place of the *Racing Calendar*, which regulates the lives of racehorses, these ceremonial horses have a routine, run of necessity with military precision, which includes Trooping the Colour, the State Opening of Parliament, State visits, the Lord Mayor's Show, international competitions and numerous other duties, and all of this work is carried out under public scrutiny. The amount of work and worry which goes into keeping the show on the road is considerable, and standards are of the highest.

My definition of real privilege does not include cavorting about in my best frock to tweak my image at Royal Ascot, but it most certainly does include being driven by Mr Arthur Showell.

At 9 a.m. sharp one January morning, Mr Showell drives Iceland and his most experienced ceremonial horse, Cardiff, under the Mews' Doric arch and out into London's morning chaos in a training session for the younger horse. Joe Day is standing behind him in the brake, forcing the traffic to submit to his hand signals.

'They try and cut you up . . .', he growls, expressing an implacable distrust of car drivers who barely know what a horse is, let alone how it works. ('Implacable?' asks Steve Matthews. '*Implacable?* Joe wouldn't know a word like that. He'd just put his foot through their windscreen.')

'The hardest thing about driving horses,' says Arthur Showell, 'is to get their heads straight. Looking right to the front and pulling in a straight draught, and not laying over to the right or to the left. Iceland's inclined to turn his head to the left and push over to the right when he's still a bit fresh. If the horses are settled and you can get them to come out of the

Mews and walk quietly up to Hyde Park, then you know you're winning.'

The clatter of hooves sounds above the roar of the traffic, and somehow the pair of horses manage to hear the Head Coachman's office. Cardiff, bought by Arthur Showell from Germany in 1975, was not always the exemplary creature he is today.

'We took him to Ascot where we had him as an outrider,' recalls Mr Showell. 'And he wouldn't go up the Long Walk. He was rearing and backing into the carriages, so we had to change him over and put him in the wheel, and even then he didn't want to go. He was a real rogue. It took a few years, but he's done everything; all the weddings. Iceland will do the same – he's got a lot of quality. A lovely horse.'

Arthur Showell has been driving horses all his life. He was brought up in Jersey at a time when the Nazi occupation necessitated the use of real horsepower, and his accent becomes more pronounced as his enthusiasm rises.

'Sometimes you can yur these horses trotting and they're in rhythm with one another . . . Yur it? All together, like one horse. I'll always remember in Jersey when there were lots of pairs of horses in those days, and you could yur this lovely rhythm.'

It is indeed a wonderful noise and now, with the invisible skills of a genuine artist, he swirls the horses in and out of the trees fringing Rotten Row.

'The way to show off is to sit still,' he says. 'Surprising what you can do with a pair of horses!'

The learning of a lifetime spills from his lips and he will talk driving to even the greatest idiot with all the didactic zest of an expert. To be with him when he drives a four-in-hand through the London streets is to witness a feat of courage – never mind the skill – which takes my breath away.

'It's not twice as hard driving a team of four as driving a pair; it's *ten* times as hard,' he says. 'When you start driving with four reins, if you're honest and admit it, you feel it in your wrists and your shoulders, the weight and the pulling. When I first started driving a four-in-hand, I used to go to bed at night and I didn't know where to lay . . .'

He greets passers-by, and gives the horses a song to encourage them in their work.

'I used to bring the competition team up to Hyde Park and canter them – the four of them. And then I'd shout "Trot!" and hopefully you'd see 'em all chuck themselves into reverse, back-pedal and get themselves into a trot. And the next thing you'd go "Canter!" and away the whole lot'd go. And if you can do that with them, it gives *you* a lot of confidence because you know that if they get frightened and start to gallop, then you've still got control.' Sooner him than me.

At the end of Rotten Row, Iceland and Cardiff are drawn to a halt. They stand like statues and Arthur Showell cannot contain his satisfaction.

'This is priceless,' he says. 'When you get two horses who will stand like this knowing they're waiting to go home. Money can't buy it.'

Back at Ascot, lunch is over and the men mount up to make their way back to the Castle. Having spotted me keeping such elevated company, the police now hold up the traffic for me to cross the road alone and return to the racing and suburbia in excelsis.

A woman is staring at the twenty-nine runners for the Wokingham Stakes circling the parade ring, but her judgement is elsewhere.

'So he'll be leaving Cheshire . . . *Well*.'

'Do you think so?' queried her companion.

'Oh yes. It's been on the cards for a long time. She's such a bad picker, but then – you've only got to look at her breeding.'

I am not convinced that dressing up brings out the best in women. I turn my attention to higher things.

'One goes to Royal Ascot because it is undoubtedly the best racing in the year. The great tragedy is that half the people who go there actually don't appreciate it.'

Michael Jackson, owner of the inestimable Morley Street, is a tense individual who notices these things and reacts very strongly when asked if the racehorse owner is offered a good enough deal in this country.

'No,' he says. '*We are treated like absolute bloody dirt*. I think I was educated when we took Morley Street to Belmont and the horse and the owner were definitely the stars, and I think the greatest star of the lot was the *horse*, which was marvellous, And, rather disconcertingly, with the Americans, second is nowhere; they only *have* a number one spot. You can be second in a million-dollar race, and you're consigned to the shadows and nobody wants to talk to you. In this country, it is undoubtedly the trainer who is the star, and the press consider the owner – maybe with absolute justification – knows nothing about their horse.' He speaks with some asperity.

Do you mind that?

'Yes. I'm getting to mind it more.' His voice rises. 'It's not a bone of contention, but I've got something to say – not to project Michael Jackson – but I've got something to say about my horse. If you've been doing something for sixteen years, whatever your hobby is, and you've followed it very closely, you'll begin to know a fair amount about it.

'Part of the enjoyment in having a horse is actually knowing a lot about it, and being active and participatory, as opposed to turning up – as maybe a lot of people do – with a bunch of friends, four bottles of champagne and a nice cold salmon, getting wildly drunk and your horse comes fourteenth out of twenty-two in the Wokingham Stakes, and then you go home!'

The catalyst which propelled publisher turned paper merchant ('it's an absorbing subject,' he says: 'You can make a lot of money doing it, and that *does* interest me because it feeds other habits: horses, gardens, shooting . . .') into racehorse ownership was a girl friend who showed him his first racing yard.

'Lovely yard, saw the horses, got slightly enthused about it and rushed off to Windsor every Monday night. And then I did practically the most stupid thing in my life. I actually had a very nice Ferrari which was only brought out in dry weather and I sold it for £8,000, bought a racehorse for £5,000 and spent the other three. The racehorse was sold to me not subject to re-examination out of a well-known yard and proceeded to display a broken bone in its knee. There was I with the Ferrari standing at twice the price I'd sold it for in the showroom in the Finchley Road while I was looking at this swollen-kneed, three-legged horse not being trained! But I was completely bitten. Completely. It's the excitement of winning.'

His introduction to ownership continued to be dismal and three more horses proved no better than the first.

'Two of them ran last at Newbury within three races of each other.'

That must have been a searching test of character.

'It was. And it found me out, I can tell you! I walked up to my trainer and said, "This is *ab*solutely disgraceful, and you should never have put them on the racecourse in the first place." With that I walked off and rang her up the next day and said I was moving all three of them tomorrow. I was angry. What I wanted to be told was that if they were no good, then tell me they're no good and then I can get *rid* of them. But for God's sake don't go on spending twelve hundred a month on a horse that's no *good*.'

After a *mauvais quart d'heure* in racing, Jackson suddenly stumbled across the right trainer, and waltzed off to untold good fortune with Morley Street and Forest Sun.

'I was still spouting on about horses, and a girlfriend said, "I'll get you to this dinner party. There's a great trainer coming called Toby Balding; you'll get to sit next to him." So there I was sat next to him and it must have been like taking candy from a baby! I was really fitted up and set up

123

for this very charming and articulate man! I was completely captured from the start, and off we went. Racing is very participatory for me,' he repeats. 'But the beauty of it from my point of view is that I don't actually have to train the horses. There's always something *wrong* with them the whole time; they're a nightmare. I think *that* would seriously *get at* me if I had to take on Toby's day-to-day responsibilities of dealing with horses, and I don't think I would have a sufficient level of communication with the sort of people that he deals with in his yard – who would try my patience *in extremis*!' He laughs, revealing a nice line in self-insight.

Jackson experienced another rite of passage one November day at Ascot last year, when Morley Street was running and an official sent the owner's blood pressure pounding way above danger level.

'I had an owner's day badge, and another owner said, "Meet me in the Garden Room for a drink after our race which is two races before yours." So I went up there and walked in, and two bowler-hatted . . .'

Gestapo?

'Two bowler-hatted gestapo said, "Where are you going?" So I said, "It's pretty obvious where I'm going. I'm going *in here*," and I walked on. He said, " 'scuse me," and he grabbed me by the arm, and I said, "Will you take your hands off me?" and he said, "You're not allowed to go in there." I said, "What do you mean?" And this is the only time, I promise you, I've ever pulled rank – and I felt ashamed about it afterwards. I said, "If you don't bloody well let me go in there to have my bloody drink in your bloody rotten racecourse that I've been coming to for eighteen bloody years, I'm going to take my horse called Morley Street out of the 3.30." '

Jackson buries his face in his hands and kicks his heels in the air at the embarrassment of the memory. He may even have blushed.

'I got really white with anger, which does me no good at all. I said, "I'm not going to steal the silver or expose myself, cause a riot, smash the windows – I'm going to spend money at that bar, and I'm meeting a friend. Why can't I go in there?" America is totally different.'

He solaced himself with a drink in another bar. 'But I was simmering,' he says, 'and I said, "I'm going to find Piers Bengough and get this man fired." I was so angry, and I can't actually afford to get too worked up too often: it's bad for me. Anyway, the day was saved because the friend I wanted to see appeared.' Jackson returned to the Garden Room, past the officials, making what he thought an appropriate gesture – not quite up to the Duke of Devonshire's standard, but similar. 'Terrible!' he says 'Terrible . . .'

The two men on the door of the Annual Members' Bar did not ruffle the owner's *amour propre*; they angered the entrepreneur. More than anything else, it was a symptom of bad business practice.

'The opposite is true at Sandown,' he says. 'We went by chopper on Whitbread day last year, but having come from the inside of the course, we found we were stopped because there were no Club tickets left. In the end I said, "I am *mad keen* to see the racing today; I'm on a tight schedule; coming by helicopter is a lot more expensive than coming by car – will you take me therefore to the Clerk of the Course: I'm *demanding* to be let in." I was escorted all the way to Nick Cheyne, and I said, "Nick. I'm terribly sorry to be a nuisance . . .", and he said, "My dear fellow, here are two tickets, it's free." Of course I made a contribution to whatever, but we were *in*. And he had his staff well trained enough to know what to do in a situation of confrontation.

'But it's not like that at most racecourses. The food is appalling, the entrance prices are entirely wrong . . . You'll love Belmont,' he added. 'They go around polishing the furniture.'

Trainer Liam Codd can also be pushed beyond the point of exasperation with racecourse management. In 1989 his best horse, Madraco, fell into a black hole on Town Moor at Doncaster, taking with him a good many of Codd's hopes and plans for the future. At first, the authorities denied the existence of this black hole, which considerably angered the 35-year-old from Galway who rents a yard near Evesham.

'But I was vindicated *the next day*,' he says. 'And if Madraco had won, I had a bloody good bet on it!' He laughs. 'I'd have me own place! Me whole life went just like that!' and he snaps his fingers to demonstrate the speed with which Fate struck down his future.

The soft Galway accent takes the sting out of what he says.

'Accent? What accent . . . ?'

Being Irish also means he has a problem with the petty restrictions the English value so highly, and although he is conforming in top hat and tails today, he looks less like a man going to Royal Ascot than a man who has already been to a damn good wedding reception. In a word, dishevelled. He is happier on the gallops at home – an oval half-mile of all-weather with another half-mile shute at one end, set in the gentle Worcestershire landscape, with three mares in foal behind post and rails in the centre. Sarah, his fiancée, runs the stud end of the operation.

'She comes from a good horsey family as well,' he says. 'Her grandmother, Mrs Scott, bred Park Top. When you've got a few horses you tend to treat them as individuals really. Mostly people send horses to us; we're not in a position to be able to go and buy horses, but in saying that again, the rejects have been the luckiest ones, really.' He indicates one of the horses being ridden round the track by Sarah. Sagaman, when we got him first . . . the day I picked him up he wouldn't go in the box he was that sour. It took us an hour and a half to get him in. We just coaxed him nice and gentle – we never touched him . . . We never use a twitch; we don't have one in the yard. We don't have a Chifney in the yard and there's only a certain amount of lads I will allow to ride out with a stick unless I'm there.'

'Get that dog out!' Sarah yells for the Jack Russell to be stopped from chasing the two horses up the tan; a whistle from Liam removes him, and the horses canter past us. Sagaman, a bonny horse, takes a pull on the bend.

'He looks well, doesn't he? She's having a job there . . . look at that!' He chuckles. 'This is packed here on a Sunday. I always give the lads a day off during the week and they come in on Sundays, and a lot of the owners come then and they see their horses work and do whatever they want to do with them, really.'

He has one straight question for any prospective owner.

'Can you afford £600 a month? That's the bottom line – as simple as that. If you can't afford it, don't have a horse. Then I go up to the pub with him – it's usually a Sunday morning – and if he blends in with the rest of the owners, he's in. But if he doesn't . . . I've got some smashing owners here in the Midlands, and they backed me before I even had a winner.

'When we started training we took anything. We needed the horses; we needed the runners. When you start from nothing you can't be choosy, can you? But I soon learned me lesson with that one. I'd like to think we're pretty straight with the owners and they know everything that's going on, you know? I remember me father telling me once there's only one thing about telling lies – you've got to remember what you've said, and I haven't got the best memory in the world so I don't tell lies!

'I'm as happy as Larry doing what I'm doing. Sometimes, yes, it's a pain in the neck, but I wouldn't want to do anything else. Horses are my life and that's it.'

In the office – a converted horse box – with an assortment of tranquil dogs and cats, the Jockey Club's Rules of Racing are at his elbow.

'I've had a few runs-in with them I suppose, so I have to try and keep on top of them, really! But politics and religion I don't talk about, and I suppose you can put the Jockey Club into that category. They're a law on their own. Racing is a funny business. Funnily enough, I like David Pipe; he's a helluva nice feller.'

The casual dismantling of England's traditions holds a morbid fascination for Liam Codd, and Galway gives the lick of poetry to the stories he tells against us.

'I loved hunting when I came here; absolutely adored it. My father was Master of Hounds for twenty-two years in Ireland, and I went hunting a couple of times when I came here, and you got a hundred horses out. Fifty of those might be genuine country people who can ride horses and they know what hunting is about, and the other fifty comes out from the city. They haven't got a goddamned clue; they ride their horses into the ground, they gallop on the roads, they gallop them across the farmer's fields, and the Joint Master will be among 'em! They've *bought* themselves into the hunt, you know? I can't stand toffee-nosed buggers. That's why I *love* racing in the north; northern jump tracks are really good fun, and the jumps boys are all right. I know 'em all now – you meet 'em once and they recognize you the next time, you know?'

What do you want out of this game? I ask.

'I've achieved my ambition. My ambition was to become a racehorse trainer, and I've done it. Whatever I achieve now is a bonus. I've trained twenty winners from nothing, but in saying that again, now I'd like to buy my own place, train maybe thirty to forty horses, have maybe thirty to forty owners that I can train for and do the job properly. But I've achieved me ambition.'

Now the door is pushed open, and a couple of owners appear. As he departs to make the coffee ('Just a little drop of whisky in it?'), Liam says that one of them, Tony Waddley, is a magistrate which comes in handy, and Tony Waddley says what he wants out of racing is a winner at Cheltenham or Aintree. 'That's all!' Tim Smith, in partnership with Waddley as a property developer, immediately establishes his racing bona fides.

'Do you know Desmond Stoneham?' he asks. '*The Times* Paris racing correspondent? He almost married my cousin but they called it off on the steps of the church!' He suffers from the belief that the Establishment has a conspiracy against the small trainers, and he disliked being a syndicate member in a big Lambourn yard because his access to the horse was limited. 'You can come here whenever you want to,' he says.

Warmed up by the morning whisky, the conversation ranges far and wide but ends up where it began: castigating authority.

'I'll never forget this . . .', says Liam Codd. 'When we raffled the horse the first year, two labourers on the road won it. They became owners overnight, you know? We went racing to Newcastle. I was dressed in me rags, really: I was doing the horses, and I said to the lads, "Come with me and I'll get you your tickets for the day." They didn't know where they were going, so I went in first. The security guard looked at me, thought that's a bit strange, but once he saw me badge – in I went. And the two boys followed behind me with big long coats on, no tie, and the Secretary man put up his hand and said, "Where're you going?" Nando his name was, he was Hungarian: "Me got runner today. Me racehorse owner . . ." The guy looked at them, and said, "Do you work here?" I thought I'll leave this for a minute and see what happens. He had a right go at them. He was almost telling them to .... off. "Excuse me,' I said. "These are racehorse owners." He said, "They're what?" "Will you let them in?" I said. "They've got a racehorse."

'So when we got the badges, they said, "Oh, you can't come into the ring unless you've got a tie," so we were marched off to the Secretary's office to root around in a big box of ties. I got one a little skinny one, and the other one got a tie that wide! Well, if you had seen them, it was unbelievable . . . The horse won! They had a carriage clock at the presentation. He came down to sixteens, didn't he?'

'33–1,' says Tim Smith. "I remember that.'

'We had a good few quid on him,' continues Codd, and we went into the Champagne Bar because the boys had never had champagne before, and Jonjo O'Neill was in there. The boys were starting to get a little bit tipsy – I'd laced it with a little drop of brandy as well – and Nando said to me, 'Oh, Jonjo . . .', and he gets up with his race card and says, 'Will you sign this?' I know Jonjo fairly well, so I had a little chat and explained the case – and this is what I like about northern racing – he came down to our table and there was about eight or ten of us, and we had a really good drink. And the boys – it must've been the best day of their life. And in my opinion, that's what racing is about. Then there was a bookie just behind us, and someone said, "What sort of day've you had?" "Oh," he said, "good day bar one. Sagaman." And we had backed him, and he had got caught for a right few quid. So I tapped him on the shoulder and asked him who was backing him. It had leaked somewhere along the line because we backed him off the course, and had a chat with him, and he joined in as well. After getting skint he ended up having a right session there!'

Sagaman is back to fight another day, but this time in the Queen Alexandra Stakes, the last race of Royal Ascot. His trainer is surrounded by a troupe of his owners transfixed by the television screen in the Owners' and Trainers' Stand. The Senior Steward is at their side, but cut off from them by a glass partition as if he were the accused in some trial of international importance, and his black silk topper adorns the separate television set he is watching. Michael Doocey has owned Sagaman for two weeks. This is his first ever runner; the first time his colours have been raced.

Ridden by Steve Cauthen, Sagaman runs a thoroughly professional race and is second for a good while, even heading the field briefly, but at the end of the two-mile six-furlong trip he is short of pace.

'I thought he was going to win there for a minute!' chuckles Liam. 'He ran a great race; he didn't disappoint us, that's for sure.'

We clutter noisily down the steps at the back of the stand and charge across the winner's enclosure.

'He's going to make a nice horse next year over the jumps, isn't he, on that form?' Liam calls over his shoulder. 'He might go to the Galway, do you see – the Galway Hurdle . . .'

Lester Piggott, whose ride in the race had been Norton's Coin, winner of the previous year's Cheltenham Gold Cup, is giving his explanation to Sirrell Griffiths, his face creased into the strain of wasting, and when the Welsh farmer recounts to me what the Maestro said, even he slips into an imitation of Piggott's voice.

' "If I'd wanted to," he said, "I could've finished fourth – but what was the point of knocking the horse about?" '

In his more familiar Carmarthen tones, Griffiths adds a note of frustration.

'I could see that with my own eyes . . . I know it doesn't mean nothing to Lester at all,' he says, 'but it would have meant a lot more to me to have gone into the winner's enclosure there . . .' He gestures towards it. 'Just gone in there, although he was fourth, you know?'

Next we encounter Steve Cauthen near the top of the ring.

'Well done,' says Liam.

'He ran a blinder,' drawls Cauthen. 'He would have been suited by a stronger pace, but at the same time I didn't feel I could go on and do it by myself from a mile . . . because he likes just having a lead, doesn't he? Then when that horse went, I went with him, and he was going good – in fact I was travelling better than him turning into the straight, but then he went . . . a bit one-paced . . .'

'I'm very pleased,' says Liam.

'Yes, he ran a cracker. I thought I was going to hold on to fourth, just near the line . . .'

'Not to worry. Not to worry . . . Chuffed to bits with that. I might go chasing with him next year because he jumps really well, you know?'

'Yes? And he had plenty of weight, didn't he?' says Cauthen. 'He was equal weights with Nomadic Way. It was a good performance.'

'Thanks very much.'

'Cheers, Liam.'

Cauthen disappears towards the weighing room looking pallid and tired, like all the top jockeys, with the exception of Willie Carson.

'So what won it?' asks Liam. 'I didn't even see what won it!'

Sarah is washing the horse down in the pre-parade ring.

'I think he ran brilliantly,' she says of her favourite horse who is blowing hard, red nostrils distended, and looking as if he's been in a race. 'Steve didn't hit him, did he?'

'I think we'll probably run him in the Cesarewitch, you know? That or the Galway – one of the two. Mike'll be pleased with that run, won't he?'

Mike Doocey, the owner, and his supporters, prominent among whom is his friend Michael Fleming and a top-hatted priest with a pink rosebud in his buttonhole and a cigarette in his fingers, arrive to join the horse and trainer. They all live in Birmingham, but hail from County Mayo, and the priest has evidently appointed himself the owner's racing manager.

'I was just saying he'd win the Galway Hurdle on that run. He moved really well on the ground as well,' says the trainer.

'I think he likes a bit of good ground, y'know,' says the priest. 'Well now, that's true. It was a slow enough race for him.'

'And he had to do a little bit of donkey work there,' says the trainer.

'He had really . . . settin' the pace,' adds the friend.

'You wouldn't get a better ride on him than that jockey; he has the hands to do it well,' says the priest. 'I think he's a great jockey.'

'The trouble was there was nothing in the race to go, was there?' asks the friend.

'But if you walk for six furlongs you get a mile-and-a-half race, don't you?' says the priest.

'He'll be some 'chaser!' says the trainer, his accent becoming more pronounced by the second.

'Now, now . . . different kettle of fish, though,' cautions the priest. 'The jumpin' is what's goin' to count, y'know. But if he's a good hurdler he'll take to the jumpin' all right.' A bundle of ten pound notes is making a bid for freedom from the breast pocket of his tail coat. 'Ah, it's all right . . . I'm givin' it away today! That was to put on the horse but I couldn't get it on. It's saved.'

'Steve said he would've hung on for fourth but he really didn't want to knock him about . . .'

'That's right. You'd be gettin' the prize money all right, but you'd be doin' yourself a lot more damage . . .'

'He's got his ears pricked; he enjoyed that!' says the trainer.

'He has, he has . . . He knows he's had an ole race . . . He'll be able to go to Galway and the Cesarewitch. Galway's the end of July, and the Cesarewitch is the end of October. He'd have seven or eight weeks,' says the priest, his fervour mounting.

'That race put him spot on for the Galway,' agrees the trainer.

'Ah! we'll see the sea!' says the friend, raring to go.

'He's not an awkward horse – he's a handy enough horse, isn't he? You need to be very handy in the Galway, y'know. I don't know, Liam, he might be handicapped around eleven stone four in Galway, something like that,' calculates the priest.

'I tell you what,' says the trainer. 'He's not very highly rated on the Flat and there's a two-mile amateur race at Galway . . .'

'There is!' says the priest.

'The first day – and you get a bonus if you win the amateur Flat race and win the Galway Hurdle . . .'

'A lot of them do, actually!' says the priest.

'But he's not a horse I can run . . .'

'. . . twice in a week – no, no . . .' The priest is ready with the responses.

'He hasn't run for eight or nine weeks . . .'

'Ten weeks,' the priest corrects the trainer.

'That was probably his best race ever.'

'It is, yes,' allows the priest.

'Christ! He got in front! He had a go!' The trainer is jubilant.

'Christ! He led 'em for two miles two,' boasts the friend. 'Two miles three even!'

The owner now ventures an opinion.

'I'd say if he'd've rode him out he could've got fourth, but what's the use of that?'

'No use, no.' All of us speak as one.

'First time you've ever worn a hat like that!' the priest says to the owner.

'He'll want to go to Ascot every year!' says the trainer.

'At least next time around I'll know where I'm going!'

Thank God for the Irish at the races.

Now the company turns to the irony of Doocey deciding to become an owner during a recession.

'Ah, somebody has to buy them when they're going down!' says the friend.

At a time when racing is in the doldrums, this has been one of the best meetings for years – a meeting which no one in their right mind would have missed but for reasons to do with the Thoroughbred racehorse, and no other reason. John Dunlop tops the trainer's list and Steve Cauthen is leading jockey. The Maktoum family dominates the owners' list with seventeen placed horses, seven of them winners earning a total of £446,810; and yet not even Sheikh Mohammed has equalled the old Aga Khan's individual success in his Ascot heyday.

Summer has come at last, and the huge push of people heading for the exit is very good-natured; some are singing. Women carry their shoes, and tables in the coach park have been piled high again with salmon and champagne for another feast. The sunlight flows through the beeches and the oaks of Windsor Great Park; the bracken is curled futurist green and the corn is golden. The Castle appears grey and sudden on the horizon, and coxed fours pull along the river which takes the bright blue from the sky. A Rolls-Royce stops to give assistance to a broken-down Cortina. Women who are loath finally to remove the hats which have been their proof of importance put them on and off in the backs of cars. Early morning rain had dampened the dust so that one can see for miles, but not beyond the social imperative.

On 1 August Sagaman won the Ir£35,000 Guinness Galway Hurdle at 25–1.

CHAPTER FOURTEEN

Horses for Courses

Ascot may be Royal but Goodwood is Glorious and for me, pretty close to heaven. One of the greatest treats in store for the new owner will be the voyage of discovery around England's racecourses as he accompanies his horse in its winning endeavours. He will form attachments to specific tracks for all sorts of sentimental, superstitious and, who knows, perhaps even practical reasons.

The second day at Goodwood's July Meeting is lucid, the sun is high and the horizons are drawn by the glimmering sea and a man-made landscape of woods and fields. The delicacy and adventurous elegance of the newest stand echo the pavilions and piers of the Sussex coastline; it is a triumph. The racing Establishment all but brings its bucket and spade along to Goodwood, and the holiday atmosphere is underlined by the bare legs of the trainers' wives. Bookmaker John Cohen – son of the more famous Jack – sashays on to his front-line pitch in yet another natty get-up. He takes holidays more often than I take umbrage, pausing briefly in the ring for a spot of work before jetting back to the Mediterranean.

'It's cheaper to be there than it is to be here,' he says to explain his hedonism. 'And I'm not in love with the business like the rest of them. I don't know anything about racing; I don't have an attitude about the horses. I'm a chartered accountant.'

Luca Cumani's Second Set steals the show from Shadayid at 5–1 in the £125,000 Group 1 Sussex Stakes.

'I have been trying to win it for years!' says the trainer to a discerning crowd, his few gracious words ringing out in contrast to the surly offering from the trainer of Dilum, the two-year-old which towers above his rivals in the Richmond Stakes.

Chester is another favourite course – the horses run on two legs alongside the city walls; and at Stratford, which is an extremely well-run track, they run on Shottery Meadow on the banks of the Avon where Garrick organized the Jubilee Race in 1769 as the highlight of his Great Shakespearean Jubilee. Yarmouth is dotty and fun, and Salisbury is seriously horsey but the endless angsting about Lloyd's is a bore. Brighton is a curiosity; an extravagantly ordinary course run by the Council ('You'd think the Council could afford a bloody roller . . .', mutters Rod Simpson) and I can vouch for the fact that anyone who has seen the inside of Brixton Prison will feel at home here.

Ascot on Diamond Day is mandatory, and Generous is bewitching when he wins another £200,000 for his owner and proves he is a great racehorse. His performance tempts me to forgive the course a good deal and confirms a belief that racing at level weights is infinitely preferable to anything else. I leave immediately after it and drive like the wind to an evening meeting at Warwick with 86-year-old Nan Widdowson who sips her whisky and says no one these days can touch Gordon Richards. Another chestnut, the veteran seven-furlong specialist Helawe, wins the races and a crate of Carling Black Label for his absent trainer, Sir Mark Prescott. And I bet he drinks it too. The red brick of the old racecourse buildings, dressed overall in geraniums, nemesia and petunias, glows in the sunset; a brass band wearing bright ochre jackets plays 'Happy Birthday', and five thousand punters are happy. It is, however, essential to avert the eyes from a carbuncular new bar.

There is no Royal Enclosure at Devon's Newton Abbot track; there is not even a Members' Enclosure. Racing here is very much in touch with its roots in point-to-pointing and all the better for that. The racecourse is largely run by one of the most endearing double acts in the game, Lang and Nekola.

Secretary Carl Nekola had been involved with the course since 1932, and Clerk of the Course Ivor Lang has farmed locally for forty years. His legs are shaped to a horse and he isn't going level. A lazy Devon accent rolls around his words as he mocks the sport he loves.

'It's ridickerless that people should ever do it! No one would go racing unless they were the biggest optimists in the world. But it's great fun!'

It is August Bank Holiday, and the first meeting of the season. A light drizzle is falling.

'It's what we call racing weather,' explains Nekola briskly. 'It gets them off the beach!'

The holidaymakers and the locals mingle together with the racing community and no one cares about the weather.

'Ivor and I, we work as a team,' says Nekola.

'Well, Carl knows everything about racing, so he comes to me and says, "With your permission Ivor, I think we'll do so-and-so . . ." And then we do it!' They explode into laughter.

'It works,' says Nekola.

'Oh, it works,' agrees Lang.

It certainly does, and the welcome here is second to none.

'We pride ourselves on being a friendly track, Ivor, don't we?'

'We want them to come back . . .' endorses Lang. 'We cater for the majority, whether it be horses or patrons, rather than the minority and I think that is the direction that racing has to go.'

'We cater for the moderate horses,' says Nekola.

'Well, they are the majority, you see,' says Lang. 'We would rather spread our prize money over the whole of the card than give a lot of money for one race, and you get three horses and Jenny Pitman comes down . . . Like when Bregawn came down and cake-walked it. It's a non-event really, and a non-betting race too. We had a selling race yesterday; a very very moderate lot of horses, but there were four horses jumped the last in line and the stands *rocked*. People really enjoyed it. And there's nothing better than if you can get a crowd of people cheering; you can go away happy and think you've achieved something.'

'We want the runners at this time of year,' says Nekola when he stops coughing for long enough to croak out a few words. Lang takes over.

'I've given the ground firm today, but I err on the pessimistic side, so actually it's better than firm and people will be pleased and come again. I would rather have three horses declared for a race and they all run than have six, and then three complain and take their horses out, saying it wasn't as described. Mrs Pitman took us to Portman Square . . . That makes you nervous! But it's not such an ordeal as you imagine. We won actually . . .'

'Ivor handles her very well,' comments Nekola, and surely this emollient administrator could soothe the most savage breast.

'Let's face it,' says Lang, 'we get a lot of horses with a history of leg trouble, and then if they break down they say, "Oh, a lot of horses break down at Newton Abbot, and it's the firm ground that breaks them down . . .", but very often they've got a history and you can't always blame the course. Nothing makes me happier than to see all the horses and all the jockeys go home sound – then we've had a good day.'

The first Bank Holiday meeting after the war yielded Newton Abbot its biggest ever crowd.

'Some 16,054 paying customers,' says Nekola, whose forte is figures. 'I had a phone call from the signal box on the railway line to tell me that a boatload was coming up the river from Teignmouth. I sent somebody down to meet them with a roll of tickets!'

Last season a gatecrasher turned up in a Porsche. He gave the name of an owner so that he was issued with a free badge, but later on the real owner turned up.

'We have one or two wily security lads,' says Lang, 'and they put together the numbers of the badges and the numbers of the cars, so we were able to go back and get this chap. It wasn't his *wife* with him, it was a lady friend, and he was very embarrassed!'

'We talked to him nicely . . .', says Nekola.

'We got £50 out of him for the Injured Jockeys' Fund!' says Lang. 'Actually, he *was* an owner . . .'

Newton Abbot's supporters are very loyal. Dick Francis turns up every year for this meeting from his home in Florida.

'I did miss *one* year,' the gentle and courteous crime writer tells me with an eye to accuracy. 'I couldn't come back to England for tax reasons. When I was champion jockey I rode three winners here on the first day. They make me very welcome, and my family have stayed in the same hotel in Paignton for twenty years.'

Forty years of punting at Newton Abbot hasn't been a day too much for Betty Tracy. There were many years of foreign postings with her late husband ('Nigeria's racing is all out or dead stop!') when leave meant dashing back to Newton Abbot for a spot of the real thing. 'I'm a gambler!' she cheerfully admits; she is also a member of the South-West Racing Club which is based at the racecourse and sends its members hither and yon for good racing. 'Deauville this weekend!' It's obviously the life of Riley in Devon in the National Hunt season.

The Stewards' lunch tends towards the traumatic. First, their Secretary, Captain Stopford, stalks into the room.

'Which one of you sharks took my race card? It's the one I'd marked up . . .'

Then the mother of the Inspector of Courses sends back her chicken chasseur. The portion is too large.

'I can't bear waste. I think of all the starving people in the world . . .' she says as I hoover up the entire menu right through to the treacle tart along with Georgina Robarts of the Racecourse Association.

'I love coming here,' she says, and we fall to a heady discussion on how horses can so easily cease to be a factor in a life and become instead its structure. Like all Newton Abbot's aficionados, she is quite blind to the

136

dog track in the centre of the course, and the stock car track, and the driving range, all of which help to keep the place afloat despite the Levy Board cuts. She sees only the horses.

'Basically I work to keep my horses,' she says. 'Jimmy Frost has just backed my three-year-old, and he's just said to me, "Come up next week and ride him out with the string." I said, "You must be joking!" That really scares the . . . that really scares me!' But she will, of course.

'The horse world is a small world,' says Jimmy Frost a little later on into the afternoon. 'The people here will have watched me as a small boy on my ponies in the shows, then on in the point-to-pointing field and as I slowly progressed to here, and then climbed up the ladder and up the country to end up at Cheltenham. But it's not cut and dried even when you've got the best to ride; the good people are the ones that make the fewest mistakes.'

The most popular winner of the day is a thirteen-year-old Deep Run gelding called Mr Seagull. The stands roar the local horse home for his permit-holder owner, Jenny Hembrow, who has ridden point-to-point winners and beaten the professionals under Rules. Over copious drinks and sandwiches in the Directors' Room (*de rigueur* here for all the winners and their friends) she talks about her star.

'I never got so excited riding a winner as I do training one,' she says. 'I get more nervous as well! Because I love Gullie so, I won't put his haynet up at home before we go racing in case something happens and he has to be shot, and doesn't come back. You get so fond of them! It's always been a standing joke at home because I adore him, and one day my daughter said, "Mum, if you had to choose who to put down between Dad and Mr Seagull, what would you choose?" And I said, "It would need some thinking about . . . !"'

She gets up at 4.45 each morning to do Gullie before she goes off to ride out for a local trainer, but she prefers this to the idea of training full-time herself.

'I'm not sure I could take the hassle of the owners, and I don't care what they say, it is harder for a woman. Look at Mrs Pitman. I admire her terribly. She's very strong-willed and she puts her horses well first.'

The mirror image of Newton Abbot and Ivor Lang is Sandown Park and Nick Cheyne.

Sandown seems to have found a permanent ritzy niche as the Racecourse of the Year, and after three years as a trainee with United Racecourses, Nick Cheyne found himself its Clerk of the Course.

'To go and land the number one job was out of this world, really,' he says.

It is Sloane Ranger Evening at his racecourse, and this popular Clerk of the Course has been cast to type. He lives in Fulham, OK yah.

'I kicked off this morning at about five-thirty when the alarm went off, and I'm the fastest man on the A3 so I was here by six-fifteen. I like to check everything's all right in the stables if there have been any horses in overnight. Check the rainfall, and then ring the Weather Centre for the forecast. Then I spin round the racecourse on foot from about six-forty and there were one or two places where I just wanted to put a touch more water on this morning. At about seven-thirty I'm back, whereupon I ring the Press Association or Racecall or Radio 5 to update the going report if there's been any change. Then I'm available in the office to take calls from trainers. I try to make myself available twenty-four hours a day in the lead-up to a race meeting; my mobile telephone number is on the answering machine, or people can ring me at home. It's probably a good thing I haven't got a wife; she'd have walked out by now. The going is a pretty contentious issue. A lot of people get pretty steamed up about it.'

Jenny Pitman has a word to say on the subject.

'There are some Clerks of Courses you can trust implicitly and that is that,' she says. 'If we make a decision about running our horses, and we take them all the way to Sandown or all the way to Newton Abbot, it's cost the owners a lot of money for transport, to have the horse plated, the box driver, the lad and the rest of it all go there, and if it's like the bloody road and the horse doesn't run, I get fined. If I do decide to run the horse and it gets injured, then that horse *at best* is going to be off for twelve months. The person that pays the cost at the end of the day is not the Clerk of the Course, it's not Jenny Pitman, it's not the owner – it is the horse. He pays the ultimate price, and that for me is unacceptable. And what you're talking about for the owner . . . it ain't just the expenses of the day. That horse is worth ten grand; tomorrow morning it is worth six hundred quid.

'I actually had one good horse removed from my care because I refused to run 'im one day. I knew that the owner badly wanted this horse to run, and I had prepared it to run in the race, and on the Monday I'd rung him up and said, "I'm very worried about Saturday; they're calling that ground firm at Sandown now, and if they say at Sandown the ground is firm, they mean it's faster." And I said, "I really don't want to run your horse on that ground because it'll bugger 'im up." So now the owner's getting hot and bothered 'cos he's arranged for his friends to go to Sandown, and I said, "Look . . . there is no rain forecast, what can I do about it?" And he said to me . . .' (her words are heavy with emphasis), '"I don't know, but you'll have to do something." That was it. I said to him, "All your whingeing and whining ain't going to make things any different. I can't run that horse on that ground." So he took his horse away, which was fine. That was his decision. I'd made mine, he made his.'

David Stait backs her up.

'I try to say to owners, "Look, if you've got an asset in your company worth five, ten, fifty or a hundred thousand pounds, if one of your employees does a deliberate act and reduces that asset from £100,000 to £1,000, you wouldn't contemplate making that move. Now if you look at your horse as an asset . . ." But it never ceases to amaze me that they will not apply the same logic to their horses as they do to their businesses.'

Nick Cheyne understands all too well the importance of such considerations to trainers.

'I was at Portman Square yesterday on an appeal. An extremely nice trainer was going to run a horse here in May but he felt the ground had dried up more than would have suited his horse, so he took it out. It was a Group 3 Pattern race worth £44,000, and he was fined 1 per cent which is quite a lot of money. The Stewards felt the ground was as given. It was my first time there, and I hope possibly the last.'

Cheerfulness breaks in again.

'The first person to take me racing was a woman!' It was his grandmother. 'Women must be encouraged to come racing and see what it's all about, and to enjoy it. I think they think it's just a day out for the boys, but it's not at all.'

They get drunk and cry, I say, rather irritated because yet another girl is sobbing into the arms of her friend in the Ladies' Cloakroom. 'What else can I do for him . . .', she weeps. Leave him is the answer to that. Leave him and find a better one.

'When they see the grey horse win here, they all cry!' he laughs. 'He's been a godsend to us. But I'm not certain I agree with women coming racing with *me* when I go racing, unless they understand about it.'

Oh asserlutely, I agree, slipping into the lingo.

'I just love to be a free agent rather than hanging about because someone's nattering to some old bore who's crashing on about their great uncle's funeral or something . . . especially at Ascot or Cheltenham where I like to be on the move.'

What a challenge he must be to the gels.

'To be honest with you I'd never been racing at Sandown until I came to work here, but now I love the place. It has a special atmosphere and they couldn't've built a nicer grandstand fifteen years ago, and everything is so compact. You can have a drink on the terrace, look at the horses and have a bet all at the same time, then whip straight back to see the horses go down to the start without having to wear your shoe leather out. The whole thing about racing is it's meant to be fun, and I think so many people lose sight of that.'

This evening meeting is doubtless fun for Barney Curley. His horse Threshfields lands a major gamble in the twenty-runner Harpers and Queen Handicap and takes more than £90,000 out of the ring. The apprentice down to ride the horse in the newspapers had been replaced by the venerable John Reid, and this caused some consternation.

'The government told racing it must help itself,' says Curley, 'and I was just helping myself.'

'Fun?'' says owner Frank Hill. 'Look at the training bills; you can hardly treat racing as all fun when you're paying out sums like that. Mind you . . .', he pauses for maximum effect, 'I must be the only man in England who tells his trainer he should put his prices up! I pay my bill within an hour of receiving it; when I have to wait a week I'll get out. Short credit makes long friends. But I've cut my horses in training down from five to four now . . . *and* I've finished with Sophia Loren and Gina Lollobrigida. Too expensive!'

Mr Hill has developed a practical approach towards horse racing.

'I've *had* to,' he insists. 'But I would never have a share in a horse. My father gave me some advice once: "You only want one partner – the one you sleep with," and I don't think he meant a different one every week!'

This tiny, feisty horse-lover ('I've always been a cocky devil!'), on whom the patina of amateurism shines very brightly, has had 117 winners during his career as an owner, and he is going to win the 1993 Cheltenham Gold Cup with his horse, Be Surprised.

'I've called him that because I shall be surprised if he wins, and I shall be surprised if I'm there to see it.'

Frank Hill is eighty-nine years old.

'I can remember Tunbridge Wells when there were four motor cars and at least four hundred horses . . .' His father had a meat business – or rather, *the* meat business in the town, and horses were used for delivery. 'One day he had the bright idea of buying a Thoroughbred for me to deliver meat on horseback. I had to put up my leathers four holes and rest a damn great butcher's basket weighing thirty pounds across my knees! Those were the days when they used to come from Millionaire's Mile to the shop with a coach and pair and the lady never got out of the carriage, and the coachman never got off the box. He would summon attention by waving his whip.

'Swank is what I can't abide in racing today. We had a lot of the *nouveaux riches* after the first War. I do detest people who have little or no knowledge about racing, airing it. It's all boloney; they don't know which end the oats go in, and they change their trainer as often as they change their shirts! They should blame themselves and sell the horse – that's where the trouble lies. Robert Sangster was the first person to disturb racing by spending money like water, and now the blinking Arabs . . .'

Frank Hill bought his first horse in 1921 and he asked Len Hammond in Lewes to train it for him.

'"How much do you charge, Mr Hammond?" I asked.

'"£3 10s 0d a week," replied the trainer. "But in your case I think we'll say ten shillings a day." I suppose he thought I wouldn't last.'

Seventy years later the very idea amuses him, and he has recently double-checked that he is still good for £50,000 at Tattersalls should the fancy take him to buy any more horses.

'I've bought every horse I've ever owned bar one, and I think I hold the record for buying one of the cheapest horses. I paid £7 11s 9d for a horse whose sire Grand Parade won the 1919 Derby. He was a gentleman, and the 11s 9d was the cost of the rail transport from Lewes to Tunbridge Wells. I bought it without seeing it. We had a little gang in Lewes in the old days when it was a real training centre and we used to meet in The White Hart at twelve o'clock on Sundays, after we'd come out of church . . . One Sunday, Towser Gosden kept missing his round because he was haggling over this horse with a riding-school master, so *I* bought it to get my whisky! I trained him on a bicycle; you couldn't ride him – his legs would hardly stand his own weight! But I finished up winning two races on him, and the greatest thrill without doubt is *riding* winners for me.'

He recalls being ushered out of the weighing room as a gentleman rider, along with the future Duke of Norfolk and the Hon. Gerald Wellesley, son of the Duke of Wellington, by a laconic voice which said, "You're certainly not gentlemen, and you'll never be bleedin' jockeys . . ."

'I preferred to ride against professionals,' he says. 'It's safer. I once beat Piggott over hurdles . . . at Folkestone.' He pauses. 'It was Keith Piggott; the father.' He also hunted regularly. 'I gave that up about ten years ago.'

This enthusiast is a tremendous connoisseur of racecourses.

'I've won a race on nearly every racecourse in England. That's saying something, isn't it? Gatwick was the toughest course to ride around; the fences were next to the National, and I hit the deck several times.'

141

It was Lingfield which saw the debut of the five-year-old Be Surprised, and Frank Hill recounts the details with relish.

'Sea Bird II is his grandsire – not bad, not bad . . .', he says with heavy irony. 'He stands 17.2 if he stands an inch; tremendous heart room, and I think he's got everything I want. Very good temperament, the backside of a cook, and he's a courageous monkey. I took him to Lingfield in March this year, and I told the jockey, "On the outside; don't you get into any sort of trouble, I want this horse to see everything." I didn't say don't *try* . . . but he's got to jump and that's that. There were about eight runners, just the normal jumping field, and I always watch my horses now in the Stewards' room on the courses all round here – that's arranged, and I was in there with the Steward who was watching on television. And this old boy (about twenty years younger than me!) was getting a bit excited. They went off like scalded cats, and after about a mile and a half as they very often do, two went on the floor; come to the next one, and another went on the floor and the Steward said, "You'll be placed, you'll be placed . . . !" He was getting more excited than I was, 'cos I didn't expect anything with the instructions I'd given. Anyway – went to the last fence and there was only one in front of me, and he fell at the last. I won three thousand two hundred quid, and I'm ashamed to say, I won another four hundred because there was no third!

'Well, I've jumped one hurdle, haven't I? I've seen him win, so that's one thing I shan't be surprised about . . . The poor silly horse had never seen a racecourse before, and when I took the reins from the lad for the photograph, he trod on my foot – he must weigh three-quarters of a ton – and he broke my toes! I said he can do it again as long as he promises to win first!'

CHAPTER FIFTEEN

'For the love
of the game'

Eileen Butler is the very model of a trainer's wife. Her involvement with Paddy Butler's yard is total.

'She's up to her neck!' laughs Roland Dubey the farrier as he enlists her help to get hold of a horse evading everyone else as it prances about in the paddock's long grass and the sunshine. Eileen dashes off, and in a trice she catches hold of the animal's headcollar.

'There you are, you see?' says Roland. 'It took the man to catch it!' The horse calls loudly in protest at his lost honour. The Alsatian guard dog at the end of a piece of twine stares vacantly until the commotion is over; his synapses rarely connect to produce the right reaction at the right time.

Paddy Butler trains on the edge of disaster near Plumpton.

'We've been in the racing a long time now, and I wouldn't be in it but for her, and there are days when she wouldn't be in it but for me,' says Paddy candidly, County Cork teasing the English language into idiosyncrasy. 'I would never have succeeded in anything only for Eileen. She would be a much better person than I am as far as business, and I am not a very good judge of people: Eileen would be more of a judge of people. She would carry on here the very same as if I were not here.'

What a mercy he found her.

'And I've got another problem,' he confesses. 'I can't watch the races. This is as sure as you're sitting on that settee. If a horse hasn't got much of a chance, I can actually *watch* it. If a horse has got a real chance, then I go into the toilet until it's over. If you go to the races and you think you should definitely win, my God, I tell you what – you get pretty worried! So

I head for the toilet, and I let Eileen out. I can guarantee every time I have a winner at Plumpton, I have to watch the tape a day or two later. And even then I get worried!'

Paddy and Eileen had their best season three years ago – seven winners and fourteen seconds. Paddy had been driving taxis at night to make enough money to pay the two lads they employed.

'Next thing,' he says, 'out of the blue this owner arrived, and he had nine horses with us, and that was about three thousand pounds a month!' There is wonder in his voice. 'It just goes to show where you can go from absolutely nothing in this game to something, just on a phone call. The only thing about this level, you haven't got far to go to go back to nothing. No one is going to be a millionaire out of this job; all you want is a sort of half-decent living.'

If Paddy Butler is struggling he knows exactly to whom the blame attaches, and it is not Fate, nor the government, nor the Jockey Club.

'I blame myself,' he says quickly. 'I blame myself. I'm not a very good mixer to get owners, and if you keep yourself to yourself, it's the wrong thing to do.'

Paddy and Eileen converted their small establishment from the derelict outbuildings of a Sussex farmhouse; it is decked out with flowers and bright paint, but their home and children are five miles away in Lewes, so if there is a problem in the yard, one of them sleeps on the sofa in the office.

'We all muck in here,' says Michelle, one of the two staff. 'It works . . .,' she adds, 'and Paddy and Eileen ride out.'

'We own this place,' says Paddy, 'but it's been by hard work. I've been at it since '77 – too long! When you look back, you're such an idiot to start with! Running horses in totally the wrong kind of race because you've got horses belonging to people that they paid peanuts for, and you're trying to win a novice hurdle with it. And they're not good enough. Because you're frightened or you're dominated or you don't know enough about it, you do totally the wrong thing. The kind of people I've had, they won't let you put the horses in sellers – in the kind of races they would be capable of winning. They won't let you do that: they want 'em in better races. So before you go to the races – you're beaten!'

Ha from the Jockey Club, Paddy found that he had an owner.

'I got horses that belonged to that Dorothy Squires. She had three or four horses with Mrs Pitman and she sent them to me. You don't get too many people better than Mrs Pitman to train a horse, but anyway, she sent them to me. One was an old horse called Walberswick – a dirty rogue, oh, a dirty rogue!' The Jockey Club inspector arrived to see the yard. 'She was here exactly the day they came. So she said to this guy, "If this yard is good enough for my horses, it's good enough for the Jockey Club," so he passed it and away he went.' The histrionic singer behaved true to form. 'She used to give me some stick! Some abuse . . . Oh, she would ring me up at one o'clock by night and tell me I was like all the rest of the trainers – but she paid me. There's no question; she paid me.'

There is never any sense of hungry futility about the game for Eileen and Paddy.

'I love the horses,' he says. 'At this level you only meet all the real characters, and I've been involved in the bottom all through the time.'

Another owner had provided a diversion a couple of days before.

'I went racing on Saturday at Warwick. I drove the lorry myself and I took this guy who wanted to go with me. He's a Kerry man. So, we left here – this takes some believing – we left here . . . and we were only about a mile from here and he came into the cab from the back, and he said to me, "There's something wrong here," he said. "There's too much pressure on the horse's feet," he said. "Travelling all the way to Warwick. Is there any chance we could make him lie down?" So I said, "Nah, you couldn't make him lie down; he'll be all right." So after about another ten minutes he came back in again and he had no shirt and trousers on 'im. This guy had no shirt and trousers on 'im. I thought to myself, "There's something funny around this place . . ." This is gospel, I'm telling you, he got a pair of overalls out of a bag and he put on the pair of overalls over him, like a boiler suit. I said to him, "Where is your shirt and trousers?" He said, "I've wrapped my trousers and shirt around each of his shoes," he said, "to take the pressure off his feet." I just sat there laughing. So . . . I was nearly at Oxford on the M40, and he hadn't come near me for about an hour and a half, and I got a fright: I thought, "He's doing something in the back all right." So I pulled in and I went back to see where he was, and he was underneath the horse's belly, with the belly on his back and he's keeping the pressure off his legs! I am not joking: that's as true as you're sitting down there. He's a Kerry man; he's as wild as a March hare he is. Eileen will tell you. That's the horse out there – Prince Rooney.' The big gelding is bucking and kicking in a field. 'He's only a three-year-old; he's a fair horse he is, as quiet as a mouse.'

In the tradition of the Irish ballads, pinpointing the emotion is what matters in Paddy's stories; narrative is of no real importance. He sits on a straight-backed chair – no one lounges about in this yard – and meanders into another tale.

'I came from Castletownroache, the same village as Jonjo O'Neill; we went to school together. I came from a very poor background . . . Do I come from a poor background?' He looks to Eileen for confirmation, she agrees and he continues. 'Very poor background – there was about eight of us, wasn't there? And for a mattress we had straw tick . . . I was going to call one of them horses out there Straw Tick. When it was oaten straw it was beautiful. It was in bran bags; they used to sew the bran bags together and fill 'em with straw.' The farrier is now at the mug of tea stage in his work and he adds his confirmation.

'I can tell when Patrick's levelling,' he says, and Paddy is off again.

'You nistled down into it, 'cos me sisters and brothers we used to sleep all in one bed – about six or seven of us. But then there'd be no oaten straw so you'd have barley straw, and that would *eat* you alive, that would. Jonjo's about two years younger than me, and as a matter of fact, the first bird he ever went with . . . There was another feller from the Mallow area, a little apprentice who worked for Emco Cleaners and Dyers who would put a crease in your trousers. They went to the pictures and I was on my own, and one of them had a bird at the back behind me, and another had a bird in front. And Jonjo said to me, "What will I do?" I said, "Put your arm around her." "Will I put my arm around her?" I said, "Yes, put your arm around her." So he goes back and he puts his arm around her. About ten minutes came by and he was back. "I've done that; what will I do now?" I said, "Put your hand inside her knickers . . .", and the next think there was a mighty scream! That was the end of him.'

Now forty-one years old, Paddy Butler arrived in England twenty years ago.

'I'd got eighteen quid from my last weeks' wages in Ireland, and it cost me thirteen quid to fly to Birmingham and I had five pounds left. I paid one pound fifty for a blue suitcase, and in that suitcase I had my good trousers wrapped around my Wellingtons. I had no job, nothing. I got a lift to Lambourn and I knocked on a guy's door to give me a place to sleep. And it was a guy who's back in training now, Pat Haslam – it was his mother and father. Just knocked on the door. They took me in, cooked me a big meal, put me up in a bunk bed, and I was there for about four weeks, and then I got a job at Peter Walwyn's. I thought it was Flook Walwyn.

'I asked him for a job with rides, because I wanted to ride over the jumps, so he said fine. The next thing was when I got out the following morning I seen there was about forty two-year-olds and the only jumper there was was used to lead them, and it was Mill House. At about twelve

146

o'clock I went up to him and I said, "I'm in the wrong place." So I stayed there about a year and a half. He was a terrific bloke. There was horses there I thought would never win a race in a hundred years, but he'd win races with 'em. Little skinny fillies and stuff like that. He was a good trainer, yes.'

Eventually Paddy moved from riding to training via a series of bad falls, and he rubs his head like an old boxer in an effort to remember events in their chronological order. He makes several stabs at beginning a sentence, only allowing himself to continue when he gets the right feel back from it.

'When you want to start training you meet these type of people that say they've got places and they can set you up . . . and it's downhill you're going from there on. If you took a hundred people applying for their licence, I would say nearly fifty of 'em would be people who didn't have money but wanted to do it. So I got this guy – Eileen didn't want to know about it, but anyway she was with me and any money I had saved up and any money she had saved up went into this thing. And it was a total disaster. It was way down in No Man's Land in Cornwall, and the travelling gets you so much the heart goes.'

Somehow they managed to extract themselves and rented the place they now own at Plumpton. They have achieved a very great deal, but the gods have never smiled quite as broadly as they might have done. Paddy, however, is philosophical.

'I think the pressure at the top is probably as great as it is at the bottom,' he says. 'The hardest thing is when an owner thinks some guy can do it better. They'd still leave the horse with you . . . they'd be very bad at paying you, they'd be owing you three months maybe . . . You actually get in the state where you have to say, "Well, give me one more chance." You can imagine what that's like and there isn't too many people that would do that, but *I* would do that.'

'You usually find that the nicest of horses are owned by the wrong owners,' says Eileen, 'and you've got some really super owners and you can't get a winner for them. They always seem to have the horses that get problems.'

'Publicans are the hardest of the lot to keep happy,' says Paddy. 'They've got punters coming in to them who are betting men, and of course they can train all the horses under the sun once they've got a couple of pints in.'

There is racing at Plumpton today, and the ground is officially firm.

'I didn't use to like Plumpton,' Paddy admits. 'It's only over the field there, but I didn't use to like it at all. Then, all of a sudden, we've had seven or eight winners there over the last year or two, so now it's become the favourite! And I think they run better because we don't have to keep the pressure off their legs!'

Ted Whatmough, a Surrey insurance broker, is here at the yard to arrange a mortgage for one of Paddy's regular jockeys, to check up on his horse and to go racing with his trainer. Over coffee and ham sandwiches served up as a pre-race snack by Eileen, he enthuses about the yard.

'This is the kind of stable that people feel comfortable with,' he says. 'I wouldn't make a nuisance of myself here, but it's nice to know the door is open any time. My horse is called Cotton Bank. He's a three-year-old . . . I think . . .' He admits his knowledge of horseflesh is limited, but he has observed a thing or two about his fellow owners. 'For a lot of them a horse is just a capital sum invested for possible entertainment. They don't seem to care much about the animal. The horses are characters, that's what I like.'

He was introduced to ownership by clients who took him along to the sales at Newmarket.

'There was a horse there, a dead ringer for Red Rum. Ginger McCain was there and he said it was. You know at the sales there are people who are prepared to put up 800 guineas for a horse and it goes straight to the knacker's yard, and there was this guy there they pointed out to me that does this, and I said I know nothing about horses but I've got a few pounds I can spend, and he's not going to get this one! It was the only one that hadn't tried to bite me or kick me in the whole day, so I bid for it!

'It was the first time I'd been a registered owner,' he says, punctuating his story with a smoker's cough. The only wonder is that it was not also his last.

'It had injections and the vet and a tooth withdrawn. Only one stable girl could handle it and when they put it out on the gallops and a jockey rode him out prior to racing, it put him straight through a fence and down a sheer drop. The horse gets something into its head, they said, and it just does it. It's in the breed. They said they could take it to a horse psychiatrist in Newmarket, but we put it back in the sales and it's show jumping now. Then I had another horse, but poor thing, she'd had a virus and when she raced her back legs weren't co-ordinating . . . and now I've ended up with this gelding. He's out to grass at the moment and I've been round there. He's been dribbling all over me!' He proudly presents the green-stained shoulder of his short-sleeved shirt. 'He's going over hurdles. I think the jumps are really dangerous. Sometimes I cringe when I see some of the big jumps. It's frightening when you see half a ton of horse coming down on those legs that are not much thicker than my arm . . .'

Michelle has been grooming Malsman for his debut over hurdles. He is boxed up and we all decamp for the races.

It is just a few days after Glorious Goodwood and the mood, and indeed many of the punters, are recognizable from that elegant meeting; never has Plumpton looked so smart as it basks in hot sunshine. Alan Baldry, another of Paddy's owners, regards the scene with suspicion.

'No wind? No rain? Spoiled, isn't it? Must be left over from that other meeting . . .'

The restrained brilliance of Richard Dunwoody will be on show and Jimmy Frost looks every inch the farmer, while Steve Smith-Eccles could be auditioning for a part in a raunchy novel as he flaunts the sun-tan beneath his singlet and stock. (When he is framed a little later in the doorway of the shower, all of us in the weighing room can see where the sun-tan stops and starts.) Trainer Charlie Moore lacks only a knotted handkerchief on his head to complete a look fit for Brighton beach as he dandles his blonde grandchildren.

Frost comes third in the first race and hurries off to supervise the running of Chummy's Staff (trained by his father) in the second, a novice steeplechase. Still in his breeches and boots, he goes into the ring to give animated instructions to the amateur rider, Mr Robin Mills, who checks the tack meticulously when the time comes to mount.

'Good luck, darling . . .' his wife calls plaintively after him.

The Test Match score is announced over the loudspeaker: England are 360 for 7, with Botham out for 31.

Chummy's Staff does a clear round, but comes in last.

'He stands up well for an amateur . . .', comments Eileen as horse and rider pass the winning post. The third race provokes the commentator into saying, 'If this is a race I'd hate to see the slow-motion replay,' and Charlie Moore, unhappy with ending up third out of four, stomps off to consult with Ken Higson.

'We wanted a big field . . .'

By the fourth race, England are 400 for 8 and Tony Budge's racing manager, Tony Murray – sleek as a water rat – is explaining that this is a tricky track: something of an understatement. Eileen watches Malsman go round the pre-parade ring.

'He's compact, he's 100 per cent genuine and hopefully he'll enjoy his day out over hurdles,' she says, County Cork omitting the 'd' from the last word.

In the saddling box, with Eileen on one side of the horse and Paddy on the other, Paddy makes an ominous remark.

149

'This isn't a toilet job . . .' he says.

'He hasn't had much racing, has he?' says Eileen. 'Four times in his life.'

'We've kept him in cotton wool!'

Into the ring, and Eileen is still assessing the animal.

'I usually get put on for the last piece of work to say whether they should run or not. We had him as a two-year-old but he was terribly colty so we cut him and turned him away. He eats well but he never carries any condition because he sweats up at the least little thing, gets excited.'

'He'll be expecting to see the stalls out here in a minute. Wait till he sees the obstacles!' Paddy tells jockey Martin Jones he would like the horse to finish; Eileen calls out 'Good luck,' and hurries off to the Tote to put £2 on him each way.

'Just for the sake of it! I'm hoping for miracles!'

Malsman's progress in the race goes from bad to worse and Eileen is concerned.

'I don't think he's enjoying it somehow. He'll probably pull him up – he's not going anywhere on the ground.'

It proves to be a race of short duration for the horse, and Tony Budge takes the honours.

Eileen goes to find the jockey for a post-mortem.

'That's probably his first and last run. I'd say sell him – he'd make a lady's hack. I don't think he's a racehorse; it's as simple as that.'

'The first couple he pinged, you know?' reports Martin Jones. 'But as soon as he thought he was in a race . . . I was at him already going to the third. It wouldn't have helped him going down the far side . . .' He leaves to weigh in.

'He wasn't doing a tap, was he?' says Eileen.

'He only needed half an excuse to get away from it. It's the same on the Flat: he'll ride well enough, but he just won't do it,' says Paddy.

'Well, we knew he wouldn't have a lot, but we just hoped!'

'No, he's a clever bugger . . .'

'Yes, he thinks too much. It's no good when they're like that. And he's so well *bred* – he's by Mansingh . . . you wouldn't believe he'd run so bad. And we had him blood tested, and the vet said he couldn't be any better . . . What can you do when they won't do it?' Eileen is at a loss.

'I don't think we've ever had a three-year-old run as bad as that,' says Paddy. 'I don't think he'd be fast enough for dressage!'

On a Sunday morning in early September, the sun is still as hot as fire, and a group of horses which includes two greys is turned out behind trainer John Spearing's American barns. They all make the small movements which discourage flies and snort down at the patch of baked ground by the gate, sending up eddies of dust.

One essential for a racing yard's well-being is a horse which keeps it in the news and attracts potential owners. This year's star for Spearing is Lucedeo, the darker of the two greys in the field, while the pale, almost white horse with a long straggling mane and stiff legs is On Edge, his star of yesterday. Now seventeen-years-old, On Edge was bought by a jobbing builder from Birmingham for 750 guineas in 1979. Within the space of three years the horse had won £23,000, and this was precisely the measure of success which can turn a man's head. He plunged into ownership way beyond his means.

'He was getting in too deep,' recalls Spearing. 'He's the only man who owes me money; he owes me a lot too. He used to have five or six horses here, and there was only one that didn't win. He had one in partnership with a very nice Irishman – easy-going – and he sold quarter shares in this horse, over the Irishman's head, to about ten people! There were about ten people with a quarter share each! He liked his horses, and the only way he could do it was to con people, you know? Of course, when the horse won at Market Rasen, there were all these people in the winner's enclosure and they all got talking together ... and saying, "Well, you don't own it, do you?" And I didn't even know. People were coming up to me and saying, "How's it going to go today?" and I'd say, "What's it got to do with you?" Racecourse Security came in, and they had a big enquiry at Portman Square. The owner obviously didn't go because he knew that was it. He got warned off for five years.'

Spearing took On Edge.

'I said, "I'll have him, and I'll knock three hundred quid off your bill;" he was retired and only worth meat money, but I knew where he'd go if he had him. He'd go straight down to Bristol to be shot, you see. Down to the abbatoir.'

'All the staff are very sentimental in this yard,' says owner Stephen Foster, who is leaning over the paddock gate.

'We can't help it,' smiles Spearing's daughter Teresa, who hopes eventually to take over from her father.

'It's why they look after the horses so well,' rationalizes Foster. 'I can't contemplate going anywhere else. John is very laid back and flexible.'

Dr Stephen Foster is Director of Group 1 Racing (1991) Ltd, and some of the members of this club are, *pace* Thatcherite principles, over-awed by the winner's enclosure and reluctant to demonstrate their status as victors, but Foster pushes them forward to have their photograph taken. Trophies, however, are another matter.

'We've had so many winners,' he says, 'but I'm still quite happy picking up the cups!' He masks his vanity with a shout of ululating laughter which must come close to frightening the horses.

This small man with a wispy beard and long hair, whose physical presence has all the force of a question mark, exhibits in his dealings with the company's horses the persistence and application which might be expected from someone who took thirteen years to complete the Ph.D. given to him by the University of Lancaster for a thesis with the title: 'A qualification of the effectiveness of television advertising and its inter-action with other marketing variables by the use of microanalytical marketing simulation.' His interaction with John Spearing's Alcester yard, where the company has ten horses, would appear to be a complete success for all the parties concerned, and the laughter continued to echo around the yard even after his wife pranged his car within earshot.

'My foot slipped off the brake . . .', she reports solemnly, 'and on to the accelerator.' She pauses. 'I've done a lot of damage.' Another pause. 'Stephen was in the lounge doing his VAT.' How cruel can a woman be?

An owner's experience in racing depends very largely on his approach to the game. The recklessness of On Edge's one-time owner and the methodical approach adopted by Group 1 Racing are worlds apart, but whatever their ethos, John Spearing reckons that a lifetime with horses and their owners has prepared him for most eventualities.

'You learn by experience . . . You've got to try and please people because they're in it for pleasure and it's costing them a lot of money, but at the same time the most important thing is the horse. You've got to get the two together, really.'

Practicality is ever the answer for this immensely self-contained and reticent man whose posture is so perfect he might be dangling from a plumb line. He achieves his serenity not by recourse to any of the more vulgar temptations, but by sheer hard work.

It's the best way to get through, isn't it? I hear myself say with sickening piety. To work so hard you don't know whether it's Christmas or Piccadilly . . .

'Beryl . . .' he calls to his wife as a smirk spreads across his face. 'Come here and listen to this.' Evidently being married to a trainer is not all milk and honey.

Born of farming stock in Moreton-in-Marsh, Gloucestershire, John

Spearing took the usual route to training via hunting and point-to-pointing, although he never quite expected to achieve his goal.

'I thought I'd never get to it really, but I used to ride as an amateur jockey and a certain owner asked me to ride his horses for him, and then he said would I train them – so I started training.'

He is entirely self-taught.

'I just picked it up. I used to ride out for different trainers – small trainers – and ride races, and if you keep your eyes open and take everything in ... Especially riding the horses, knowing how they go. You've got to have a feel for a horse, you know – what each horse needs; you've got to be able to work it out – if it comes naturally. If you're brought up to farming it does come a bit natural.'

Use the word 'job' to him, and the calm is interrupted.

'Job?' he queries, looking somewhat put out. *'I've* never had a job. I couldn't work for anyone else. I'd disagree with them very quickly. I don't look on it as a job. A lot of people are stuck in a factory or an office and they hate it, don't they? But they can't do anything else. If you love horses, and love racing, you don't look on it as work, you know.'

He began with six horses.

'I did it all myself – the whole lot. Led 'em round as well at the races!'

He achieved eight wins from those six horses and now, twenty-two years later, he has forty boxes and a full complement of horses.

'We've got very few in the yard that haven't been in the first four; very few. They're all capable of running close – I'm not saying *win*, it's very hard to say that. It's always been like that because we don't keep the rubbish. If it's not good enough, it's not good enough and we tell the owners. Some of them don't like being told; they still want to run it again, or take it somewhere else because they think they're going to do better. What we try to do is get the best out of every horse we've got.'

The day before Infeb, a four-year-old grey filly belonging to the 1991 company, had come second of fifteen in a handicap 'chase over two miles and six furlongs at Stratford, and there were more of her supporters in the winner's enclosure than there were around Martin Pipe's winner, Timid. Mr Pipe was proving that he is a man without aesthetic fear by wearing the tie of Pipe-Scudamore Racing Plc, and novelist Dick Francis was proving that literature (like training) is now all about business and not art by patiently signing copies of his latest book. Spearing sent Beryl into the ring for the celebrations.

'It's not my scene ...' he said, taking off pretty smartly to saddle his runner in the next.

153

Back in her box, Infeb is a little sore but otherwise suffering no ill-effects.

'How are you, sweetie pie?' asks Dr Foster. 'Didn't you do well, eh? We're quite used to beating Mr Pipe now; it's not impossible by any means. Infeb's beaten Timid on the Flat at Wolverhampton.' The company bought the filly on 11 June and she had won for them a week later. 'It was the first time she'd ever won, and she's won £8,500 since then, and she cost £3,000! We're well ahead!'

Accompanying Foster on his Sunday morning tour of the yard are two club members, Martin Tunley and his wife, who live just outside Birmingham. Tunley is as pale as can be.

'I'm a civil servant,' he says, and hearing the sharp intake of breath which went along with the suspicion he is with the Inland Revenue, he quickly adds, 'I give it out rather than take it in. I work for Social Security.'

Tunley's initial stab at group ownership with another trainer had given him a taste for success.

'We've had a bite at the cherry and we can't go back.' He eliminated the other clubs one by one, concluding that they were either ego trips for the man behind them or merely tipping services. 'One of the things which attracted us to Group 1 as opposed to some of the other clubs is that the management team do not take a salary from the funds; they do it for the love of the game, for the love of the sport.'

'If you were going to take a salary,' says Foster, 'with most of the racing clubs there would be no money left to buy or train any horses – which is what happens. And you can see that the trainers who set them up, they're just trying to get horses in their yard – you can see their angle. I take nothing at all . . . Look at the pleasure of getting these horses and organizing them!' His voice rises getting dangerously near more manic laughter. 'I enter 'em, book the jockeys, instruct the jockeys . . . I'm used to the trainer never turning up because, as he says, he's trained the horse and he can do no more. Some owners wouldn't be happy about that, but we are.'

'It's a waste of my time going racing,' says Spearing. 'You can watch it all on SIS and see a lot more.'

Foster concedes that it is very difficult to launch a racing club.

'We were still trying to find our first winner when John and I bought Basic Fun at the Doncaster sales out of Peter Walwyn's yard for 3,500 guineas, but a month later she won at Ludlow, and we needed that.'

Aside from the problems of finding the all-important first winner to set the ball rolling, the club experienced some teething troubles with Customs and Excise.

'What we say in our brochure and advertising is that the purpose of the company is to buy and improve racehorses, some of which we sell. John's got a track record of improving horses – like Lucedeo which he bought for 2,800 guineas – and we've done that with most of the horses we've had to date, and some of them we've sold on. The important point I won with the Customs and Excise, who de-registered us, and then finally eighteen months later conceded and re-registered the company, was that it is possible to improve horses, and that all horses don't depreciate. They were saying you buy yearlings and they depreciate from £100,000 to nothing in the first sixty seconds when it's palpably obvious that they haven't got the speed, which is of course true. What they couldn't accept was that there is a niche you could find where you can improve horses, and this meets the members' objectives as well because they improve not by being left in a field or a stable, but by being raced, which is what we do.'

Foster reaches up to a bay gelding to illustrate his point. King William just about tolerates the attention.

'This is the star, aren't you, sweetheart? Now I bought him', he boasts, 'all on my own. I went up to Doncaster sales all on my own – John couldn't go – and I walked into his box, stroked him and I thought, "My, apart from being a good horse, this is a lovely horse." Timeform said he was a big, robust gelding, carries condition, and I looked at his form and tried to work out why someone would sell a horse like that. Well, he'd been beaten favourite three times running over hurdles; he'd run second or third, and by our standards at that time, that would have been pretty good! But you could see why, when you've got a horse 6–4 favourite and it hits every alternate flight, why you might be prepared to sell it. It'd only run third three weeks previously, so I thought it's unlikely to be unsound – it's much more likely that the owners are disillusioned. I had to pay 8,000 guineas – he wasn't cheap, but he's won five races for us, and been placed about fifteen times, and won about £18,000.

'He'd be worth about £20,000 in the market now as a 'chaser – he's had one run over fences.' He raises his voice to carry over to Teresa who is mucking out the paper beds. 'And it's Teresa's favourite horse! She won the amateur race at Beverley on him three weeks ago. She looks after him; most people won't go into his box. I asked John why he was so good when I went in at the sales, and he said it was most likely because he was off his own territory.'

155

'He's very naughty when you're grooming him,' Teresa confirms cheerfully. 'He's a bit evil, but he's not too bad if you know him . . .' In other words, King William bites and kicks at every opportunity.

The club is getting closer to breaking even and making money; their dream is to have a Group horse.

'We might even do it this year!' whoops Foster, keen to take advantage of low bloodstock prices to make a killing for his members, who form their major decisions at the AGM held in Alcester Town Hall, a couple of miles from the yard. 'We try to make the evening social as well,' says Foster. 'Some of the jockeys come along, and we have a karaoke evening afterwards.' He pauses. 'Couldn't get John on the karaoke . . .'

CHAPTER SIXTEEN

'No airs and graces'

Gary Cooper is at Doncaster for the 215th running of the St Leger, the final Classic of the season. But this is not the 'High Noon' Gary Cooper, it is the racehorse owner Gary Cooper and it is fairly simple to spot the difference, particularly when one of them is in the noisy, crowded bar at the St Leger Sales making his comparison between trainers.

' 'e 'ad my 'oss banged up to 'ell. It's eyes were bulgin' owt . . . It's true! It's true! And if Siddall ent better than 'im, I'll sell my backside under t'Town 'all clock!'

A heavy, four-square and rumpled man, he is standing in the centre of a group of owners and trainers, and the pint glass in his hand trembles very slightly as the words tumble out an enthusiasm for the game which is almost overpowering. His expression follows every nuance of his story-line and is as sunny as can be when things are going right. He has a Mansingh colt in the last today.

'The Saturday before last it worked with a three-year-old at Wetherby and give it two stonn and finished upsides after seven furlongs. It ent a good 'un but it ran in a 0–70 and finished second 'cos eez run just in sellers up to now, apart from that nursery. It depends if eez got the pace; they might be a bit too quick for 'im at this level, but Siddall's very good at Donnie; she's 'ad a lot of luck there, ent she? But she wanted to go to Leicester, but arm not goin' to *Leicester*; I'm not into this gamblin' lark – can't be bothered. Leicester, Wolver'ampton – I'm norrinto it.' There is a slight pause, then the next phrase is delivered legato. 'I want to go to Cheltenham, Sandown, Doncaster, Newbury . . .' Now he returns to normal speed. 'And if they ent good enough, thee does sell 'em. There's no arguin' then in between. It's true, ent it?' The Tadcaster trainer, Lynn Siddall – short and blonde – is trying to attract his attention across the bar, but he is in mid-flow and resolutely ignores her. 'Ooh Christ! I've left 'er thirty-four times, but she's very good with the 'ooses, anyway . . .' He continues with the pungent descriptions.

'She's got this chestnut colt, this two-year-old by Be My Guest; I paid twenty-five thousand quid for that and my . . . *what* a bloody nice 'oss. It'll run probably in Franz towards back end. I 'ad 'im with somebody else who jarred 'im oop to bloody 'ell, but eez all right now. Mr Secreto? The filly? Oh . . .' He spirals into despair. 'It's useless. Useless. That is useless. That is absolutely useless. I don't rate Secreto's. Bought it in America; I couldn't go; paid fifty-odd thousand quid and I was let down badly. Ooh, I've 'ad an 'orrific time. It's cost me two hundred thousand quid.'

Someone asks him about his pride and joy and the light leaps back into his eyes.

'It's 16.1 – at the moment – and it looks just like Arkle! 'ey, it dooz! And the boogers that 'ad it on this stud . . . you've never seen such a rip-off in your life. You can see all 'is ribs . . . acksherly, if aad've coom t'sales it would've been an RSPCA job. Eez a disgrace. They 'adn't fed 'im; 'e 'ad thrush on 'is feet. It's an absolute disgrace. Do you know what they did to me? They bought me a mare in foal to Nishapour and put it on their tab; no need to 'cos I 'ad a tab at Tattersalls. I've paid 'em end of January, and on 12 February it was still on their tab. It 'ad a colt foal and they registered it on 18 February in their name. A month later it were booked for Petoski – four thousand quid which I've got to pay for 1 October – and they covered it with their stallion. It's no wonder folk don't come into it, is there?' He shakes his head. 'You don't usually get them as bad as that . . .' Another blast of ebullience quickly drags away the despair. 'I shall still be 'ere when they're all dead!' And off he strides with a laugh to see the Midian colt he is selling, its box door emblazoned with encouragement to prospective buyers in his own hand.

A middle-aged woman with pebble glasses, slightly over-sized false teeth and a track suit is standing by the door. She is clutching a skipping rope and with ecstasy in her voice she lets us into a secret.

'They're going to let me put in for my First Aid certificate. I don't expect I'll get it, but I'll try . . .'

A trainer's wife, Vanessa Haigh, looks on impassively.

'It's the horses,' she says. 'They get you like that eventually.'

Another owner jerks a thumb in the direction of Charles Booth.

'He's got a particular talent for training fillies. There's nobody else would train any of my fillies.'

Henry Cecil . . . ? I murmur.

'*WHO?*' The chorus is deafening. This is Yorkshire and I should have known better.

'It's a bloody nonsense that everybody's spending money on colts,' continues the owner. 'If you get a good filly, you can't do any better. Not in my book. If a colt's no good, what do you do with it? Geld it. What do you do with him after that?'

'To be perfectly frank,' says a trainer, 'the sort of 'osses we get, people like Henry Cecil wouldn't have in their yards because they wouldn't know how to get 'em on the racecourse.'

A man who turned in his licence explains what forced him to give up.

'I had to. I went through a bad time; I got too many people syndicated from the mining fraternity, and when they all went out on strike . . .' He had worked hard in his local community to build up a larger ownership and to get across-the-board involvement. But his resourcefulness ultimately went unrewarded, and it brings home how a blip in the economy – never mind a global recession – can wipe out small businesses. A despondent comment from a top trainer comes back to me.

'Sad to say, there are a lot of trainers who probably shouldn't be training for various reasons; basically they can't afford to, and I think there are some very unattractive relationships with owners . . . The trainers are so vulnerable; they have no choice.'

Outside, the dust swirls around the ring and the auctioneer's voice cajoles and bullies over the loudspeaker to a counterpoint of calling horses and their soft, unshod footfalls.

'Can I see you out, please!' a trainer calls to one of the lads leading a horse which had interested him as it walked around the ring. The animal emerges, slipping and sliding on the tarmac until it is stood up properly. The trainer walks around it to see if he can find any faults: he inspects the legs and watches carefully as it walks in a straight line away from him, and then returns.

'I look at these yearlings as if they were a field of two-year-olds,' he says, 'and I wonder which one is going to win the race. If you ever buy a yearling that you're iffy about, you are on a hiding to nothing. You go into it's box every day and you think, "Christ! Why did I buy this?" And the longer you keep the horse, the more you hate it. They have to jump out at you; you have to be certain.'

Jimmy FitzGerald has called out Lot No. 471.

'We call 'im the Jenny Pitman of the North . . .' says a fellow trainer. 'It's a nice colt; well presented, but a bit slack in his pasterns. He's too far off his job for me and a little bit straight as well in his off fore – but it's his type of horse. He looks at them in a dual-purpose light.'

Jack Berry, Matt McCormack, Bill O'Gorman and Richard Hannon all dodge in and out of the sale ring. Paul Kelleway is wearing running shoes. Tony Murray is keeping an eye on things for A.F. Budge (Equine) Ltd. The faces (well known and otherwise) seated or standing around the ring at a sale of horses fire the imagination more than anywhere else with the exception of a court of law. The atmosphere is good-natured, hard-working and intense, and wholly absorbing.

'This is Yorkshire,' one of the group reminds me. 'It's not Newmarket. We're different up here.'

How any one of them could extricate himself from this life – a trainer give up his licence, for example – is almost impossible to suppose. It must be a terrible thing to do.

The mood is equally appealing across the road at the races; the staff seem pleased to see the punters, but this is hardly a surprise since England's natural democrats live in the north. Everything is accessible and twenty thousand people are set to have a good time. The place has been brought alive again through a joint venture between the local authority and Tony Budge, with the help of the much-admired Clerk of the Course, John Sanderson.

'It's the likes of those two who should be running racing,' I am told authoritatively. 'The rest of the Jockey Club should have a bomb up their bloody arses.' This is Yorkshire. It's different up here.

In the vast and Stygian betting hall there is a perfume counter selling all the big-name scents. The assistants are wearing hats. This is unquestionably Yorkshire. The Channel Four team are mucking about like school-boys in the Annual Members' room (they pull themselves together to be deferential to Major Dick Hern) and old-age pensioners are trotting after Willie Carson for his autograph as he makes his way towards the elephant-coloured weighing room. A list of racing definitions printed in the race card helps the uninitiated, and a woman with Elastoplasts on her blistered heels is getting to grips with the concept of an each-way bet.

'Does that come cheaper?' she enquires, perking up. Yorkshire.

Wearing a boater, a baggy, rather modish double-breasted suit and a scarlet bow tie, Woodrow Wyatt with his knees slightly bent gives a totally convincing Groucho Marx impression as he pursues his cigar through the crowds until he reaches a door marked Tote. He bangs on it with his fist until it opens, and then he vanishes. Shirt-sleeved men accost the aloof Henry Cecil and ask for his autograph; he smiles broadly and for the first time this season gives every indication of enjoying himself. He refuses to sabotage the cut of his jackets with binoculars dangling from his shoulder, so God knows what he ever sees of the racing.

A woman is sweeping the grass in Members with a long-handled dustpan and brush; now I have seen everything. This management certainly deserves to succeed.

Outside Tony Budge's box virtually opposite the winning post for the Coalite St Leger is a sign which says, 'First Aid Post', and judging from the speed with which champagne is dispensed inside the box it could well be speaking the truth. Tony Budge is an ample figure, immediately likeable and slightly shy, and if he were a stick of seaside rock, 'Captain of Industry' would be printed all the way through. Moreover, unlike the rest of us, he speaks not only in sentences, but in sentences with punctuation.

And he must be a trainer's dream.

'I approach racing from a businessman's perspective,' he says. 'I've never been to the sales in my life. Never, ever. And I've only been to Richard Hannon's yard the first time I met him. We bought three horses that day, two of which are still running, and in fact one of them, Savahra Sound, won the Sprint at Haydock last week. He's now a six-year-old, and I've never been back since.

'We work on the basis that the trainers choose the horses they would like to train; we set a price, and if we can buy it for that price, we do. If we don't, we wait for the next one to come along. If I went to the sales and I bought the horse and it turned out to be not any good, the trainer would give me a rather doleful look and say, "Well, I didn't choose the horse, sir . . .", so the trainers buy the horses.'

Should you like to have more involvement?

'I don't know. The relationship works well, and as the Americans say, "If it ain't bust, don't fix it." Right now it ain't bust, so . . .'

Tony Budge's forty-six horses are split between National Hunt and the Flat and they run in the colours of A. F. Budge (Equine) Ltd, which will end this season tenth in the leading owners' table with £214,132 in win and place money, an improvement of five places on the 1990 performance; but despite three more wins the prize money takes a dive of some £50,000. His annual training fees are in the region of £400,000. He has two ambitions in racing: one is to win the Cheltenham Gold Cup (since winning the Derby is now, he calculates, an unrealistic goal), and the other is to avoid being Senior Steward of the Jockey Club – 'too many brickbats'.

161

'I enjoy National Hunt; it's very exciting,' he says. 'A three-mile 'chase is very exciting when the horse is doing well, and jumping and really enjoying himself. But after four or five months of that you're ready for the Flat again. A whole new season opens up and out come the two-year-olds until you're looking round to September, October and the horses are beginning to lose their coats and it's time to think about the Mackeson at Cheltenham, and another season begins.

'Our original involvement started about six years ago. It was my brother's idea; we're in the coal-mining business and he thought to try to find a way round a landowner in Shropshire which nobody else in the industry could do: we would approach the landowner's son, who was a trainer, to buy us a horse. It didn't do very well, and after a year he said, "Sorry the horse isn't very good but I don't know whether you know, we've got some coal under our fields – will you mine the coal?" From the profit on the coal-mine, we bought a better horse – which won – and we've gone on from there.

'A meteoric rise to the top? Oh yes. Within three years of being in racing we'd won the Gimcrack. And now we've won it three times in the last four years. Very meteoric.'

Tony Budge's Gimcrack speeches have been oases of good sense, and he feels that they were instrumental in his election to the Jockey Club.

'It was a great honour; a great thrill; and at the same time I was elected a member, Sir Ernest Harrison of Racall was elected, so there's two people with a fairly wide business experience becoming members, and I think this is the new direction Lord Hartington is taking now.

'Racing takes commitment. You have to *want* to do it. I don't see a lot of racing myself; I see it on Saturdays, and we do a certain amount of corporate sponsorship which gives us an opportunity to entertain business clients, but it's really done by professionals. I think racing has to have a business approach. It can never be run exactly "as a business" – certainly as an owner you can't run it "as a business", but you can put business principles to work: it you've got to take a loss, if you've got a bad horse, then the sooner you recognize that the better. There is no point in paying training fees if the horse isn't going to win.'

Richard Hannon will close the season at number two in the table with 126 winners, and with no Arab force behind his soaring success, the Budge connection has been the catalyst which took him to racing superstardom, enabling him to build on the Classic success he had gained previously for the Horgans of County Cork. Hannon has no truck with the superficial elitism which can bedevil racing, and his feet are planted firmly on the ground.

'It's always a bloody struggle in this game,' he has admitted. 'You can be flying one minute and the next it all comes crashing down around you.'

Budge says that his relationship with Hannon works well, and it is easy to understand why.

'I think Richard Hannon puts it very succinctly,' he says. "As long as he keeps buying 'em, I'll keep training 'em," and I think it's as fundamental as that. Enthusiasm and enterprise is what I want from my trainers, with the combination of Tony Murray as racing manager standing one step sideways so that he can look at it slightly more objectively. It's all about placing horses right.'

Tony Murray won the St Leger in 1975 on Bruni, and now the team has just watched its colt Power Lake take £8,645 for second place in the Group 2 Flying Childers Stakes. This owner came as near to wild enthusiasm as he is able with an articulate appraisal of the situation.

'Our second in a Group 2 to probably the best five-furlong horse in Europe this year was a great race in which to run second. It would have been a great race to have won, but none the less, a great race to have come second. You've got to put a value on the horses because it's a long-term commitment, and it isn't just going to run for us this year, it's what we do with him. Savahra Sound now, we're trying to place him in a stud. He's run for us for four years and we need to find a nice home for him. It's not appropriate just to put him in the sales and let him go for a few hundred pounds.' Long and faithful service to this company is rewarded with more than a gold watch and a word of thanks from the chairman to precede an uncaring farewell. Furthermore, the chairman may not throw his brown hat in the air and whoop with delight, and he is more or less silent on racing's heart-stopping moments, but he does care about his horses.

'The horse doesn't like coming at the back and getting his bottom smacked, so we place him in the company in which he can do well. It's all about placing them,' he reiterates. 'I think with Jimmy FitzGerald we've hardly had a horse run this year; he would rather not give a horse a hard time, and more of his are dual-purpose so they can go on and hurdle, and he can place them where they can win. There's no point in giving a horse a hard race otherwise he equates being put in a box and going to the races with an unpleasant occasion.

'Clearly if you win it's better than coming second; you have to pay the bills; but the more important aspect is we recognize the horses are individuals and we've got to bring them on so they think it's fun, so that they can win. The mental aspect from the horse's point of view is just as important as the owner's commitment. The horse has got to think he can win because if he does, he'll do his best. We tend not to give the horses hard races; they go as well as they can within their ability, but we don't dull their appetite for racing. They need to enjoy it; if they're having fun, they'll do well.'

Little is left to chance in Tony Budge's strategy, and when he sets his sights on the future of racing it is not only the champagne which is lifting my spirits, for here is a man who does more than hanker after a better yesterday.

'It needs a team approach,' he says. 'At the moment so many people are playing to their own corner. We couldn't run a business this way and we *are* a business; we're a multi-million-pound business. The Jockey Club's role historically has been that of maintaining integrity, which they do very well: we're second to none on that. They are becoming more commercial, but we still have a stand-off at the moment between the Jockey Club and the bookmakers. We have to become as one. I agree with the Home Secretary – there has to be one body in racing. The people are there to do it; it's just getting the attitude that now is the time. I think something like Sunday racing might be an issue round which we might be able to try and unite, and try to go forv·d.

'Everywhere else in Europe has Sunday racing and I really don't understand why we don't. Well, I do . . . at the moment it's illegal to bet on a Sunday, but there has to be a will. I think one of the most reprehensible things of the past was when the vote was held on Sunday racing and half the members of the Jockey Club were out at dinner, and didn't vote in the House of Lords.

'I think we've moved on since then,' says the reformer, before mentioning the stumbling block of the Levy. 'I think a more reasonable Levy is also important – but not to the detriment of the bookmaker. I think competition is our way of life in the UK; I think a more invigorated Tote because the Tote ploughs a lot of their money back – and with the bookmakers paying a little more Levy.'

By now more accustomed to hearing the sentiments expressed to me by a leading trainer: 'Nobody trusts the bloody bookmakers – *I* don't believe them; I don't think anybody does, and they've never come clean as to what their profits are – they've never published them accurately . . .' I can barely believe my ears. The Jockey Club is used as a metaphor for arrogance, naivety and defensive aggression, but this member confounds the imagery. The off-course bookmakers have a legal duty to their shareholders and to assume that they also have a moral duty to give away more of their profits than the Levy demands is to demonstrate a singular inability to grasp the fundamental tenets of capitalism. The basis of the Levy may well be vague; the original figure may have been plucked out of the air; but racing is not, as I understand it, a charity.

It is no wonder the St Leger meeting is a triumph, and Tony Budge is rightly proud of the entertainment.

'I think here at Doncaster we've got a great team. The sponsor of the St Leger today, David McErlain, is a close personal friend, and we first discussed this walking along the seafront at Torquay, October last year, and within six weeks we were signed up! John Sanderson has lots of contacts in racing and I've got lots of contacts within business, and we're trying to put the two together here. There's lots of companies here today, so we'll get one or two of those to sponsor a race at Doncaster . . . And there's more here today than just being a casual observer,' he stresses. 'There's a huge crowd around the weighing room listening to the jockeys' comments – they've all got their ears tuned in which is fine . . . We might get somebody to become an owner, and build on it . . .'

The appreciative Yorkshire crowd shout home the impressive French horse Toulon in the St Leger, and after a momentary hiccup when Farfelu clipped Plain Fact's heels in the Tote Portland Handicap and came down, recalling that chilling moment when Madraco fell two years before, the quality of the racing matched the superb organization. Morley Street ran a magnificent race in the Doncaster Cup; Lester Piggott on Bog Trotter, by his son-in-law, William Haggas, waited in front to beat Satin Flower in the Kiveton Park Stakes; and on the day before the St Leger, Rodrigo de Triano swept from last to first to take the Champagne Stakes and claim favouritism for next year's Two Thousand Guineas.

This victory was the latest in a first season of colossal success for trainer Peter Chapple-Hyam, and both he and the horse deserve every moment of their glory. Barely out of short trousers, he trains at Manton, which was established as one of the finest training centres by Alec Taylor in the 1860s and celebrated its first Classic win in 1873 when Gang Forward won the Two Thousand Guineas. The Manton House Estate on the Marlborough Downs covers two thousand acres, of which about four hundred are devoted to the exceptional equestrian facilities, and the rest are farmed in hand. It is designated an Area of Outstanding Natural Beauty and offers the joy of seeing real farming, not Mr Gummer's apologetic fantasy, stewardship of the countryside.

A month before the St Leger meeting, the beauty of the Downs is veiled in rain, making the photographer's task all the more tricky.

Gerry Cranham, doyen of racing photographers, is in Manton's state-of-the-art forty-box Astor Yard, running off pictures of Peter Chapple-Hyam and his other dazzling two-year-old – one of Robert Sangster's home-breds – Dr Devious. This is a sure sign that the trainer has arrived. The colt exudes star quality, primping and posing and sticking his tongue out.

'He does nothing but improve all the time,' says his trainer, 'and he's a happy little horse; he loves life, he really does.'

Posing with a stunning accessory like the Doctor is one thing, but posing alone is something else altogether. Chapple-Hyam rises to the challenge with a wry grin, obediently wiping the rain off his face and hair for the close-ups at the command of the photographer to take his place in the Gerry Cranham Library. Nevertheless, not yet armed with the polished platitudes that keep the press at bay, he is wary of what they get up to.

'I don't usually like talking to the press very much because some of them say things I haven't actually said, and get things mixed up a little bit.'

They began gunning for him when it was discovered he is married to Sangster's step-daughter, née Jane Peacock, whose politician father is himself a considerable racehorse owner in Australia, and it was deduced that Chapple-Haym had borrowed her silver spoon to ease himself into top-level training. This was not the case.

Born in the village of Bishops Itchington near Warwick, he had one goal as a child.

'All I ever wanted to do was train. Don't ask me why . . .', he says, unable to account for the dream, 'but what I was hoping to do was one day take over my uncle's yard in Leamington Spa – that Mecca of English racing!' His uncle, Wilmer Mann, has a permit and trains a few, and his cousin Robert used to ride for Martin Tate. 'Anywhere they had rides, I used to go with them and my grandfather from when I was about nine.'

Instead of cosy obscurity in Royal Leamington Spa, Chapple-Hyam began training at the legendary Manton in the full glare of Mr Sangster's reflected glory.

'I can't believe it in my wildest dreams, really,' he says, and when the mask of driving ambition is let slip, he can seem almost nonplussed by his success and good fortune.

There is, of course, a downside.

'To fail in a place like Manton would absolutely kill me,' he admits.

'And everyone kept telling me if you can't train winners at Manton, you wouldn't train winners anywhere – which really helps!' Most training debutants have the bank manager on their back, but Chapple-Hyam is saddled instead with tradition, and the full magnificence of Manton. On balance, I myself might prefer the bank manager. 'So might I sometimes,' he says and chuckles ruefully.

He left home at sixteen and began his career with Fred Rimell.

'He was with us at Kinnersley for three years,' remembers the decisive Mrs Mercy Rimmel, now retired after fifty years of racing. 'He was just an ordinary lad in the yard when he was with us! And then he was with Barry Hills for several years, so he's had a very good grounding. A very good grounding. He'd gone up the ladder a bit then – he was Barry's assistant.'

'I was pupil assistant for four years,' says Chapple-Hyam, 'and Mr Hills taught me most about training; there's not much wrong with B. Hills as a trainer. A very clever man. He can do anything in a yard – still rides one through the stalls now and again, and loses his temper with it . . . "Let me get on the effing thing!" We worked all day long for him; you did your two, and I used to look after a horse called Gildoran; the only time I got to the track was when he ran. He won two Ascot Gold Cups, and my real ambition is to train a Gold Cup winner so that I can be interviewed on television and say it's as good as Gildoran, because no one ever thought he was any good!'

When Mr Hills took over Manton, Peter Chapple-Hyam was put in charge of Barton House Yard with Billy Keenan as his head lad.

'Mr Hills left us alone a lot more,' he says, 'but if he said "jump", we jumped, and if there was any problem, you told him straight away. Ben Sangster came here about two years ago; he'd been more into the breeding side and he wanted to get into the racing side a lot more, and Ben, Joe Naughton who was in charge of another yard here and myself all lived together and the three of us became very good friends. Then when Mr Hills went, I was approached by Mr Sangster who said Ben had put my name forward to take over last August.

'Then I didn't hear much, and I was getting pretty worried, with the press bothering me, and it wasn't until Christmas Eve that I actually found out I was taking over properly. I'd got married in the June, and Jane's been here longer than anyone. She worked here for Mr Dickinson and for Mr Hills, so we've known each other for four or five years. It's a partnership; she rides out every morning, and if we're short she'll do two or three horses. We've got no airs and graces – neither of us . . .'

In his office complex, which is so bleak and uncompromising in design

Sir Basil Spence could have been the architect, Peter Chapple-Hyam is equipped with a boardroom and every possible mod. con.; but the building echoes with emptiness. The desk is bare and a couple of sets of Sangster silks hang forlornly in the cupboard. He troops off to make the coffee; Manton holds its breath as it adjusts from the personality of one trainer to another. There are just thirty-eight horses rattling around in the vast set-up, but next season the story will be different, with the number rising to some seventy or eighty.

'The horses arrived on 7 January; they had to be fished out from everywhere and 90 per cent of them had problems – hobdayed, or due to have operations, things like that, and when I saw them I thought to myself, "What am I doing . . . ?' But we took them along steadily, and then a few of them started to show a little bit . . . a few of the two-year-olds (they're all two-year-olds bar five), and so I thought, right, we'd better wind a few up! Our best-bred is a half brother to Observation Post by Sadlers Wells actually, but *someone* said he'd never stand training! He's our best-bred, but he's not the best by a long way. All the others are by middle-of-the-road sires: Night Shift, Ahonoora, Commanche Run. There's a couple of nice El Gran Senors which everyone would like to have but they were May foals, so that's why they came to me.

'Noble Flutter was my first winner – on April Fool's Day, at Warwick! It was a Bank Holiday Monday (and it was Warwick) and there had been an earlier race, but I thought if I send her there no one'll know! There's another sixteen meetings on – I'll sneak her in there, and if she wins all well and good, and if she loses I might be able to get away with it! But she duly went and won by seven lengths. Paul Eddery rode her. I was very nervous, actually, but then when she came round the bend I always thought she was going to win, but when she kicked clear, I couldn't *believe* it. And then the next day we went back again – on my birthday actually – and the big horse Papal Legate went and won as well, and I thought, "This can't last . . ." But it did.' He sounds amazed. 'We kept on and on and on. We've had seventeen winners actually . . .'

Chapple-Hyam will finish the season with two Group 1 successes. Dr Devious and Rodrigo de Triano will bring his brilliant first season to a climax with victories in the Dewhurst Stakes and the Middle Park Stakes, and with a 24 per cent strike rate Manton's new star has helped to put Robert Sangster sixth in the leading owners' table and in excellent heart to topple the five Arabs above him.

'Suddenly he's back,' acknowledges the young trainer. 'In this yard at the moment we've got the second and third best two-year-olds in the country – or supposed to be – and Cambrian Hills: I still think she's better than all of them. I was disappointed at Ascot, but she came back with a big joint and she's just swimming at the moment, but I still think she's the best of the lot.

'I've just followed along Mr Hill's lines really, but I have tried, I suppose, to put a bit more speed into the horses because we've got a couple of gallops that are flat which he didn't use too often, and normally first time out I take them up there for their last piece of work to get a bit of speed into them. Here at Manton it's all up hills and you can take the speed out of them, I think. I've been to Australia a lot of times, and I always like to follow the Australian way as well. I think the true Flat horse is a miler. They're all trying to breed a mile-and-a-half horse, but after you get the mile and a half, they all want two miles anyhow. It'd give me more pleasure than anything to have a champion miler. But if a horse shows speed, nine times out of ten, they'll get any trip; they will do.'

The Manton gallops were laid out over a hundred years ago and they extend to about 286 acres, offering a variety of ground which enables the horses to be worked throughout the year in near ideal conditions. Chapple-Hyam stands in the centre of the all-weather covered round canter of one and a half furlongs to watch Spanish Grandee and Cocherbamba being given a spin.

'We could get a football pitch in the middle here . . .' says the West Bromwich Albion supporter. He uses the classic Victorian stable yard at Manton House as an isolation yard; ravishingly pretty, and with not a soul in sight, it has an air of artificiality, as if it were a film set. It comes to life in the evenings, however, with a pub and a disco for the lads who live in the various cottages on the estate.

In the old days – and, indeed, until comparatively recently – the top trainers were men in their seventies, but now the average age is tumbling and with the strain of modern-day training becoming ever more intense, they will be forced to retire rather than waiting for compulsory retirement when they drop dead on the gallops.

'It does get a bit of a strain every now and again,' says Chapple-Hyam. 'You do get a bit worried – or I do.' That, one feels, is a considerable understatement.

'We were snowed in for a week once,' he says, driving on towards the gallops, 'but when the weather gets it right, it's beautiful. It's very quiet indeed and I like that. And we don't have to fight for gallops. The one place I never hope to go to is Newmarket; I won't even stay there. If I had a horse it's the last place on earth I'd get it trained. If I had a horse I'd sent it to John Hills, I really would.' The Establishment has its own way of dealing with a new boy. 'Some of the trainers are all right,' he says with a laugh; 'some of them don't speak to me! Richard Hannon is the best one, and when we go to Salisbury we always pop back and have a drink with him. He's a super chap.'

Up on the famous Clatford complex, he explains how it works.

'Six spurs come on to it and you can get anything from five furlongs to two miles, and on the skyline is what they call the Derby gallop and it's a mile and a half but it bears no resemblance to Epsom whatsoever, although George Todd and all the rest of them, ten days before they were going to run a horse in the Derby, they used to take them up there for their last serious piece of work. We take them up there in the early part of the year to get a bit of ground work into them. We've flown over Guy Harwood's place on the way to France, and I always get the pilot to go down a bit lower so I can have a look, and see if we can improve anything!'

Billy Keenan, his head lad from the Hills' days, has stayed here with Peter Chapple-Hyam.

'I'd be lost without him. We both started at the same time with B. Hills. He rode a second and third in the Ayr Gold Cup . . .' he adds proudly. 'We've got fifteen lads and I wouldn't swap any of them for all the tea in China.'

Having ridden out with one lot, Lucy Sangster, Ben Sangster's wife, comes up to the six-furlong oval all-weather track to watch the action.

'I ride out most days if I'm around,' she says. 'I love it.' This whole little gang is always inseparable and supportive at the races, all shaking equally with nerves and anticipation. 'There's nothing like winning,' says Lucy, 'and the second spot is the loneliest place in the world.'

The horses appear, raring to go, but the lads are all smiling.

'We bring them here when they're not doing too much, or if they're going to work they'll come here and have a little hack round before they go up to Clatford,' says the trainer, who then runs off every detail concerning the horses passing by. They are having a high old time.

'This lot haven't been doing much, as you can see! Michael's having a job with Dr Devious – look at him diving and chucking his head about . . . ! Gerry can't hold Night Duty . . . The horse in front is a three-year-old by Be My Guest called Lunar Rhythm, and he takes a *right* grip . . .' He describes the scene with such enthusiasm I should like nothing better than to be out there with them. All the lads look particularly competent, but Formal Occasion is being ridden very stylishly. 'That's Brian Chunn; he's second head lad. But they're all very good,' he says. 'They've all had rides.'

The atmosphere is terrific; relaxed enough to bring out the best in everyone, but fiercely professional, and it is a marvellous treat to see racehorses being worked at Manton when there is such promise for the future.

Peter Chapple-Hyam looks after his horses as they emerge from the gallop and walk back towards the yard.

'The best thing is', he says, 'when you see these horses – the horses you see every day – when you see them go to the races, and they win. It's fantastic . . .'

CHAPTER SEVENTEEN

'Winners are everything'

I was casting around for someone to blame.

I had heard a great many complaining voices in racing, and glimpsed the Sport of Kings being ferried nearer to apocalypse than ever before by the self-preserving stupidity of warring factions, the prodigious indifference of the government and, to some extent, by the deification of respectibility. The catalyst has been the recession.

And still the opinions roll out . . .

'There are no politics in racing,' asserts one trainer. 'There are no politics because there is no one capable of dealing with any politics!'

'It would perhaps be stretching a point to say that Cartesian men are thick on the ground in racing,' agrees an insider who is the exception to prove his own rule. 'Racing culture is fairly narrow. It is bounded on one side by the *Sporting Life* and on the other by the *Racing Post*, and what appeals to the people in this game is craftiness, not intellect.'

Another trainer simply waved the white flag. 'The Jockey Club has got it all sewn up. They're not earning their living from it. They're either lords or retired Army people. They're like a bank manager inside his little square who's never been out in the rain. What do they care about the small trainers?'

Nicky Henderson knows exactly how to set about that kind of inertia.

'I'm not a great believer in whingeing and whining about everything and waiting for the world to sort itself out. Christ! We're all working away – come and help us *do* something; we've got to get this show on the road. There is no easy solution, and change for change's sake is always dangerous. I am very pro the Jockey Club; I train for quite a few members

– my father's a member – and I think they do a very good job. Who's paying them? Nobody. And who ever turned round and said, "Thanks"? They're doing their very best.'

'The trouble with you is . . .' Now the advice for which I am, of course, grateful is getting personal. An owner who has complained to the Stewards of the Jockey Club about her trainer, citing Rule 51 – 'Every trainer shall conduct his business of training racehorses with reasonable care and skill and with due regard to the interests of his owners' – thinks she will identify my shortcomings as well. 'The trouble with you is you talk to too many people in the Establishment.' But where, I wonder, lies the value in ignoring the Establishment?

The Duke of Devonshire had given a personal view of the members' role.

'I was never Senior Steward, but I was a Steward, and it was *hard* work. But it is fair to say there are considerable perks (not as many as there were); but with a number of exceptions – people like the Maktoums who've been made Honorary Members – virtually all the members of the Jockey Club have worked their way to being members by being Stewards at local meetings and that is hard work – I don't think it's desperately hard work, but it's work. They've served their time.

'The Jockey Club is very like the House of Lords in that it is very easy to criticize it, but problems start arising with what you put in its place.

'My son is now *Senior* Steward – it's a devil of a job because it's every bit as bad as being Master of Foxhounds, *and* of course the international side of it has grown much more, and he's very conscious of this – almost over-conscientious – and he's either in Cincinnati lecturing on the medication of horses, or at the *Breeders* Cup or the *Japan* Cup . . . Mind you, having said that, he loves it.'

Luca Cumani has a word to add about the Establishment.

'Whilst I am very happy with the present Senior Steward, who has brought the Jockey Club out of the cave ages, and is frog-leaping over the iron age and the stone age trying to get into the twentieth century,' he says, 'there is no guarantee that the next one will be the same. He could be someone like the past ones who never did anything.'

There is no doubt that horse racing under Rules in this country is in decline; whether the decline is a trend or part of a cycle is open to question but very little, it would appear, is being done either to slow it down or to reverse it, and although there are many capable and well-meaning people involved in the business, they are allowing this situation to obtain.

I have always thought that life is too short to be hindered by ignorance or reticence, so I went to the Jockey Club and asked the Senior Steward whom I could blame.

'There is no single area of blame,' replied Lord Hartington. 'A lot of people say there's only one body to blame, and that's the Jockey Club – they've been sitting around running things for ever, and look at the state we're in ... I don't agree with that, or accept it, but I completely understand where they're coming from on that.'

Number 42 Portman Square has been done over by the decorators: its glass walls, stripped wood and discreet lighting are strangely incompatible with the role of the Jockey Club. In the Senior Steward's office, however, style and taste are salvaged by his contemporary paintings – bright as jockeys' silks and equally seductive – which crowd the walls, and although this organization is a self-perpetuating oligarchy, not a trace of pomposity clouds any issue.

The Jockey Club is remarkably unpopular, I ventured.

'I don't think it's the role of the regulatory body to be particularly popular with those it regulates. My job is deeply satisfying, and sometimes very rewarding – but sometimes very very frustrating. Everything has to be done – and quite rightly so – by endless consultation. Despite what people say, we consult with everybody all the time about any change, and it's nearly always done by consensus and that's quite hard work.

'It is quite a conservative industry. Racehorse trainers, owners, racecourse managers all tend to be conservative, and new developments like steeplechasing on sand seem to be great big mountains to climb to start with, but once they happen everybody says more or less straight away – that's fine. We use roadshows going around the country to explain what we're going to do and I think that has made changes quicker to effect, but if trainers choose not to go, then they choose not to have their voice heard. And that is why the Jockey Club can seem like some awful distant body; somebody's got to make a decision. The Jockey Club is only mandated by our Charter to run the rules, discipline and licensing; we are not mandated by any legislation to *control* the industry,' he reminds me. 'We can't tell racecourses how much to charge; we can't tell trainers what the maximum training bill should be . . . We don't have any control over how clean the loos are, or how much the sandwiches cost. I judge our success on the integrity of racing, and although there is always a *little* element of cheating in racing, by and large, most of the industry seems pretty satisfied with the way the integrity of racing is managed; that's the principal benchmark we're judged by. When something goes wrong people turn to the Jockey Club and ask why we haven't done something about it, but if it's not our direct concern we have to say it's not our business, and it's not what people want to hear.

'The racing industry was perhaps slow in the past to appreciate the changes that have come about since the 1961 legislation. Up until then it was a pure sport. I think it quite wrong to think that in 1961 there was a real possibility of a Tote monopoly, but people love to say if only the Jockey Club had gone for that, the government would have given it to them; a lot of people say it, so many more people believe it. I think the possibility had gone many years before, in about 1928. Since 1961, the racing industry has enabled the bookmakers to exist legally, and initially the Jockey Club wanted twice as much from the annual Levy as they were given, and ever since there has been an historic underfunding of racing which has resulted in our present calamitous state and hand-to-mouth existence.'

Would a Labour government regard racing any differently? I asked.

'Well, I'm not entirely aware of how the Conservative Party treat racing . . .' the Senior Steward said with a degree of bitterness (or it may have been resignation) in his voice. I think it is important for us now to make it aware that the racing industry, the betting industry and the government have a common interest in a thriving racing industry. The government gets irritated by racing because, I'm afraid, it is still comparatively divided .

'Trainers are free agents, and so long as the horses are looked after properly, and so long as they run their yards in an honest way, we have no further part in it. If there were a central body in racing it would mean that the constituent parts of that body would have to give up quite a lot of their own power. In the same way, the Jockey Club would have to give up its power voluntarily, and I am sure it would not do that unless it was very convinced indeed that what it was giving up was going to be taken over by something which would be better.'

Sunday racing?

'The Home Office is absolutely adamant that we wouldn't get Sunday racing without bookmakers being open, and it is their premier role to stop the law being broken. I think they're wrong; I don't think there would be much illegal betting, but I can't prove it. We are beginning to test with them a little to see if the Chapel vote is still as strong as ever in Parliament. I have a feeling it is possibly stronger than one thinks, and one has to respect that.

'I think the government's stance on the stimulation of betting is pretty ridiculous. Although they make a great deal of money out of it, it's in some way naughty and therefore can't be stimulated.'

Prostitution again.

'They know it goes on; they're perfectly happy for the need to be satisfied, but not for it to be stimulated: a very fine line. And it is a great flaw. I was at an international conference in America last week, and I was saying that one of the difficulties we had in promoting racing was that we are not allowed to promote betting, and they all looked at me as if I were mad.'

Finally the conversation took a less theoretical turn, and the spotlight moved on to all those people who perform with deliberate perversity in the great game of horse-racing.

'I think training must be the most desperate profession,' says Lord Hartington. 'They go from one disappointment to another. It's twenty-four hours a day and much too much like hard work, I would have thought. I think that's why they spend a lot of time in each other's company because they understand, without having to explain. And jockeys are unbelievably philosophical. You hardly ever see a jockey being angry when he's stood down – perhaps unfairly, and Stewards do make mistakes very occasionally. When they're in the Stewards' room they're unfailingly polite. Some are more helpful than others . . . but they're not obliged to be helpful. They're doing something which is difficult, dangerous; they're often tired and have had nothing to eat and I think they're wonderful people, and remarkably resilient.

'And the whole thing would grind to a halt without the owners. They are the main investors in racing, and there are 25 per cent fewer owners coming into racing than last year. That is partly the recession, perhaps partly Lloyd's, but it must be partly due to the level of prize money, I think.

'I don't think there should be more prize money because the owners get a rough deal; but racing should get more from the betting industry, and no doubt out of that increased fee – the price of the product – prize money would increase.'

Since giving his speech in the House of Lords on the prize money profits for owners, the Duke of Devonshire has refined his arguments. 'The tail of betting is wagging the body of racing,' is what he says now, and with this sentiment the Senior Steward would agree whilst conceding that rational considerations about cash go out of the window when a winner is in sight.

'There is something magically exciting which makes people come back for more despite what the bank manager continues to tell them! Winning is a great ego trip, and the owners who disappear quickest are the ones for whom the anticipation of *not* losing outweighs the fact of actually losing.

It sounds crazy,' he says, 'but getting beaten can still be great fun, and a modern owner who wouldn't probably recognize his racehorse in a field amongst other horses can still be immensely excited by their achievements. It's like people who buy art: you don't have to be a scholar to buy a picture.'

So who bore the blame?

Quite clearly, everybody bears the blame, and it is impossible not to be struck again by the lunacy of fragmentation and its consequences. Although the personal popularity of the present Senior Steward is high, it would smack of the miraculous if his reputation were burnished by his proposed British Horseracing Board, with its apparent snub to the trainers who have long subsidized the game. A rear-guard action more than a serious commitment to power sharing and progress, it is a gift to the Jockey Club's critics.

As racing is an excellent short-cut to the depths of the human psyche, so flippancy sets in. I embroider a fantasy in which the Senior Steward, the Home Secretary, Christopher Haines, J.J. Warr and Sir John Sparrow together with representatives from the owners, the trainers and the bookmakers are taken to a place where they can do themselves no harm until such time as their minds meet on a solution for the problems which beset their industry. Tony Budge – a sounding-board of good sense – will be in the chair to manipulate everyone and solve everything, and he will have Jenny Pitman's pet Rottweiler in attendance to focus everyone's attention, and bring them to heel. Or perhaps Mrs Pitman (with her rusticities) could be persuaded to do the job herself? The only company they shall have is a quotation from Archbishop Temple: 'The art of government is the art of so ordering life that self-interests governs what justice demands,' and their only entertainment will be to watch Flat racing on an all-weather track in mid-winter: that would bring anyone to their senses.

'Steady on . . .' Now the advice comes from John Dunlop. 'Don't overdo this – the all-weather tracks serve a very useful purpose.'

This trainer has achieved a rare degree of authority and respect in his profession; the *insouciance* and the humour are a bonus. He is sitting in his Shogun ('the van') watching second lot have a pick at grass before returning to the stables at Arundel Castle. It is nearing the end of the season and this is his first day back after a week at the sales. Pheasants in gaudy plumage stride crowing along the grass gallops, still safe from the guns. Autumn and Embassy cigarettes scent the air.

It has been another memorable season for John Dunlop. Marju is off to stand at stud next day; his injuries have been a constant problem.

177

'He's been a great frustration to me; an awful frustration,' he says, but Shadayid, the stable pet, is a star. 'She's had the most remarkable year, really. The only regret I have with her is that I think she should have won the Sussex Stakes. I think that's the one regret.

'The only one thing that's certain about racing is that if you're ever dogmatic about any aspect of it, almost certainly you're always proven wrong. Because it's animals; they're not machines. One of the great fascinations about Flat racing in particular is that every year we have this input of fresh blood, any one of which – *any* one, even the ones with the most obscure credentials – *could* be the best horse that's ever trodden on the Turf. *Could* . . . and it's a billion to one that it's not going to be, but there is always that possibility. And that is the excitement; that is the fascination of it, really. Equally, of course, it does make it the most frustrating, disappointing business you can possibly be involved in. Most horses don't win. That's a fact of life – more horses don't win than do!'

Now it is his turn to ask a question. He lights another cigarette, and starts to laugh.

'I suppose you realize by now that we all train racehorses because we can't do anything else . . . ?'

Still in Sussex, over at Plumpton where the National Hunt season is well under way, Paddy Butler is bustling out of the weighing room carrying a neat leather briefcase.

'It's the money!' he grins. 'I've got the money in here!'

The day has been good to him. His magnificent looking chestnut novice 'chaser by Le Moss has made a very promising racecourse debut. A six-year-old ('They couldn't catch 'im in Ireland until he was four or five; they *couldn't* catch 'im!') has jumped clear and run on gamely to capture the £235 third prize in his race. Paddy and Eileen are delighted for the horse, and for his owner, local farmer John Patty who had spotted him by chance and then bought him over in Ireland.

'He's a genuine owner,' says Paddy, imparting a wealth of meaning with those few words.

Up at the two-mile start, a hare skids to the safety of her ditch across the damp turf of the track as a handful of hurdlers canter in front of the buxom Downs for the start of a seller. The light is fading into blue afternoon mist, October is putting a chill into the air and the light rain dampens the jockeys' silks. Starter Sir John Guise walks into the centre of the course.

'All the horses at the start!' is the message sent back to the stands and the yellow elastic is pulled taut across the starting line. The horses are snorting and straining to be off. Sir John is tightening a girth when the usual shout goes up from one of the jockeys.

'Anybody making it?'

'Yeah! I'll be very handy . . .' comes a reply as they jostle for position, and the Starter takes the rostrum.

'Hold on, sir!' comes a shout from Gary Moore.

'I can see you, Gary,' Sir John assures him in a stentorian voice as the horse wheels round and turns his back on the proceedings.

Richard Dunwoody is looking as calm and collected as ever.

'Winners are everything to me, you know,' he has told me. 'A winner round here means as much as a winner at Newbury or Kempton. I can get a big kick if I feel I've ridden a good race on a horse to go and win.' Now he's on the rails and ready for the off.

'Are you all right back there!' roars Sir John to a jockey holding his horse up.

'Yes, sir! Thank you, sir!' he replies as he fights his mount.

Now the Starter lets rip with his final roar.

'COME ON!'

With that, the elastic snakes free and the horses jump into their strides. Sir John stands stock still and looks down the hill after them, and then he takes his place in the jeep and lights up the inevitable cigarette.

'That's more like it, isn't it?' he says quietly, signalling his love of National Hunt. There is a moment of prim silence as he inhales, and then the rasping, roguish and very infectious chuckle starts up. 'I work *bloody* hard!' he announces to no one in particular. 'Wincanton tomorrow . . .'